RECESSION-PROOF YOUR LIFE
The Ultimate Guide to
Financial Stability During
Economic Downturns

LUNA Z. RAINSTORM

Get A Free Book At: BornIncredible.com/free-book-offer/[4]

---

1. https://BornIncredible.com

2. https://BornIncredible.com

3. https://BornIncredible.com

4. https://bornincredible.com/free-book-offer/

Table of Contents

Introduction

Introduction to Recessions

A recession is a period of economic decline that lasts for several months, or even years, characterized by a decrease in Gross Domestic Product (GDP), employment, income, and trade. Recessions are caused by various factors, including supply and demand imbalances, financial crises, global shocks, government policies, and other external factors that disrupt the normal functioning of the economy. The impact of a recession can be felt across different sectors and industries, leading to widespread job losses, bankruptcies, and reduced consumer spending.

History of Recessions

Recessions have occurred throughout history, with the earliest recorded recession dating back to the 1st century AD, during the reign of Emperor Augustus in Rome. Since then, several significant recessions have taken place, including the Great Depression of the 1930s, the oil crisis of the 1970s, and the Global Financial Crisis of 2008-2009.

The Great Depression, which began in 1929 and lasted for ten years, was one of the worst economic crises in modern history, leading to massive job losses, bank failures, and a decline in international trade. The crisis was caused by a combination of factors, including overproduction, speculative investments, and a decline in consumer spending, which led to a severe downturn in the economy. The government response to the Great Depression was to implement Keynesian economic policies, including increased government spending and reduced interest rates, to stimulate economic growth and employment.

The oil crisis of the 1970s was caused by a sudden increase in the price of oil due to the decision by the Organization of Petroleum Exporting Countries (OPEC) to limit oil production. The crisis led to a recession in many countries, particularly those heavily dependent on oil imports. The crisis also led to an increased focus on energy efficiency and the development of alternative energy sources.

The Global Financial Crisis of 2008-2009 was caused by a collapse of the housing market and the subprime mortgage industry in the United States, leading to a crisis in the financial sector and a global recession. The crisis was exacerbated by the interconnectedness of the global financial system, which led to a rapid spread of the crisis to other countries. The government response to the crisis included measures such as bailouts of banks and other financial institutions, increased regulation of the financial sector, and fiscal stimulus to support economic growth.

Causes of Recessions

Recessions can be caused by various factors, including:

Supply and Demand Imbalances: Recessions can occur when there is a mismatch between supply and demand in the economy. This can happen when there is overproduction or oversupply in certain industries, leading to reduced prices and profits. Alternatively, a recession can occur when demand for goods and services declines, leading to reduced production and employment.

Financial Crises: Recessions can also be caused by financial crises, such as bank failures, stock market crashes, or debt crises. These crises can lead to a loss of confidence in the financial system, leading to reduced investment and economic activity.

Global Shocks: Recessions can also be caused by global shocks, such as natural disasters, pandemics, or political crises. These events can disrupt trade and supply chains, leading to reduced economic activity.

Government Policies: Government policies can also contribute to recessions. For example, restrictive fiscal policies, such as increased taxes or reduced government spending, can lead to reduced economic activity. Similarly, tight monetary policies, such as increased interest rates, can reduce investment and consumer spending.

Effects of Recessions

Recessions have significant economic and social effects, including:

Job Losses: Recessions lead to a decline in employment as businesses reduce production and cut costs. This can result in job losses, particularly in industries that are particularly affected by the recession. Workers who lose their jobs may face financial difficulties and may need to rely on government support or other forms of assistance.

Reduced Consumer Spending: During a recession, consumers may become more cautious with their spending as they face uncertainty about their financial future. This can lead to a decrease in consumer spending, particularly on non-essential goods and services. This reduction in spending can further exacerbate the economic downturn.

Business Failures: As demand for goods and services decreases during a recession, businesses may struggle to make a profit. This can lead to business failures, particularly among small and medium-sized enterprises (SMEs) that may have less financial resilience than larger companies.

Decreased Investment: Recessions can also lead to a decrease in investment as individuals and businesses become more risk-averse. This can result in a reduction in the number of new businesses being created, as well as a decrease in investment in infrastructure and other long-term projects.

Housing Market Decline: Recessions can have a significant impact on the housing market, with house prices falling and the number of new homes being built decreasing. This can result in a decline in the construction industry, which can have knock-on effects on other sectors of the economy.

Mental Health Issues: Recessions can also have a significant impact on mental health, particularly for those who have lost their jobs or are struggling financially. The stress and anxiety associated with financial uncertainty can lead to mental health issues such as depression and anxiety, which can have long-term effects on individuals and communities.

Explanation of a recession

A recession is a period of economic decline where there is a significant decrease in the Gross Domestic Product (GDP), employment, income, and trade. It is a significant decline in economic activity that lasts for several months or even years. Recessions are caused by various factors, including supply and demand imbalances, financial crises, global shocks, government policies, and other external factors that disrupt the normal functioning of the economy.

One of the key indicators of a recession is a decline in GDP, which measures the total value of goods and services produced in an economy. When GDP declines, it means that there is less economic activity and production, which can lead to a decrease in employment and income.

Another important indicator of a recession is a rise in unemployment rates. During a recession, businesses tend to reduce production and cut costs, which often means laying off workers. This can lead to a decrease in consumer spending, which can further exacerbate the economic decline.

A recession can also have an impact on the stock market, with prices falling as investors become more cautious about the future of the economy. In some cases, a recession can lead to a financial crisis, where banks and other financial institutions fail, and there is a significant reduction in the availability of credit and loans.

Recessions can be caused by various factors, including supply and demand imbalances, financial crises, global shocks, government policies, and other external factors. Supply and demand imbalances occur when there is a mismatch between supply and demand in the economy, which can lead to reduced production and employment. For example, if there is an oversupply of goods and services, prices can fall, and businesses may reduce production and lay off workers.

Financial crises can also lead to a recession, as was the case during the Global Financial Crisis of 2008-2009. The collapse of the housing market and the subprime mortgage industry in the United States led to a crisis in the financial sector and a global recession. The crisis was exacerbated by the interconnectedness of the global financial system, which led to a rapid spread of the crisis to other countries.

Global shocks can also lead to a recession. For example, a natural disaster or a pandemic can disrupt trade and supply chains, leading to reduced economic activity. Similarly, political crises or international conflicts can lead to a decline in trade and investment, which can further exacerbate the economic decline.

Government policies can also contribute to recessions. For example, if the government implements restrictive fiscal policies, such as increased taxes or reduced government spending, this can lead to reduced economic activity. Similarly, if the government implements tight monetary policies, such as increased interest rates, this can reduce investment and consumer spending.

The effects of a recession can be significant and widespread. Job losses are one of the most significant impacts of a recession, with many businesses reducing production and cutting costs by laying off workers. This can lead to a decrease in consumer spending, which can further exacerbate the economic decline.

A recession can also have an impact on the stock market, with prices falling as investors become more cautious about the future of the economy. This can lead to a reduction in investment, which can further exacerbate the economic decline.

In some cases, a recession can lead to a financial crisis, where banks and other financial institutions fail, and there is a significant reduction in the availability of credit and loans. This can have a significant impact on businesses and consumers, who may struggle to access the credit they need to operate or make purchases.

Prevalence and impact of recessions

Recessions are a prevalent economic phenomenon that occurs across different countries and regions. They are periods of significant economic decline characterized by a decrease in Gross Domestic Product (GDP), employment, income, and trade. Recessions can have a significant impact on individuals, businesses, and society as a whole. Below we will discuss the prevalence and impact of recessions.

Prevalence of Recessions

Recessions are not rare events, and they have occurred throughout history. In the United States, there have been 33 recessions since 1854, with the most recent being the COVID-19 recession, which began in February 2020. Other countries have also experienced significant recessions, including the Great Depression in the 1930s and the Global Financial Crisis in 2008-2009.

The duration and severity of recessions vary depending on the underlying causes and the government's response. Some recessions are relatively short-lived, lasting only a few months, while others can last for several years. Similarly, the severity of a recession can range from a minor decline in economic activity to a significant economic crisis.

Impact of Recessions

Recessions can have a significant impact on individuals, businesses, and society as a whole. The effects of a recession can be widespread and long-lasting, and they can take a toll on people's physical, mental, and financial well-being.

Job Losses

One of the most significant impacts of a recession is job losses. During a recession, businesses tend to reduce production and cut costs, which often means laying off workers. This can lead to a decrease in consumer spending, which can further exacerbate the economic decline. Job losses can have a significant impact on individuals and their families, leading to financial stress, reduced quality of life, and even homelessness.

Income Reductions

Recessions can also lead to a reduction in income for individuals and businesses. This can occur due to a decline in demand for goods and services, which leads to reduced prices and profits. In some cases, wages and salaries may also be reduced, particularly if businesses are struggling to remain profitable. Reduced income can lead to financial stress, which can have a negative impact on mental and physical health.

Bankruptcies and Business Closures

During a recession, businesses may struggle to remain profitable, leading to bankruptcies and business closures. This can have a significant impact on the economy, as businesses play a critical role in providing goods and services, creating jobs, and contributing to economic growth. Business closures can also have a ripple effect on other businesses, particularly those that are dependent on the closed business for their supply chain or customer base.

Stock Market Declines

Recessions can also have an impact on the stock market, with prices falling as investors become more cautious about the future of the economy. This can lead to a reduction in investment, which can further exacerbate the economic decline. Stock market declines can also have a significant impact on individuals' retirement savings and investment portfolios.

Mental and Physical Health Impacts

Recessions can have a significant impact on individuals' mental and physical health. Financial stress and job loss can lead to depression, anxiety, and other mental health conditions. Similarly, reduced access to healthcare and social services can lead to physical health problems, particularly for those who are already vulnerable.

Government Responses

Governments often respond to recessions by implementing fiscal and monetary policies aimed at stimulating economic growth and employment. These policies can include increased government spending, tax cuts, and reduced interest rates. While these policies can be effective in mitigating the effects of a recession, they can also lead to increased government debt and inflation.

Importance of understanding the history of recessions and how to survive them

Understanding the history of recessions and how to survive them is crucial for individuals, businesses, and governments. Recessions are periods of economic decline characterized by a decrease in Gross Domestic Product (GDP), employment, income, and trade. They can have a significant impact on people's physical, mental, and financial well-being. Below we will discuss the importance of understanding the history of recessions and how to survive them.

Importance of Understanding the History of Recessions

Learning from Past Mistakes

Studying the history of recessions can help individuals, businesses, and governments learn from past mistakes. By understanding the causes and effects of previous recessions, they can identify warning signs and take appropriate measures to mitigate the impact of future recessions. This can help prevent the same mistakes from being repeated and ensure a faster recovery.

Identifying Economic Trends

Studying the history of recessions can also help individuals, businesses, and governments identify economic trends. By analyzing patterns and trends from past recessions, they can make informed decisions about investments, employment, and other financial decisions. This can help them prepare for future recessions and minimize the impact on their financial well-being.

Evaluating Government Policies

Studying the history of recessions can also help evaluate the effectiveness of government policies. By analyzing the policies implemented during past recessions, governments can identify what worked and what did not work. This can help them develop better policies to mitigate the impact of future recessions and ensure a faster recovery.

How to Survive Recessions

Reduce Debt

Reducing debt is one of the most important steps individuals and businesses can take to survive a recession. This can help minimize financial stress and ensure a stable financial position during a recession. Paying off high-interest debt, such as credit card debt, can be particularly important as it can save money in the long run.

Build an Emergency Fund

Building an emergency fund can also help individuals and businesses survive a recession. This can help cover unexpected expenses and provide a cushion during a financial crisis. Experts recommend having three to six months of living expenses saved in an emergency fund.

Diversify Investments

Diversifying investments can also help individuals and businesses survive a recession. This can help minimize risk and ensure that investments are not overly dependent on a single industry or sector. Investing in a mix of stocks, bonds, and other assets can help ensure a stable financial position during a recession.

Cut Costs

Cutting costs is another important step individuals and businesses can take to survive a recession. This can include reducing discretionary spending, negotiating lower rates for services, and finding ways to reduce fixed expenses. By cutting costs, individuals and businesses can minimize financial stress and ensure a stable financial position during a recession.

Stay Educated

Staying educated about the economy and the job market can also help individuals and businesses survive a recession. This can include following news and economic reports, networking with other professionals, and learning new skills that can help in a changing job market. By staying educated, individuals and businesses can identify opportunities and adapt to changing economic conditions.

Conclusion

Understanding the history of recessions and how to survive them is crucial for individuals, businesses, and governments. Studying the causes and effects of past recessions can help identify warning signs, identify economic trends, and evaluate government policies. To survive a recession, individuals and businesses can reduce debt, build an emergency fund, diversify investments, cut costs, and stay educated. By taking these steps, individuals and businesses can minimize the impact of a recession and ensure a stable financial position during difficult economic times.

History of Recessions:

Recessions are periods of economic decline characterized by a decrease in Gross Domestic Product (GDP), employment, income, and trade. They are not rare events and have occurred throughout history. Below we will discuss the history of recessions, including significant events, causes, and impacts.

The Early History of Recessions

The earliest recorded recession dates back to the 1st century AD, during the reign of Emperor Augustus in Rome. The recession was caused by a decline in trade and agricultural productivity, leading to a decrease in economic activity. Similar recessions occurred throughout the Middle Ages, including the Great Slump of the 14th century and the Great Depression of the 17th century.

The Industrial Revolution and Recessions

The Industrial Revolution in the 18th and 19th centuries led to significant economic growth and development. However, it also led to several significant recessions, including the Panic of 1819, the Panic of 1837, and the Panic of 1873.

The Panic of 1819 was caused by a decline in international trade and a decrease in agricultural prices, leading to a significant decline in economic activity. The Panic of 1837 was caused by a speculative bubble in land and railroad investments, which led to a significant decline in economic activity. The Panic of 1873 was caused by a decline in railroad investment and a decrease in international trade, leading to a significant decline in economic activity.

The Great Depression

The Great Depression of the 1930s was one of the worst economic crises in modern history. It was caused by a combination of factors, including overproduction, speculative investments, and a decline in consumer spending, which led to a severe downturn in the economy. The government response to the Great Depression was to implement Keynesian economic policies, including increased government spending and reduced interest rates, to stimulate economic growth and employment.

The Oil Crisis of the 1970s

The oil crisis of the 1970s was caused by a sudden increase in the price of oil due to the decision by the Organization of Petroleum Exporting Countries (OPEC) to limit oil production. The crisis led to a recession in many countries, particularly those heavily dependent on oil imports. The crisis also led to an increased focus on energy efficiency and the development of alternative energy sources.

The Global Financial Crisis

The Global Financial Crisis of 2008-2009 was caused by a collapse of the housing market and the subprime mortgage industry in the United States, leading to a crisis in the financial sector and a global recession. The crisis was exacerbated by the interconnectedness of the global financial system, which led to a rapid spread of the crisis to other countries. The government response to the crisis included measures such as bailouts of banks and other financial institutions, increased regulation of the financial sector, and fiscal stimulus to support economic growth.

Causes of Recessions

Recessions can be caused by various factors, including supply and demand imbalances, financial crises, global shocks, government policies, and other external factors. Supply and demand imbalances occur when there is a mismatch between supply and demand in the economy, which can lead to reduced production and employment. For example, if there is an oversupply of goods and services, prices can fall, and businesses may reduce production and lay off workers.

Financial crises can also lead to a recession, as was the case during the Global Financial Crisis of 2008-2009. The collapse of the housing market and the subprime mortgage industry in the United States led to a crisis in the financial sector and a global recession. The crisis was exacerbated by the interconnectedness of the global financial system, which led to a rapid spread of the crisis to other countries.

Overview of the history of recessions

Recessions are periods of economic decline characterized by a decrease in Gross Domestic Product (GDP), employment, income, and trade. They have occurred throughout history and have had significant impacts on individuals, businesses, and society as a whole. Below we will provide an overview of the history of recessions, including significant events, causes, and impacts.

Early Recessions

The earliest recorded recession dates back to the 1st century AD, during the reign of Emperor Augustus in Rome. The recession was caused by a decline in trade and agricultural productivity, leading to a decrease in economic activity. Similar recessions occurred throughout the Middle Ages, including the Great Slump of the 14th century and the Great Depression of the 17th century.

Industrial Revolution and Recessions

The Industrial Revolution in the 18th and 19th centuries led to significant economic growth and development. However, it also led to several significant recessions, including the Panic of 1819, the Panic of 1837, and the Panic of 1873.

The Panic of 1819 was caused by a decline in international trade and a decrease in agricultural prices, leading to a significant decline in economic activity. The Panic of 1837 was caused by a speculative bubble in land and railroad investments, which led to a significant decline in economic activity. The Panic of 1873 was caused by a decline in railroad investment and a decrease in international trade, leading to a significant decline in economic activity.

Great Depression

The Great Depression of the 1930s was one of the worst economic crises in modern history. It was caused by a combination of factors, including overproduction, speculative investments, and a decline in consumer spending, which led to a severe downturn in the economy. The government response to the Great Depression was to implement Keynesian economic policies, including increased government spending and reduced interest rates, to stimulate economic growth and employment.

Post-World War II Recessions

Following World War II, several significant recessions occurred, including the recession of 1949, the recession of 1953, and the recession of 1958. These recessions were caused by various factors, including government policies, inflation, and changes in consumer spending.

Oil Crisis of the 1970s

The oil crisis of the 1970s was caused by a sudden increase in the price of oil due to the decision by the Organization of Petroleum Exporting Countries (OPEC) to limit oil production. The crisis led to a recession in many countries, particularly those heavily dependent on oil imports. The crisis also led to an increased focus on energy efficiency and the development of alternative energy sources.

The Early 1980s Recession (1980-1982)

The Early 1980s Recession, also known as the Reagan Recession, was a significant economic downturn that occurred in the United States from 1980 to 1982. The recession was caused by a combination of factors, including high inflation, high interest rates, and a decline in consumer spending.

One of the primary causes of the Early 1980s Recession was high inflation. In the 1970s, inflation in the US had reached double-digit levels, and the Federal Reserve had responded by raising interest rates to try to control inflation. However, high interest rates led to a decline in consumer spending, which contributed to the recession.

Another factor that contributed to the recession was a decline in manufacturing and other industries. In the late 1970s and early 1980s, many US manufacturers faced stiff competition from foreign companies, particularly in the automotive industry. This led to job losses and a decline in economic growth.

The Early 1980s Recession had a significant impact on the US economy. The unemployment rate peaked at 10.8% in late 1982, the highest level since the Great Depression. The recession also had a significant impact on the US housing market, with home prices declining and many homeowners struggling to make mortgage payments.

To address the recession, President Ronald Reagan implemented a range of economic policies, including tax cuts and deregulation. These policies were designed to stimulate economic growth and reduce government intervention in the economy. The policies eventually led to a period of sustained economic growth in the US, known as the "Reagan Recovery."

The dot-com Recession

The dot-com recession, also known as the dot-com bust or the tech bubble burst, was a period of significant decline in the value of internet-based companies and technology stocks. The recession began in early 2000 and lasted until 2002, resulting in a significant impact on the US economy and the global technology industry.

The dot-com recession was caused by a combination of factors, including:

Over-investment in technology companies: Many investors poured large amounts of money into internet-based companies, leading to a significant increase in the valuation of these companies. However, many of these companies had no real business model or revenue stream, and the valuations were based on hype and speculation rather than actual financial performance.

Lack of profitability: Many of the dot-com companies were not profitable and were burning through cash. As investors became more cautious and demanding, many of these companies were unable to secure additional funding or investment, leading to their collapse.

Bursting of the tech bubble: The dot-com recession was part of a larger tech bubble that had been building since the mid-1990s. The bubble was created by the rapid growth of the technology industry and the high valuations of tech companies. However, the bubble eventually burst, leading to a significant decline in the value of technology stocks.

Economic downturn: The dot-com recession was also exacerbated by the general economic downturn that began in 2001, following the September 11th terrorist attacks. The economic downturn led to reduced consumer spending and lower demand for technology products and services.

The dot-com recession had significant effects on the US and global economy, including:

Job losses: The dot-com recession resulted in significant job losses, particularly in the technology sector. Many internet-based companies went bankrupt, leading to layoffs and unemployment.

Stock market decline: The dot-com recession led to a significant decline in the stock market, particularly in the technology sector. Stock prices for many technology companies plummeted, leading to significant losses for investors.

Business failures: Many dot-com companies went bankrupt during the recession, leading to a decline in the number of new technology companies being created.

Investment decline: The dot-com recession led to a decline in investment in the technology sector, as investors became more cautious and risk-averse.

Economic impact: The dot-com recession had a significant impact on the US and global economy, leading to a slowdown in economic growth and reduced consumer spending.

Global Financial Crisis

The Global Financial Crisis of 2008-2009 was caused by a collapse of the housing market and the subprime mortgage industry in the United States, leading to a crisis in the financial sector and a global recession. The crisis was exacerbated by the interconnectedness of the global financial system, which led to a rapid spread of the crisis to other countries. The government response to the crisis included measures such as bailouts of banks and other financial institutions, increased regulation of the financial sector, and fiscal stimulus to support economic growth.

The COVID-19 Pandemic Recession (2020-2021)

The Pandemic Recession, also known as the COVID-19 recession, was a global economic downturn that began in early 2020 and was caused by the outbreak of the COVID-19 pandemic. The pandemic led to widespread lockdowns and a significant decline in economic activity, resulting in high unemployment rates and a significant decline in economic growth.

The COVID-19 pandemic had a significant impact on the global economy, particularly in the service sector, which was hit hard by the lockdowns and social distancing measures. Restaurants, hotels, airlines, and other industries that rely on in-person interaction were particularly affected. Many businesses were forced to close temporarily, while others were forced to permanently shut down.

The pandemic recession also had a significant impact on the labor market. Unemployment rates reached historic highs in many countries, with millions of workers losing their jobs or experiencing reduced hours. The pandemic recession also had a disproportionate impact on low-income workers and workers in industries that were most affected by the pandemic.

Governments and central banks around the world responded to the pandemic recession with a range of measures designed to mitigate the impact on individuals and businesses. These measures included massive government spending programs, low-interest rates, and other forms of economic stimulus. In some countries, governments also provided direct financial support to individuals and businesses impacted by the pandemic.

As vaccination rates have increased and lockdowns have been lifted, the global economy has begun to recover from the pandemic recession. However, the pandemic and its economic impact are ongoing, and the long-term effects of the pandemic recession are still uncertain.

Major recessions throughout history

Recessions are periods of significant economic decline characterized by a decrease in Gross Domestic Product (GDP), employment, income, and trade. Throughout history, there have been several major recessions that have had significant impacts on individuals, businesses, and society as a whole. Below we will discuss some of the major recessions throughout history, including the Great Depression and the 2008 financial crisis.

The Great Depression

The Great Depression of the 1930s was one of the most severe economic crises in modern history. It was caused by a combination of factors, including overproduction, speculative investments, and a decline in consumer spending. The stock market crash of 1929 is often cited as the beginning of the Great Depression, but the decline in economic activity had already begun before the crash.

The Great Depression led to significant job losses, bank failures, and a decrease in consumer spending. The government response to the Great Depression was to implement Keynesian economic policies, including increased government spending and reduced interest rates, to stimulate economic growth and employment. The Great Depression had a lasting impact on the United States and the world, leading to significant changes in economic policy and increased government regulation of the economy.

The Oil Crisis of the 1970s

The oil crisis of the 1970s was caused by a sudden increase in the price of oil due to the decision by the Organization of Petroleum Exporting Countries (OPEC) to limit oil production. The crisis led to a recession in many countries, particularly those heavily dependent on oil imports. The crisis also led to an increased focus on energy efficiency and the development of alternative energy sources.

The oil crisis of the 1970s had significant impacts on the global economy, leading to a decrease in economic activity and an increase in inflation. The crisis also led to increased geopolitical tensions and a shift in global power dynamics.

The Dot-Com Bubble Burst of 2000

The dot-com bubble burst of 2000 was caused by a speculative bubble in the technology sector, particularly in internet-related companies. The bubble was fueled by excessive investments in internet-based businesses, many of which had little to no revenue or profit. The burst of the bubble led to significant losses for investors and a decrease in economic activity.

The dot-com bubble burst of 2000 had significant impacts on the technology sector, leading to a decrease in investments and a shift in focus towards more sustainable business models. The burst of the bubble also had significant impacts on the broader economy, leading to a decrease in consumer spending and a decrease in economic growth.

The 2008 Financial Crisis

The 2008 financial crisis was one of the most significant economic crises in modern history. It was caused by a collapse of the housing market and the subprime mortgage industry in the United States, leading to a crisis in the financial sector and a global recession. The crisis was exacerbated by the interconnectedness of the global financial system, which led to a rapid spread of the crisis to other countries.

The 2008 financial crisis led to significant job losses, bank failures, and a decrease in economic activity. The government response to the crisis included measures such as bailouts of banks and other financial institutions, increased regulation of the financial sector, and fiscal stimulus to support economic growth. The 2008 financial crisis had significant impacts on the global economy, leading to changes in economic policy and increased government regulation of the financial sector.

Causes and consequences of past recessions

Recessions are periods of economic decline characterized by a decrease in Gross Domestic Product (GDP), employment, income, and trade. They have occurred throughout history and have had significant impacts on individuals, businesses, and society as a whole. Below we will discuss the causes and consequences of past recessions.

Causes of Recessions

Recessions can be caused by various factors, including supply and demand imbalances, financial crises, global shocks, government policies, and other external factors.

Supply and demand imbalances occur when there is a mismatch between supply and demand in the economy, which can lead to reduced production and employment. For example, if there is an oversupply of goods and services, prices can fall, and businesses may reduce production and lay off workers.

Financial crises can also lead to a recession, as was the case during the Global Financial Crisis of 2008-2009. The collapse of the housing market and the subprime mortgage industry in the United States led to a crisis in the financial sector and a global recession. The crisis was exacerbated by the interconnectedness of the global financial system, which led to a rapid spread of the crisis to other countries.

Global shocks can also lead to a recession. For example, the oil crisis of the 1970s was caused by a sudden increase in the price of oil due to the decision by the Organization of Petroleum Exporting Countries (OPEC) to limit oil production. The crisis led to a recession in many countries, particularly those heavily dependent on oil imports.

Government policies can also have an impact on the occurrence and severity of recessions. For example, during the Great Depression of the 1930s, the government implemented Keynesian economic policies, including increased government spending and reduced interest rates, to stimulate economic growth and employment.

Consequences of Recessions

Recessions can have significant economic, social, and political consequences.

Economically, recessions can lead to significant job losses, a decrease in consumer spending, and a decrease in economic growth. The Great Depression of the 1930s led to significant job losses and a decrease in consumer spending, which led to a severe downturn in the economy. The 2008 financial crisis also led to significant job losses and a decrease in consumer spending, which led to a global recession.

Socially, recessions can lead to an increase in poverty and inequality. Job losses and a decrease in economic activity can lead to a decrease in income and an increase in poverty. The 2008 financial crisis led to an increase in poverty and inequality in many countries.

Politically, recessions can lead to a shift in power dynamics and changes in economic policy. The Great Depression of the 1930s led to significant changes in economic policy, including increased government spending and regulation of the economy. The 2008 financial crisis also led to changes in economic policy, including increased regulation of the financial sector and fiscal stimulus to support economic growth.

Understanding the causes and consequences of past recessions can help individuals, businesses, and governments identify warning signs and take appropriate measures to mitigate the impact of future recessions.

Lessons learned from past recessions

Recessions have occurred throughout history and have had significant impacts on individuals, businesses, and society as a whole. While each recession is unique, there are lessons that can be learned from past recessions that can help individuals, businesses, and governments prepare for and mitigate the impact of future recessions. Below we will discuss some of the lessons learned from past recessions.

Lesson 1: The Importance of Diversification

One of the most significant lessons learned from past recessions is the importance of diversification. Recessions can have a significant impact on specific industries, and businesses that are overly dependent on a single industry or market can be particularly vulnerable. For example, during the dot-com bubble burst of 2000, many businesses in the technology sector suffered significant losses due to the collapse of the speculative bubble in internet-based companies.

Businesses can mitigate the impact of future recessions by diversifying their operations and investments across multiple industries and markets. This can help reduce the risk of significant losses in any one area and provide a more stable source of revenue during economic downturns.

Lesson 2: The Importance of Risk Management

Another lesson learned from past recessions is the importance of risk management. Recessions can expose weaknesses in a business's operations and financial management, and businesses that have not adequately prepared for the possibility of a recession can be particularly vulnerable.

Businesses can mitigate the impact of future recessions by implementing effective risk management practices, such as regularly reviewing financial performance and identifying potential risks, developing contingency plans for economic downturns, and maintaining sufficient reserves to weather periods of economic decline.

Lesson 3: The Importance of Government Intervention

Past recessions have shown that government intervention can play a critical role in mitigating the impact of economic downturns. During the Great Depression of the 1930s, the government implemented Keynesian economic policies, including increased government spending and reduced interest rates, to stimulate economic growth and employment. The government response to the 2008 financial crisis included measures such as bailouts of banks and other financial institutions, increased regulation of the financial sector, and fiscal stimulus to support economic growth.

Governments can prepare for and mitigate the impact of future recessions by implementing effective economic policies, such as targeted fiscal stimulus and increased regulation of the financial sector. Governments can also provide support to individuals and businesses that are particularly vulnerable during economic downturns, such as providing unemployment benefits and small business loans.

Lesson 4: The Importance of Innovation

Past recessions have also shown the importance of innovation in mitigating the impact of economic downturns. Innovation can lead to the development of new industries and markets, creating new opportunities for employment and economic growth.

During the Great Depression of the 1930s, the government invested in infrastructure projects, such as the construction of highways and bridges, which led to the development of new industries and markets. During the 2008 financial crisis, businesses that were able to adapt to new market conditions and innovate were more likely to weather the economic downturn.

Individuals, businesses, and governments can prepare for and mitigate the impact of future recessions by investing in research and development and supporting innovation in key industries and markets.

What is a Recession:

A recession is a period of economic decline characterized by a decrease in Gross Domestic Product (GDP), employment, income, and trade. It is typically defined as a decline in economic activity that lasts for at least two consecutive quarters.

During a recession, businesses may reduce production and lay off workers, leading to a decrease in employment and income. Consumers may also reduce spending, leading to a decrease in trade and economic growth. Recessions can have significant impacts on individuals, businesses, and society as a whole.

Causes of Recessions

Recessions can be caused by various factors, including supply and demand imbalances, financial crises, global shocks, government policies, and other external factors.

Supply and demand imbalances occur when there is a mismatch between supply and demand in the economy, which can lead to reduced production and employment. For example, if there is an oversupply of goods and services, prices can fall, and businesses may reduce production and lay off workers.

Financial crises can also lead to a recession, as was the case during the Global Financial Crisis of 2008-2009. The collapse of the housing market and the subprime mortgage industry in the United States led to a crisis in the financial sector and a global recession. The crisis was exacerbated by the interconnectedness of the global financial system, which led to a rapid spread of the crisis to other countries.

Global shocks can also lead to a recession. For example, the oil crisis of the 1970s was caused by a sudden increase in the price of oil due to the decision by the Organization of Petroleum Exporting Countries (OPEC) to limit oil production. The crisis led to a recession in many countries, particularly those heavily dependent on oil imports.

Government policies can also have an impact on the occurrence and severity of recessions. For example, during the Great Depression of the 1930s, the government implemented Keynesian economic policies, including increased government spending and reduced interest rates, to stimulate economic growth and employment.

Consequences of Recessions

Recessions can have significant economic, social, and political consequences.

Economically, recessions can lead to significant job losses, a decrease in consumer spending, and a decrease in economic growth. The Great Depression of the 1930s led to significant job losses and a decrease in consumer spending, which led to a severe downturn in the economy. The 2008 financial crisis also led to significant job losses and a decrease in consumer spending, which led to a global recession.

Socially, recessions can lead to an increase in poverty and inequality. Job losses and a decrease in economic activity can lead to a decrease in income and an increase in poverty. The 2008 financial crisis led to an increase in poverty and inequality in many countries.

Politically, recessions can lead to a shift in power dynamics and changes in economic policy. The Great Depression of the 1930s led to significant changes in economic policy, including increased government spending and regulation of the economy. The 2008 financial crisis also led to changes in economic policy, including increased regulation of the financial sector and fiscal stimulus to support economic growth.

Definition of a recession

A recession is a period of significant economic decline, characterized by a decrease in Gross Domestic Product (GDP), employment, income, and trade. It is typically defined as a decline in economic activity that lasts for at least two consecutive quarters, or six months.

Recessions are cyclical in nature and can be caused by various factors, including supply and demand imbalances, financial crises, global shocks, government policies, and other external factors. Recessions can have significant impacts on individuals, businesses, and society as a whole.

Causes of Recessions

Recessions can be caused by various factors, including supply and demand imbalances, financial crises, global shocks, government policies, and other external factors.

Supply and demand imbalances occur when there is a mismatch between supply and demand in the economy, which can lead to reduced production and employment. For example, if there is an oversupply of goods and services, prices can fall, and businesses may reduce production and lay off workers.

Financial crises can also lead to a recession, as was the case during the Global Financial Crisis of 2008-2009. The collapse of the housing market and the subprime mortgage industry in the United States led to a crisis in the financial sector and a global recession. The crisis was exacerbated by the interconnectedness of the global financial system, which led to a rapid spread of the crisis to other countries.

Global shocks can also lead to a recession. For example, the oil crisis of the 1970s was caused by a sudden increase in the price of oil due to the decision by the Organization of Petroleum Exporting Countries (OPEC) to limit oil production. The crisis led to a recession in many countries, particularly those heavily dependent on oil imports.

Government policies can also have an impact on the occurrence and severity of recessions. For example, during the Great Depression of the 1930s, the government implemented Keynesian economic policies, including increased government spending and reduced interest rates, to stimulate economic growth and employment.

Consequences of Recessions

Recessions can have significant economic, social, and political consequences.

Economically, recessions can lead to significant job losses, a decrease in consumer spending, and a decrease in economic growth. The Great Depression of the 1930s led to significant job losses and a decrease in consumer spending, which led to a severe downturn in the economy. The 2008 financial crisis also led to significant job losses and a decrease in consumer spending, which led to a global recession.

Socially, recessions can lead to an increase in poverty and inequality. Job losses and a decrease in economic activity can lead to a decrease in income and an increase in poverty. The 2008 financial crisis led to an increase in poverty and inequality in many countries.

Politically, recessions can lead to a shift in power dynamics and changes in economic policy. The Great Depression of the 1930s led to significant changes in economic policy, including increased government spending and regulation of the economy. The 2008 financial crisis also led to changes in economic policy, including increased regulation of the financial sector and fiscal stimulus to support economic growth.

Causes and indicators of a recession

A recession is a period of significant economic decline, characterized by a decrease in Gross Domestic Product (GDP), employment, income, and trade. It is typically defined as a decline in economic activity that lasts for at least two consecutive quarters, or six months. There are several causes and indicators of a recession that can help identify when an economy is entering a downturn.

Causes of a Recession

Recessions can be caused by various factors, including supply and demand imbalances, financial crises, global shocks, government policies, and other external factors.

Supply and demand imbalances occur when there is a mismatch between supply and demand in the economy, which can lead to reduced production and employment. For example, if there is an oversupply of goods and services, prices can fall, and businesses may reduce production and lay off workers.

Financial crises can also lead to a recession, as was the case during the Global Financial Crisis of 2008-2009. The collapse of the housing market and the subprime mortgage industry in the United States led to a crisis in the financial sector and a global recession. The crisis was exacerbated by the interconnectedness of the global financial system, which led to a rapid spread of the crisis to other countries.

Global shocks can also lead to a recession. For example, the oil crisis of the 1970s was caused by a sudden increase in the price of oil due to the decision by the Organization of Petroleum Exporting Countries (OPEC) to limit oil production. The crisis led to a recession in many countries, particularly those heavily dependent on oil imports.

Government policies can also have an impact on the occurrence and severity of recessions. For example, during the Great Depression of the 1930s, the government implemented Keynesian economic policies, including increased government spending and reduced interest rates, to stimulate economic growth and employment.

Indicators of a Recession

There are several indicators that can signal the onset of a recession. These indicators include:

1. Gross Domestic Product (GDP) Growth: A decrease in GDP growth, particularly if it lasts for two consecutive quarters, can indicate the onset of a recession.

2. Unemployment Rate: An increase in the unemployment rate can signal a decrease in economic activity and a potential recession. If unemployment remains high for an extended period, it can be an indicator of a prolonged economic downturn.

3. Consumer Spending: A decrease in consumer spending can indicate a slowdown in economic activity and a potential recession. If consumers are not spending, it can lead to a decrease in production and employment.

4. Business Investment: A decrease in business investment can signal a decrease in economic activity and a potential recession. If businesses are not investing in new projects or expanding their operations, it can lead to a decrease in production and employment.

5. Interest Rates: A decrease in interest rates can indicate that the government is trying to stimulate economic activity and avoid a recession. If interest rates remain low for an extended period, it can be an indicator of a prolonged economic downturn.

The impact of a recession on the economy and individuals

A recession is a period of significant economic decline, characterized by a decrease in Gross Domestic Product (GDP), employment, income, and trade. Recessions can have a significant impact on both the economy and individuals.

Impact on the Economy

During a recession, businesses may reduce production and lay off workers, leading to a decrease in employment and income. This can lead to a decrease in consumer spending, which can further reduce economic growth. The decrease in economic activity can also lead to a decrease in trade, as businesses reduce their imports and exports.

Recessions can have significant impacts on various sectors of the economy. For example, during the 2008 financial crisis, the housing market collapsed, leading to a significant decrease in construction activity and employment in the construction sector. The financial sector was also heavily impacted, as banks and other financial institutions faced significant losses and had to be bailed out by the government.

The impact of a recession can be long-lasting, as it can take several years for the economy to recover. For example, the Great Recession of 2008-2009 led to a prolonged period of slow economic growth and high unemployment.

Impact on Individuals

Recessions can have significant impacts on individuals, particularly those who lose their jobs or experience a decrease in income. Job losses can lead to a decrease in income and an increase in poverty. This can have significant impacts on individuals and families, as they may struggle to pay for basic necessities such as housing, food, and healthcare.

Recessions can also lead to a decrease in social mobility, as individuals who lose their jobs may struggle to find new employment opportunities. This can lead to a decrease in upward mobility, as individuals may be unable to obtain the education and skills necessary to advance their careers.

The impact of a recession can be particularly severe for vulnerable populations, such as low-income individuals and minorities. These groups may be more likely to experience job losses and poverty during a recession, exacerbating existing inequalities in society.

Policy Responses

Governments can respond to a recession in several ways, including monetary policy and fiscal policy. Monetary policy involves changing interest rates to stimulate economic growth. During a recession, central banks may decrease interest rates to encourage borrowing and investment.

Fiscal policy involves changes in government spending and taxation to stimulate economic growth. During a recession, governments may increase government spending on infrastructure projects and provide financial assistance to individuals and businesses.

These policies can help to mitigate the impact of a recession on the economy and individuals. For example, during the Great Recession, the U.S. government implemented fiscal stimulus measures, including the American Recovery and Reinvestment Act, to support economic growth and job creation.

Understanding the difference between a recession and a depression

A recession and a depression are both periods of significant economic decline, but they differ in their severity, duration, and impact on individuals and the economy. Understanding the difference between a recession and a depression is important for individuals, businesses, and policymakers to prepare for and mitigate the impact of economic downturns.

Recession

A recession is a period of significant economic decline, characterized by a decrease in Gross Domestic Product (GDP), employment, income, and trade. It is typically defined as a decline in economic activity that lasts for at least two consecutive quarters, or six months.

Recessions can be caused by various factors, including supply and demand imbalances, financial crises, global shocks, government policies, and other external factors. During a recession, businesses may reduce production and lay off workers, leading to a decrease in employment and income. This can lead to a decrease in consumer spending, which can further reduce economic growth.

The impact of a recession can be long-lasting, as it can take several years for the economy to recover. For example, the Great Recession of 2008-2009 led to a prolonged period of slow economic growth and high unemployment.

Depression

A depression is a severe and prolonged economic downturn that is characterized by a significant decrease in economic activity, employment, income, and trade. Depressions are typically more severe and longer-lasting than recessions, lasting for several years or even a decade or more.

Depressions are typically caused by major financial crises or structural imbalances in the economy. During a depression, the economy may experience a significant decrease in GDP, employment, and income. The impact of a depression can be devastating, leading to widespread poverty, unemployment, and social unrest.

One of the most well-known examples of a depression is the Great Depression of the 1930s. The Great Depression was caused by a combination of factors, including the stock market crash of 1929, a decline in consumer spending, and a decrease in international trade. The Depression lasted for several years and had a significant impact on individuals and the economy, leading to widespread poverty and unemployment.

Difference between Recession and Depression

The primary difference between a recession and a depression is the severity and duration of the economic downturn. While both periods are characterized by a decrease in economic activity, a depression is typically more severe and longer-lasting than a recession.

In a recession, economic activity may decrease for several quarters, but it typically recovers within a year or two. In a depression, economic activity may decrease for several years or even a decade or more, with significant impacts on individuals and the economy.

Another key difference between a recession and a depression is the impact on individuals. While both periods can lead to job losses and a decrease in income, a depression can lead to widespread poverty and social unrest. During the Great Depression, for example, many individuals were unable to afford basic necessities such as food, shelter, and healthcare.

A recession and a depression are both periods of significant economic decline, but they differ in their severity, duration, and impact on individuals and the economy. While a recession is typically defined as a decline in economic activity that lasts for at least two consecutive quarters, a depression is a severe and prolonged economic downturn that can last for several years or even a decade or more. Understanding the difference between a recession and a depression is important for individuals, businesses, and policymakers to prepare for and mitigate the impact of economic downturns.

The Economic Cycle

The economic cycle is the pattern of growth and contraction in the economy over time. It is typically characterized by periods of expansion, where the economy grows, and periods of contraction, where the economy slows down or goes into recession. Understanding the economic cycle and the factors that lead to recessions is important for individuals, businesses, and policymakers to prepare for and mitigate the impact of economic downturns.

The Economic Cycle

The economic cycle is often depicted as a series of phases, including expansion, peak, contraction, and trough. During the expansion phase, the economy grows, and economic indicators such as GDP, employment, and consumer spending increase. As the economy continues to grow, it reaches a peak, which is the highest point in the economic cycle. After the peak, the economy enters a contraction phase, where economic indicators begin to decrease. This contraction phase can lead to a recession, which is a prolonged period of economic decline.

Causes of Recessions

There are several factors that can lead to a recession, including:

Overproduction and Overcapacity: Overproduction occurs when businesses produce more goods and services than consumers are willing or able to purchase. This can lead to a decrease in prices, which can cause businesses to reduce production and employment. Overcapacity occurs when businesses have more production capacity than is necessary to meet consumer demand. This can also lead to a decrease in production and employment.

Financial Crises: Financial crises can lead to a recession by disrupting the financial system and reducing the availability of credit. This can make it difficult for businesses to obtain the financing they need to invest and grow.

External Shocks: External shocks, such as natural disasters, geopolitical events, or pandemics, can also lead to a recession by disrupting supply chains, reducing trade, and causing businesses to reduce production and employment.

Changes in Government Policy: Changes in government policy, such as tax increases or spending cuts, can also lead to a recession by reducing consumer spending and business investment.

Asset Bubbles: Asset bubbles occur when the prices of assets such as real estate, stocks, or commodities become inflated beyond their intrinsic value. When the bubble bursts, it can lead to a decrease in asset prices, which can cause businesses to reduce production and employment.

Impact of Recessions

Recessions can have a significant impact on both the economy and individuals. During a recession, businesses may reduce production and lay off workers, leading to a decrease in employment and income. This can lead to a decrease in consumer spending, which can further reduce economic growth. Recessions can also lead to a decrease in trade, as businesses reduce their imports and exports.

Individuals who lose their jobs or experience a decrease in income may struggle to pay for basic necessities, leading to an increase in poverty. Recessions can also lead to a decrease in social mobility, as individuals who lose their jobs may struggle to find new employment opportunities. This can lead to a decrease in upward mobility, as individuals may be unable to obtain the education and skills necessary to advance their careers.

Policy Responses

Governments can respond to a recession in several ways, including monetary policy and fiscal policy. Monetary policy involves changing interest rates to stimulate economic growth. During a recession, central banks may decrease interest rates to encourage borrowing and investment.

Fiscal policy involves changes in government spending and taxation to stimulate economic growth. During a recession, governments may increase government spending on infrastructure projects and provide financial assistance to individuals and businesses.

These policies can help to mitigate the impact of a recession on the economy and individuals. For example, during the Great Recession, the U.S. government implemented fiscal stimulus measures, including the American Recovery and Reinvestment Act, to support economic growth and job creation.

The role of interest rates in the economic cycle

Interest rates play a critical role in the economic cycle, particularly in the context of recessions. Central banks around the world use interest rates as a tool to manage economic growth, with the goal of keeping inflation in check and ensuring economic stability. Understanding the role of interest rates in the economic cycle and their relationship to recessions is essential for individuals, businesses, and policymakers.

Interest Rates and the Economic Cycle

Interest rates are the cost of borrowing money, and they affect the behavior of consumers and businesses. Lower interest rates encourage borrowing and spending, while higher interest rates discourage borrowing and spending. Central banks use interest rates as a tool to manage economic growth by adjusting the cost of borrowing money.

During an economic expansion, central banks may increase interest rates to slow down borrowing and spending, which helps to control inflation. This is because as economic growth accelerates, demand for goods and services increases, which can lead to higher prices. By raising interest rates, central banks make it more expensive to borrow money, which can reduce demand and help to keep inflation in check.

During an economic contraction or recession, central banks may decrease interest rates to stimulate borrowing and spending, which can help to boost economic growth. Lower interest rates make it cheaper to borrow money, which can encourage businesses to invest in new projects and hire more workers. This can help to increase consumer spending and overall economic activity, leading to a recovery in the economy.

The Role of Interest Rates in Recessions

Interest rates play a particularly important role in recessions. During a recession, central banks may lower interest rates in an effort to stimulate economic growth. By making it cheaper to borrow money, businesses may be more willing to invest in new projects and hire more workers, which can help to increase economic activity.

Lower interest rates can also make it more affordable for individuals to borrow money, which can increase consumer spending. This can help to boost demand for goods and services, which can lead to an increase in production and employment.

However, there are limitations to the effectiveness of interest rate policy during a recession. When interest rates are already low, there may be limited room for further reductions, which can limit the impact of monetary policy on the economy. In these situations, governments may need to use fiscal policy, such as increased government spending or tax cuts, to stimulate economic growth.

Understanding the role of interest rates in the economic cycle is essential for individuals, businesses, and policymakers to prepare for and mitigate the impact of economic downturns.

The business cycle and recessions

The business cycle is the pattern of growth and contraction in the economy over time. It is characterized by periods of expansion, where the economy grows, and periods of contraction, where the economy slows down or goes into recession. Understanding the business cycle and its relationship to recessions is essential for businesses to prepare for and mitigate the impact of economic downturns.

The Business Cycle

The business cycle is often depicted as a series of phases, including expansion, peak, contraction, and trough. During the expansion phase, the economy grows, and economic indicators such as GDP, employment, and consumer spending increase. As the economy continues to grow, it reaches a peak, which is the highest point in the economic cycle. After the peak, the economy enters a contraction phase, where economic indicators begin to decrease. This contraction phase can lead to a recession, which is a prolonged period of economic decline.

The business cycle is driven by various factors, including changes in consumer behavior, business investment, government policy, and external shocks. For example, during an expansion phase, consumer spending typically increases, leading to higher demand for goods and services. This increase in demand leads to an increase in business investment, which further stimulates economic growth.

Impact of Recessions on Businesses

Recessions can have a significant impact on businesses. During a recession, businesses may reduce production and lay off workers, leading to a decrease in employment and income. This can lead to a decrease in consumer spending, which can further reduce economic growth. Recessions can also lead to a decrease in trade, as businesses reduce their imports and exports.

Businesses that are heavily reliant on credit may find it more challenging to obtain financing during a recession, as banks become more risk-averse. This can make it difficult for businesses to invest in new projects or make necessary upgrades to their operations.

However, recessions can also present opportunities for businesses that are well-prepared. For example, businesses that have a strong balance sheet and a diversified customer base may be better able to weather economic downturns. Additionally, businesses that can adapt to changes in consumer behavior or market conditions may be able to take advantage of new opportunities.

Indicators of a Recession

A recession is a period of significant economic decline that is characterized by a reduction in economic activity, including a decline in GDP, employment, and consumer spending. Recognizing the signs of an impending recession is essential for individuals, businesses, and policymakers to prepare for and mitigate the impact of economic downturns.

There are several key indicators that economists and policymakers use to determine whether an economy is in a recession. These indicators can help to provide insight into the state of the economy and identify potential areas of weakness.

Gross Domestic Product (GDP)

GDP is one of the most widely used indicators of economic activity. It measures the total value of goods and services produced within a country's borders during a specific period, typically a quarter or a year. During a recession, GDP will typically decrease or grow at a slower rate than during an economic expansion.

A decline in GDP can be a sign that the economy is slowing down, as businesses produce fewer goods and services and consumers spend less. However, it is worth noting that a decline in GDP can also be caused by factors such as a natural disaster or a decline in exports.

Employment

Employment is another critical indicator of economic activity. During a recession, employment typically declines as businesses reduce their production and lay off workers. High unemployment rates can also lead to a decrease in consumer spending, which can further exacerbate economic decline.

Unemployment rates are typically calculated by dividing the number of unemployed individuals by the total labor force. During a recession, unemployment rates may increase significantly, which can be a sign that the economy is in trouble.

Consumer Spending

Consumer spending is a significant driver of economic activity, and changes in consumer behavior can be an important indicator of economic health. During a recession, consumers may reduce their spending as they become more cautious about their financial future. This can lead to a decrease in demand for goods and services, which can further contribute to economic decline.

Consumer spending can be measured in several ways, including retail sales, consumer confidence, and personal income. Retail sales data can provide insight into how much consumers are spending on goods and services, while consumer confidence surveys can provide insight into how confident consumers feel about the economy. Personal income data can provide insight into how much income individuals have available to spend.

Business Investment

Business investment is another critical indicator of economic health. During a recession, businesses may reduce their investment in new projects or upgrades to their operations as they become more cautious about the future. This can lead to a decrease in economic activity and employment.

Business investment can be measured in several ways, including capital expenditures, business confidence surveys, and stock prices. Capital expenditures data can provide insight into how much businesses are investing in new projects or upgrades, while business confidence surveys can provide insight into how confident businesses feel about the economy. Stock prices can also be an indicator of business investment, as companies that are expected to perform well may see their stock prices increase.

Interest Rates

Interest rates can also be an indicator of economic health, particularly in the context of recessions. During a recession, central banks may lower interest rates to stimulate borrowing and spending, which can help to boost economic growth. Lower interest rates can make it cheaper for businesses to borrow money, which can encourage businesses to invest in new projects and hire more workers. This can help to increase consumer spending and overall economic activity, leading to a recovery in the economy.

By monitoring these indicators, individuals and businesses can make informed decisions about their financial future, while policymakers can take appropriate action to stimulate

Leading economic indicators

Leading economic indicators are statistics or measures that provide insight into the direction of the economy, often before changes in economic activity are reflected in other indicators. Understanding leading economic indicators is important for individuals, businesses, and policymakers, as they can help to anticipate changes in the economy and identify potential areas of weakness.

There are several leading economic indicators that are closely monitored by economists and policymakers, including:

Stock Market Indexes

Stock market indexes, such as the S&P 500 or the Dow Jones Industrial Average, can be a leading indicator of economic activity. The stock market is often viewed as a reflection of investor confidence in the economy. During a recession, stock market indexes will typically decline as investors become more cautious about the future.

Building Permits

Building permits are a measure of the number of new construction projects that have been approved by local authorities. An increase in building permits can be a leading indicator of economic growth, as it indicates that businesses and individuals are investing in new construction projects. Conversely, a decrease in building permits can be a sign that the economy is slowing down.

Purchasing Managers Index (PMI)

The Purchasing Managers Index (PMI) is a survey of purchasing managers in the manufacturing sector. The PMI provides insight into the health of the manufacturing sector and can be a leading indicator of economic activity. During a recession, the PMI will typically decline as manufacturing activity slows down.

Consumer Confidence Index (CCI)

The Consumer Confidence Index (CCI) is a survey of consumers that measures their confidence in the economy. An increase in the CCI can be a sign of economic growth, as consumers are more likely to spend money when they feel confident about the future. Conversely, a decrease in the CCI can be a sign that consumers are becoming more cautious about their financial future.

Initial Jobless Claims

Initial jobless claims are a measure of the number of individuals who have filed for unemployment benefits for the first time. A decrease in initial jobless claims can be a sign of economic growth, as it indicates that fewer individuals are losing their jobs. Conversely, an increase in initial jobless claims can be a sign that the economy is slowing down and that more individuals are losing their jobs.

Yield Curve

The yield curve is a measure of the difference in interest rates between short-term and long-term government bonds. During a recession, the yield curve will typically flatten or invert, meaning that long-term interest rates are lower than short-term interest rates. This is often viewed as a sign of economic weakness, as investors become more cautious about the future.

By monitoring these indicators, individuals and businesses can make informed decisions about their financial future, while policymakers can take appropriate action to stimulate economic growth and mitigate the impact of economic downturns.

Lagging economic indicators

Lagging economic indicators are economic indicators that change after the economy has already begun to change. These indicators are used to confirm changes in economic activity that have already occurred. Lagging indicators can be important in understanding the full extent of an economic downturn, but they are not useful for predicting future economic changes.

Understanding lagging economic indicators is important for individuals, businesses, and policymakers, as they can help to provide a more complete picture of the state of the economy.

Some of the lagging economic indicators that are closely monitored by economists and policymakers include:

Unemployment Rate

The unemployment rate is a measure of the percentage of the labor force that is unemployed but actively seeking employment. The unemployment rate is a lagging indicator because it changes after the economy has already begun to change. During a recession, the unemployment rate will typically increase as businesses reduce their production and lay off workers.

Corporate Profits

Corporate profits are a measure of the profitability of businesses. Changes in corporate profits are a lagging indicator of economic activity because they often reflect changes in economic activity that have already occurred. During a recession, corporate profits will typically decline as businesses reduce their production and sales.

Gross Domestic Product (GDP)

Gross Domestic Product (GDP) is a measure of the total value of goods and services produced within a country's borders during a specific period. Changes in GDP are a lagging indicator of economic activity because they often reflect changes that have already occurred. During a recession, GDP will typically decline as economic activity slows down.

Consumer Price Index (CPI)

The Consumer Price Index (CPI) is a measure of the average price of a basket of goods and services purchased by households. Changes in the CPI are a lagging indicator of economic activity because they often reflect changes in economic activity that have already occurred. During a recession, the CPI will typically decline as businesses reduce their production and sales, leading to a decrease in demand and lower prices.

Personal Income

Personal income is a measure of the income received by individuals from all sources. Changes in personal income are a lagging indicator of economic activity because they often reflect changes in economic activity that have already occurred. During a recession, personal income will typically decline as businesses reduce their production and lay off workers, leading to a decrease in employment and income.

Lagging economic indicators are an important tool for individuals, businesses, and policymakers to understand the full extent of an economic downturn. Indicators such as the unemployment rate, corporate profits, GDP, CPI, and personal income can provide valuable insight into the direction of the economy and identify potential areas of weakness. By monitoring these indicators, individuals and businesses can make informed decisions about their financial future, while policymakers can take appropriate action to mitigate the impact of economic downturns. However, it is important to note that lagging indicators are not useful for predicting future economic changes and should be used in conjunction with leading indicators to get a complete picture of the state of the economy.

Coincident economic indicators

Coincident economic indicators are statistics or measures that reflect the current state of the economy. They change simultaneously with changes in the economy and provide a real-time snapshot of economic activity. Understanding coincident economic indicators is important for individuals, businesses, and policymakers to monitor the state of the economy and make informed decisions.

There are several coincident economic indicators that are closely monitored by economists and policymakers, including:

Industrial Production

Industrial production is a measure of the output of the manufacturing, mining, and utilities sectors. Industrial production is a coincident indicator because it changes simultaneously with changes in economic activity. During a recession, industrial production will typically decline as businesses reduce their production and sales.

Nonfarm Payrolls

Nonfarm payrolls are a measure of the number of individuals employed in the economy, excluding farm workers and certain other types of workers. Nonfarm payrolls are a coincident indicator because they change simultaneously with changes in economic activity. During a recession, nonfarm payrolls will typically decline as businesses reduce their production and lay off workers.

Retail Sales

Retail sales are a measure of the total amount of goods sold by retailers. Retail sales are a coincident indicator because they change simultaneously with changes in economic activity. During a recession, retail sales will typically decline as consumers reduce their spending and become more cautious about their financial future.

Personal Income and Spending

Personal income and spending are measures of the income received by individuals and the amount spent on goods and services. Personal income and spending are coincident indicators because they change simultaneously with changes in economic activity. During a recession, personal income and spending will typically decline as businesses reduce their production and lay off workers, leading to a decrease in employment and income.

Business Sales

Business sales are a measure of the sales made by businesses. Business sales are a coincident indicator because they change simultaneously with changes in economic activity. During a recession, business sales will typically decline as businesses reduce their production and sales.

Coincident economic indicators are important tools for individuals, businesses, and policymakers to monitor the state of the economy and make informed decisions. Indicators such as industrial production, nonfarm payrolls, retail sales, personal income and spending, and business sales can provide valuable insight into the current state of the economy and identify potential areas of weakness. By monitoring these indicators, individuals and businesses can make informed decisions about their financial future, while policymakers can take appropriate action to stimulate economic growth and mitigate the impact of economic downturns.

Types of Recessions

Recessions are periods of significant economic decline characterized by a reduction in economic activity, including a decline in GDP, employment, and consumer spending. While all recessions share some common characteristics, there are different types of recessions that can occur. Understanding the different types of recessions is essential for individuals, businesses, and policymakers to prepare for and mitigate the impact of economic downturns.

Cyclical Recession

A cyclical recession is the most common type of recession and is caused by a downturn in the business cycle. During the business cycle, there are periods of expansion and contraction. When the economy experiences a contraction, it is referred to as a cyclical recession. Cyclical recessions are often caused by a decline in consumer spending, which leads to a decrease in demand for goods and services. This can lead to a decrease in production and employment, which further exacerbates the economic decline.

Structural Recession

A structural recession is caused by changes in the economy's structure, such as changes in technology, industry consolidation, or shifts in global trade. These changes can lead to the decline of certain industries or regions and create economic imbalances. Structural recessions can be difficult to recover from because they require significant changes in the economy's structure, such as investment in new industries or retraining workers.

Seasonal Recession

A seasonal recession is caused by changes in the demand for certain goods and services due to seasonal factors. For example, the tourism industry may experience a recession during the off-season when demand for travel and tourism-related services is low. Seasonal recessions can be mitigated by businesses that anticipate the seasonal changes and adjust their operations accordingly.

Secular Stagnation

Secular stagnation is a long-term economic decline that is caused by a combination of demographic and economic factors. These factors can include an aging population, declining productivity, and weak investment. Secular stagnation can lead to persistently low economic growth, high unemployment, and increasing inequality.

Financial Crisis

A financial crisis is a severe economic downturn caused by a collapse of the financial system or significant disruption in financial markets. Financial crises can be caused by factors such as excessive lending, speculative bubbles, or the failure of financial institutions. Financial crises can have a significant impact on the economy and can lead to a deep and prolonged recession.

Understanding the different types of recessions is essential for individuals, businesses, and policymakers to prepare for and mitigate the impact of economic downturns. Cyclical, structural, seasonal, secular stagnation, and financial crises are all different types of recessions that can occur. By recognizing the specific characteristics and causes of each type of recession, individuals and businesses can make informed decisions about their financial future, while policymakers can take appropriate action to stimulate economic growth and mitigate the impact of economic downturns.

Demand-side recessions

Demand-side recessions are a type of economic downturn that occurs due to a decrease in demand for goods and services in the economy. These recessions are often caused by a decline in consumer spending or a decrease in business investment, which can lead to a reduction in production and employment.

Demand-side recessions can have a significant impact on the economy, and understanding their causes and characteristics is essential for individuals, businesses, and policymakers.

Causes of Demand-Side Recessions

Several factors can cause a demand-side recession, including:

Tight Monetary Policy

Tight monetary policy, such as increasing interest rates, can decrease the amount of money that individuals and businesses have to spend. This can lead to a decrease in consumer spending and business investment, which can cause a demand-side recession.

Asset Bubble Burst

An asset bubble occurs when the price of a particular asset, such as real estate or stocks, rises to an unsustainable level. When the bubble bursts, individuals and businesses who have invested in the asset may lose money, leading to a decrease in consumer spending and business investment.

External Shocks

External shocks, such as a global pandemic or a significant natural disaster, can lead to a decrease in demand for goods and services. These shocks can cause consumers to become more cautious about their spending, leading to a reduction in consumer spending and a demand-side recession.

Characteristics of Demand-Side Recessions

Demand-side recessions are often characterized by:

Decline in Consumer Spending

A decline in consumer spending is a hallmark of a demand-side recession. When consumers become more cautious about their spending, it can lead to a reduction in demand for goods and services, which can cause a recession.

Decrease in Business Investment

A decrease in business investment is another characteristic of a demand-side recession. When businesses become more cautious about their investment, they may reduce production and employment, leading to a decrease in economic activity.

Increase in Unemployment

Demand-side recessions often lead to an increase in unemployment as businesses reduce their production and lay off workers. This can lead to a decrease in consumer spending and a further decline in economic activity.

Demand-side recessions are a type of economic downturn that occurs due to a decrease in demand for goods and services in the economy. These recessions are often caused by factors such as tight monetary policy, asset bubble bursts, or external shocks. Understanding the causes and characteristics of demand-side recessions is essential for individuals, businesses, and policymakers to prepare for and mitigate the impact of economic downturns. By recognizing the specific characteristics of demand-side recessions, individuals and businesses can make informed decisions about their financial future, while policymakers can take appropriate action to stimulate economic growth and mitigate the impact of economic downturns.

Supply-side recessions

Supply-side recessions are a type of economic downturn that occurs due to a decrease in the supply of goods and services in the economy. These recessions are often caused by factors such as a decrease in production capacity, a shortage of raw materials, or disruptions to supply chains.

Understanding the causes and characteristics of supply-side recessions is essential for individuals, businesses, and policymakers to prepare for and mitigate the impact of economic downturns.

Causes of Supply-Side Recessions

Several factors can cause a supply-side recession, including:

Reduction in Production Capacity

A reduction in production capacity can occur due to factors such as factory closures, a decrease in workforce, or damage to production facilities. This can lead to a decrease in the supply of goods and services, which can cause a supply-side recession.

Shortage of Raw Materials

A shortage of raw materials, such as oil or steel, can lead to a decrease in production capacity and a reduction in the supply of goods and services. This can cause a supply-side recession.

Disruptions to Supply Chains

Disruptions to supply chains can occur due to factors such as natural disasters, political instability, or global pandemics. These disruptions can lead to a decrease in the supply of goods and services, which can cause a supply-side recession.

Characteristics of Supply-Side Recessions

Supply-side recessions are often characterized by:

Increase in Prices

A decrease in the supply of goods and services can lead to an increase in prices as consumers compete for limited resources. This can lead to inflation and a decrease in consumer spending.

Decrease in Output

A supply-side recession can lead to a decrease in output as businesses reduce their production capacity or are unable to access necessary raw materials. This can lead to a decrease in employment and economic activity.

Increase in Unemployment

A supply-side recession can lead to an increase in unemployment as businesses reduce their production capacity and lay off workers. This can lead to a decrease in consumer spending and a further decline in economic activity.

Supply-side recessions are a type of economic downturn that occurs due to a decrease in the supply of goods and services in the economy. These recessions are often caused by factors such as a reduction in production capacity, a shortage of raw materials, or disruptions to supply chains. Understanding the causes and characteristics of supply-side recessions is essential for individuals, businesses, and policymakers to prepare for and mitigate the impact of economic downturns. By recognizing the specific characteristics of supply-side recessions, individuals and businesses can make informed decisions about their financial future, while policymakers can take appropriate action to stimulate economic growth and mitigate the impact of economic downturns.

Financial crises

Financial crises are periods of significant economic decline characterized by disruptions in the financial system or significant problems in financial markets. These crises can have a severe impact on the economy, leading to a decrease in economic activity, a decline in GDP, and high levels of unemployment.

Understanding the causes and consequences of financial crises is essential for individuals, businesses, and policymakers to prepare for and mitigate the impact of economic downturns.

Causes of Financial Crises

Several factors can cause financial crises, including:

Speculative Bubbles

A speculative bubble occurs when the price of an asset rises to an unsustainable level due to speculation and investor hype. When the bubble bursts, individuals and businesses who have invested in the asset may lose money, leading to a decline in the financial system.

Excessive Lending

Excessive lending by financial institutions can lead to a buildup of debt and create a risky financial system. If borrowers default on their loans, it can cause a chain reaction of financial losses, leading to a financial crisis.

Systemic Risk

Systemic risk refers to the risk that a failure in one part of the financial system can lead to a broader economic crisis. For example, if a major financial institution were to fail, it could cause a chain reaction of financial losses that could lead to a financial crisis.

Consequences of Financial Crises

Financial crises can have severe consequences for the economy, including:

Economic Downturn

Financial crises often lead to a significant economic downturn, characterized by a decline in GDP, employment, and consumer spending.

Bank Failures

Financial crises can lead to bank failures as financial institutions become insolvent and are unable to repay their debts.

Stock Market Decline

Financial crises often lead to a decline in stock markets as investors become more cautious and sell off their stocks.

High Levels of Unemployment

Financial crises often lead to high levels of unemployment as businesses reduce their production and lay off workers.

Financial crises are periods of significant economic decline characterized by disruptions in the financial system or significant problems in financial markets. These crises can have severe consequences for the economy, leading to a decline in GDP, employment, and consumer spending. Understanding the causes and consequences of financial crises is essential for individuals, businesses, and policymakers to prepare for and mitigate the impact of economic downturns. By recognizing the specific characteristics of financial crises, individuals and businesses can make informed decisions about their financial future, while policymakers can take appropriate action to stimulate economic growth and mitigate the impact of economic downturns.

The Great Recession of 2008

The Great Recession of 2008 was a severe global economic downturn that began in the United States and quickly spread to other countries. The recession was characterized by a significant decline in economic activity, a sharp increase in unemployment, and a widespread banking and financial crisis.

Causes of the Great Recession

The Great Recession was caused by a combination of factors, including:

Housing Bubble

The housing bubble, which began in the early 2000s, was a significant contributor to the Great Recession. Banks and other financial institutions were offering subprime mortgages to individuals who did not have the financial means to repay them. As the housing market continued to grow, many individuals took out mortgages they could not afford, leading to a housing bubble.

Financial Deregulation

Financial deregulation in the 1990s and early 2000s allowed financial institutions to engage in risky lending practices, such as offering subprime mortgages and securities backed by these mortgages.

Excessive Leverage

Many financial institutions became highly leveraged, meaning they borrowed large sums of money to finance their investments. This left these institutions vulnerable to financial shocks and increased the risk of financial collapse.

Consequences of the Great Recession

The Great Recession had severe consequences for the global economy, including:

High Unemployment

The Great Recession led to a sharp increase in unemployment rates as businesses reduced their production and laid off workers.

Financial Crisis

The Great Recession was characterized by a widespread banking and financial crisis, as many financial institutions became insolvent and were unable to repay their debts.

Decline in Economic Activity

The Great Recession led to a significant decline in economic activity, including a decline in GDP and a decrease in consumer spending.

Government Bailouts

To prevent a complete collapse of the financial system, governments around the world had to provide massive bailouts to financial institutions.

Policy Responses to the Great Recession

Governments around the world implemented various policy responses to mitigate the impact of the Great Recession, including:

Fiscal Stimulus

Governments implemented fiscal stimulus programs, including increased government spending and tax cuts, to stimulate economic growth and reduce unemployment.

Monetary Policy

Central banks around the world implemented monetary policy measures, such as lowering interest rates and implementing quantitative easing, to stimulate lending and boost economic growth.

Financial Regulation

Governments implemented new financial regulations, such as the Dodd-Frank Act in the United States, to prevent similar financial crises from occurring in the future.

The Great Recession of 2008 was a severe global economic downturn that had significant consequences for the global economy. The housing bubble, financial deregulation, and excessive leverage were among the primary causes of the recession. Governments implemented various policy responses to mitigate the impact of the recession, including fiscal stimulus, monetary policy, and financial regulation. The Great Recession serves as a reminder of the importance of responsible financial practices and effective policy responses to mitigate the impact of economic downturns.

Causes of the Great Recession

The Great Recession of 2008 was a severe economic downturn that had a significant impact on the global economy. The recession was characterized by a sharp decline in economic activity, a spike in unemployment, and a widespread banking and financial crisis. Several factors contributed to the Great Recession, including:

Housing Bubble

One of the primary causes of the Great Recession was the housing bubble, which began in the early 2000s. Lenders offered subprime mortgages to individuals with poor credit histories, which allowed people who could not afford a mortgage to purchase homes. These subprime mortgages were then bundled into complex financial products and sold to investors around the world. As the housing market continued to grow, the demand for these mortgages increased, and lenders became increasingly reckless in their lending practices.

Financial Deregulation

Financial deregulation in the 1990s and early 2000s allowed financial institutions to engage in risky lending practices, such as offering subprime mortgages and securities backed by these mortgages. The repeal of the Glass-Steagall Act in 1999 also allowed commercial banks to engage in investment banking activities, leading to an increase in risky investments.

Excessive Leverage

Many financial institutions became highly leveraged, meaning they borrowed large sums of money to finance their investments. This left these institutions vulnerable to financial shocks and increased the risk of financial collapse.

Credit Default Swaps

Credit default swaps (CDS) played a significant role in the Great Recession. CDS are financial instruments that provide insurance against default on bonds and other investments. Financial institutions were using CDS to hedge against the risk of default on subprime mortgages. However, these CDS were not regulated, and many institutions did not have the financial resources to cover the losses.

Systemic Risk

Systemic risk refers to the risk that a failure in one part of the financial system can lead to a broader economic crisis. The interconnectedness of the financial system meant that the failure of one institution could have a domino effect on the entire system. The collapse of Lehman Brothers in 2008 triggered a widespread banking and financial crisis, as many financial institutions became insolvent and were unable to repay their debts.

Global Imbalances

Global imbalances, such as large trade surpluses and deficits between countries, played a role in the Great Recession. The US had been running a large trade deficit with China, and China was investing heavily in US government debt. This created a cycle of debt and consumption, leading to an unsustainable housing bubble and the eventual collapse of the financial system.

The impact of the Great Recession

The Great Recession of 2008 was a severe global economic downturn that had a significant impact on the global economy. The recession was characterized by a sharp decline in economic activity, a spike in unemployment, and a widespread banking and financial crisis. The impact of the Great Recession was felt in many different areas of the economy and society, including:

Job Losses

The Great Recession led to a sharp increase in unemployment rates, with many businesses reducing their production and laying off workers. The unemployment rate in the US peaked at 10% in October 2009, and other countries experienced similarly high rates of unemployment.

Decline in Economic Activity

The Great Recession led to a significant decline in economic activity, including a decline in GDP and a decrease in consumer spending. The US economy contracted by 4.3% in the fourth quarter of 2008, and the global economy as a whole contracted by 0.5% in 2009.

Banking and Financial Crisis

The Great Recession was characterized by a widespread banking and financial crisis, as many financial institutions became insolvent and were unable to repay their debts. The US government had to provide massive bailouts to financial institutions, including AIG, Citigroup, and Bank of America, to prevent a complete collapse of the financial system.

Housing Crisis

The housing bubble and subsequent collapse were at the heart of the Great Recession. Many individuals who had taken out subprime mortgages found themselves unable to repay their debts, leading to a wave of foreclosures and a collapse in the housing market.

Government Debt

Governments around the world had to provide massive fiscal stimulus programs to mitigate the impact of the Great Recession, leading to a significant increase in government debt. The debt-to-GDP ratio increased in many countries, including the US, UK, and Japan.

Income Inequality

The Great Recession had a significant impact on income inequality, with many low-income individuals and families experiencing the worst effects of the recession. The recession led to a significant increase in poverty rates, particularly among minorities and children.

The Great Recession of 2008 had a significant impact on the global economy, leading to a decline in economic activity, a spike in unemployment, and a widespread banking and financial crisis. The recession also had a significant impact on society, leading to a housing crisis, government debt, and income inequality. Governments around the world implemented various policy responses to mitigate the impact of the recession, including fiscal stimulus, monetary policy, and financial regulation. While the global economy has largely recovered from the Great Recession, the lessons learned from this period will continue to shape economic policy for years to come.

Lessons learned from the Great Recession

The Great Recession of 2008 was a severe global economic downturn that had a significant impact on the global economy. The recession was characterized by a sharp decline in economic activity, a spike in unemployment, and a widespread banking and financial crisis. The lessons learned from the Great Recession have had a significant impact on economic policy and practices in the years since.

Financial Regulation

One of the most significant lessons learned from the Great Recession was the need for stronger financial regulation. The deregulation of the financial sector in the 1990s and early 2000s allowed financial institutions to engage in risky lending practices, leading to the housing bubble and subsequent collapse. The Dodd-Frank Act, passed in the US in 2010, implemented new financial regulations, including stricter capital requirements for banks and greater oversight of derivatives trading.

Monetary Policy

Central banks around the world implemented monetary policy measures, such as lowering interest rates and implementing quantitative easing, to stimulate lending and boost economic growth during the Great Recession. The effectiveness of these measures has been debated, but they remain an important tool for policymakers to mitigate the impact of economic downturns.

Fiscal Stimulus

Governments around the world implemented fiscal stimulus programs, including increased government spending and tax cuts, to stimulate economic growth and reduce unemployment during the Great Recession. However, the long-term impact of these measures on government debt and deficits remains a topic of debate.

Risk Management

The Great Recession highlighted the importance of risk management in the financial sector. Financial institutions must take steps to manage their risk exposure, including implementing effective risk management practices and diversifying their portfolios.

Income Inequality

The Great Recession had a significant impact on income inequality, with many low-income individuals and families experiencing the worst effects of the recession. This has led to a renewed focus on income inequality in economic policy, with a growing recognition that a strong economy must also be an inclusive one.

Global Cooperation

The Great Recession demonstrated the need for global cooperation in addressing economic challenges. Governments and central banks around the world worked together to implement policy responses to the recession, and the importance of international cooperation in addressing economic challenges has only become more apparent in the years since.

The Great Recession of 2008 had a significant impact on the global economy and led to a rethinking of economic policy and practices. The lessons learned from the recession have had a lasting impact on economic policy, including the need for stronger financial regulation, the importance of risk management, and the role of global cooperation in addressing economic challenges. By recognizing the lessons learned from the Great Recession, policymakers and individuals can better prepare for and mitigate the impact of future economic downturns.

The Impact of Recessions on Employment

Recessions have a significant impact on employment, with the job market often being one of the hardest-hit areas during an economic downturn. The impact of recessions on employment is felt in many different ways, including job losses, reduced working hours, and increased underemployment. Below we will explore the impact of recessions on employment and the factors that contribute to this impact.

Job Losses

Job losses are one of the most significant impacts of recessions on employment. During a recession, many businesses reduce their production, leading to layoffs and job losses. In the US, the unemployment rate increased from 4.7% in December 2007 to 10% in October 2009 during the Great Recession. Many other countries also experienced similarly high rates of unemployment during the same period.

Reduced Working Hours

During a recession, many businesses reduce their working hours to cut costs. This has a significant impact on the income of workers who rely on full-time work to make ends meet. Reduced working hours also lead to a decline in consumer spending, which can further exacerbate the impact of the recession.

Underemployment

Underemployment is another impact of recessions on employment. During a recession, many workers who lose their full-time jobs may take on part-time or low-wage jobs to make ends meet. This leads to an increase in underemployment, where workers are employed but not in a job that matches their qualifications or experience.

Long-Term Unemployment

Long-term unemployment is another impact of recessions on employment. During a recession, many workers who lose their jobs may be unable to find new employment for an extended period. This can have long-lasting effects on their earnings and job prospects, even after the economy has recovered.

Industry-Specific Impacts

The impact of recessions on employment varies by industry. Industries that are heavily dependent on consumer spending, such as retail and hospitality, are often hit hardest during a recession. In contrast, industries that are less dependent on consumer spending, such as healthcare and education, may be less affected.

Recessions have a significant impact on employment, with job losses, reduced working hours, underemployment, long-term unemployment, and industry-specific impacts being common outcomes. Governments and policymakers have a significant role to play in mitigating the impact of recessions on employment, including implementing fiscal stimulus programs, monetary policy measures, and job training programs. By recognizing the impact of recessions on employment, individuals and policymakers can take steps to mitigate the impact of economic downturns and support workers during difficult times.

Unemployment rates during recessions

Unemployment rates are one of the most significant indicators of the impact of recessions on the economy. During a recession, job losses are common, and the unemployment rate often increases as a result. Below we will explore the impact of recessions on unemployment rates and the factors that contribute to this impact.

Job Losses

Job losses are one of the most significant impacts of recessions on unemployment rates. During a recession, many businesses reduce their production and lay off workers, leading to an increase in the number of people who are unemployed. The Great Recession of 2008 resulted in a significant increase in unemployment rates, with the US unemployment rate increasing from 4.7% in December 2007 to 10% in October 2009.

Reduced Working Hours

During a recession, many businesses reduce their working hours to cut costs. This has a significant impact on the unemployment rate, as workers who have their hours reduced may be counted as employed but are still unable to make ends meet. In addition, reduced working hours can lead to a decline in consumer spending, which can further exacerbate the impact of the recession.

Underemployment

Underemployment is another factor that contributes to unemployment rates during recessions. During a recession, many workers who lose their full-time jobs may take on part-time or low-wage jobs to make ends meet. While they may be counted as employed, they are still not working in a job that matches their qualifications or experience. This can have a significant impact on their earnings and job prospects.

Long-Term Unemployment

Long-term unemployment is another factor that contributes to unemployment rates during recessions. During a recession, many workers who lose their jobs may be unable to find new employment for an extended period. This can have long-lasting effects on their earnings and job prospects, even after the economy has recovered. The longer someone is unemployed, the more challenging it becomes to find a new job.

Industry-Specific Impacts

The impact of recessions on unemployment rates varies by industry. Industries that are heavily dependent on consumer spending, such as retail and hospitality, are often hit hardest during a recession. In contrast, industries that are less dependent on consumer spending, such as healthcare and education, may be less affected. This can lead to disparities in unemployment rates across different industries.

Unemployment rates are one of the most significant indicators of the impact of recessions on the economy. During a recession, job losses, reduced working hours, underemployment, long-term unemployment, and industry-specific impacts can all contribute to an increase in the unemployment rate. Governments and policymakers have a significant role to play in mitigating the impact of recessions on unemployment rates, including implementing fiscal stimulus programs, monetary policy measures, and job training programs. By recognizing the impact of recessions on unemployment rates, individuals and policymakers can take steps to mitigate the impact of economic downturns and support workers during difficult times.

The impact of recessions on different industries

Recessions have a significant impact on the economy, and different industries are affected in different ways. During a recession, some industries may experience significant declines in demand, while others may be more resilient. Below we will explore the impact of recessions on different industries and the factors that contribute to this impact.

Retail

The retail industry is one of the most impacted industries during a recession. Consumer spending tends to decline during an economic downturn, and retailers may struggle to maintain their sales volume. Retailers may be forced to cut prices, reduce staff, or even close their stores in some cases. The Great Recession of 2008 saw a significant decline in the retail industry, with many retailers going bankrupt or closing stores.

Hospitality and Tourism

The hospitality and tourism industry is another industry that is heavily impacted during a recession. During an economic downturn, consumers may reduce their spending on travel and tourism, leading to a decline in demand for hotels, restaurants, and other hospitality businesses. This can result in layoffs, reduced hours, and in some cases, business closures.

Construction

The construction industry is also significantly impacted during a recession. As demand for new homes and commercial buildings declines, construction companies may struggle to find work. This can lead to layoffs and reduced hours for construction workers, and can also have a ripple effect on other industries, such as building materials and equipment suppliers.

Manufacturing

The manufacturing industry is another industry that can be heavily impacted by recessions. As demand for goods declines, manufacturing companies may be forced to reduce their production, leading to layoffs and reduced hours for workers. In addition, many manufacturing companies rely on credit to finance their operations, and a recession can lead to a credit crunch that makes it more challenging for companies to obtain the funding they need to operate.

Healthcare

The healthcare industry is generally considered to be more resilient during a recession than other industries. This is because healthcare services are typically essential and have a relatively stable demand, regardless of the state of the economy. However, even the healthcare industry is not immune to the impact of recessions, and some healthcare providers may experience reduced demand or financial difficulties during an economic downturn.

Recessions have a significant impact on the economy, and different industries are affected in different ways. The retail industry, hospitality and tourism industry, construction industry, manufacturing industry, and healthcare industry are all impacted by recessions, with some industries being more resilient than others.

Governments and policymakers have a significant role to play in mitigating the impact of recessions on different industries, including implementing fiscal stimulus programs, monetary policy measures, and industry-specific support programs. By recognizing the impact of recessions on different industries, individuals and policymakers can take steps to support affected industries and minimize the impact of economic downturns.

Strategies for managing job loss during a recession

Recessions can be a challenging time for individuals who experience job loss. Losing a job can be a stressful and emotional experience, but there are strategies that individuals can use to manage job loss during a recession. Below we will explore strategies for managing job loss during a recession.

Assess Your Finances

The first step in managing job loss during a recession is to assess your finances. This includes creating a budget, identifying areas where you can cut expenses, and exploring opportunities for additional income. It may also be helpful to review your savings and investment accounts to determine how long you can sustain yourself financially.

Apply for Unemployment Benefits

Applying for unemployment benefits is another important step in managing job loss during a recession. Unemployment benefits can provide a temporary source of income while you search for a new job. Be sure to review the eligibility requirements and application process for unemployment benefits in your state or country.

Network and Seek Support

Networking and seeking support are essential strategies for managing job loss during a recession. Reach out to friends, family, and professional contacts for emotional support and job leads. Joining professional organizations or attending job fairs can also provide opportunities to connect with others in your industry and learn about job openings.

Upgrade Your Skills

During a recession, it can be challenging to find a new job in your current field. Upgrading your skills through training or education can make you a more attractive candidate for new job opportunities. Look for online courses or training programs that can help you develop new skills and make you more marketable in your field.

Consider Temporary or Freelance Work

Temporary or freelance work can provide a source of income while you search for a new job. Consider offering your services as a freelancer or exploring temporary work opportunities in your field. This can also help you build your professional network and develop new skills.

Explore Entrepreneurship

If you have an entrepreneurial spirit, a recession can be an excellent opportunity to explore starting your own business. This can be a challenging and risky endeavor, but it can also provide financial independence and career flexibility. Consider exploring small business opportunities or consulting services that align with your skills and interests.

Managing job loss during a recession can be challenging, but there are strategies that individuals can use to navigate this difficult time. Assessing your finances, applying for unemployment benefits, networking and seeking support, upgrading your skills, considering temporary or freelance work, and exploring entrepreneurship are all strategies that can help individuals manage job loss during a recession. By being proactive and taking steps to manage job loss, individuals can increase their chances of finding a new job and achieving financial stability.

The Impact of Recessions on Housing

Recessions have a significant impact on the housing market. During a recession, many homeowners may face challenges paying their mortgages, and demand for housing may decline. Below we will explore the impact of recessions on housing and the factors that contribute to this impact.

Declining Home Values

During a recession, home values may decline as demand for housing decreases. This can lead to negative equity, where homeowners owe more on their mortgages than their homes are worth. Negative equity can make it challenging for homeowners to sell their homes or refinance their mortgages, leading to financial difficulties.

Foreclosures

Foreclosures are another significant impact of recessions on the housing market. During a recession, many homeowners may struggle to make their mortgage payments, leading to an increase in foreclosures. Foreclosures can have a significant impact on communities, leading to blight and reduced property values.

Reduced Demand for New Construction

During a recession, demand for new construction may decline as potential homebuyers delay purchasing a new home. This can lead to a decline in new housing construction, which can have a ripple effect on other industries, such as construction materials and equipment suppliers. This can also lead to job losses in the construction industry.

Rental Market

The rental market can also be impacted by recessions. During an economic downturn, demand for rental housing may increase as more people are unable to afford to purchase a home. However, declining incomes and increased competition can make it challenging for landlords to maintain rental income, leading to financial difficulties.

Access to Credit

Access to credit can be another challenge for the housing market during a recession. As lenders become more risk-averse, it can be challenging for potential homebuyers to obtain a mortgage or refinance their existing mortgage. This can lead to reduced demand for housing and contribute to declines in home values.

Recessions have a significant impact on the housing market, including declining home values, foreclosures, reduced demand for new construction, challenges in the rental market, and reduced access to credit. Governments and policymakers have a significant role to play in mitigating the impact of recessions on housing, including implementing fiscal stimulus programs, monetary policy measures, and targeted support for homeowners facing financial difficulties. By recognizing the impact of recessions on housing, individuals and policymakers can take steps to mitigate the impact of economic downturns and support the stability of the housing market.

Housing market trends during recessions

Recessions can have a significant impact on the housing market, with fluctuations in home prices, changes in consumer demand, and shifts in financing options. Below we will explore the trends that emerge in the housing market during recessions and the factors that contribute to these trends.

Decrease in Home Prices

One of the most significant trends in the housing market during a recession is a decrease in home prices. During an economic downturn, demand for housing typically declines, leading to a decrease in home values. Homeowners may be forced to sell their homes at a lower price than they originally paid, leading to a decline in property values.

Increase in Foreclosures

Foreclosures are another significant trend in the housing market during a recession. When homeowners are unable to make their mortgage payments, they may be at risk of foreclosure. During an economic downturn, more homeowners may face financial difficulties and be unable to keep up with their mortgage payments, leading to an increase in foreclosures.

Shift in Housing Demand

Another trend in the housing market during a recession is a shift in housing demand. As incomes decline and unemployment rises, the demand for housing may shift from single-family homes to rental properties. This can result in an increase in rental prices and a decrease in home sales.

Tighter Credit Standards

During a recession, lenders may become more risk-averse, leading to tighter credit standards. This can make it more challenging for potential homebuyers to obtain a mortgage or refinance their existing mortgage. Tighter credit standards can lead to a decline in home sales and contribute to a decrease in property values.

Increase in Housing Inventory

An increase in housing inventory is another trend in the housing market during a recession. When homeowners are unable to sell their homes or are facing foreclosure, they may put their homes on the market, leading to an increase in housing inventory. This can result in a more significant decline in home prices, as buyers have more options to choose from.

Recessions can have a significant impact on the housing market, with trends such as a decrease in home prices, an increase in foreclosures, a shift in housing demand, tighter credit standards, and an increase in housing inventory. These trends can have a ripple effect on the economy, with declining home values contributing to a decline in consumer confidence and reduced economic activity. Governments and policymakers have a significant role to play in mitigating the impact of recessions on the housing market, including implementing fiscal stimulus programs, monetary policy measures, and targeted support for homeowners facing financial difficulties. By recognizing the trends that emerge in the housing market during recessions, individuals and policymakers can take steps to mitigate the impact of economic downturns and support the stability of the housing market.

The impact of recessions on home values

Recessions have a significant impact on the housing market, with changes in demand, financing options, and economic conditions leading to fluctuations in home values. Below we will explore the impact of recessions on home values and the factors that contribute to this impact.

Decrease in Home Values

One of the most significant impacts of recessions on home values is a decrease in home prices. During an economic downturn, demand for housing typically declines, leading to a decrease in home values. Homeowners may be forced to sell their homes at a lower price than they originally paid, leading to a decline in property values. This decline can be exacerbated by a surge in foreclosures, which can lead to an increase in housing inventory and further declines in home prices.

Negative Equity

Negative equity is another impact of recessions on home values. Negative equity occurs when a homeowner owes more on their mortgage than their home is worth. During a recession, declining home values and a decrease in demand for housing can lead to negative equity, making it challenging for homeowners to sell their homes or refinance their mortgages.

Difficulty in Selling Homes

During a recession, many homeowners may face challenges selling their homes due to a decline in demand and a surplus of inventory. Homes may stay on the market for an extended period, leading to reduced home values as sellers become increasingly desperate to make a sale.

Change in Consumer Demand

During a recession, consumer demand for housing may shift, leading to a change in home values. As incomes decline and unemployment rises, the demand for housing may shift from single-family homes to rental properties. This can result in an increase in rental prices and a decrease in home sales, leading to a decline in home values.

Tighter Credit Standards

During a recession, lenders may become more risk-averse, leading to tighter credit standards. This can make it more challenging for potential homebuyers to obtain a mortgage or refinance their existing mortgage. Tighter credit standards can lead to a decline in home sales and contribute to a decrease in property values.

Recessions have a significant impact on home values, with declining demand, negative equity, difficulty in selling homes, shifts in consumer demand, and tighter credit standards leading to fluctuations in home prices. These fluctuations can have a ripple effect on the economy, with declining home values contributing to a decline in consumer confidence and reduced economic activity. Governments and policymakers have a significant role to play in mitigating the impact of recessions on home values, including implementing fiscal stimulus programs, monetary policy measures, and targeted support for homeowners facing financial difficulties. By recognizing the impact of recessions on home values, individuals and policymakers can take steps to mitigate the impact of economic downturns and support the stability of the housing market.

Strategies for managing homeownership during a recession

Recessions can have a significant impact on homeownership, with changes in economic conditions leading to challenges in paying mortgages and fluctuations in home values. Below we will explore strategies for managing homeownership during a recession and the factors that contribute to these strategies.

Refinancing

One strategy for managing homeownership during a recession is refinancing. Refinancing involves obtaining a new mortgage with a lower interest rate, which can result in lower monthly payments and reduced financial strain. Refinancing can also allow homeowners to convert their adjustable-rate mortgage to a fixed-rate mortgage, providing stability in monthly payments.

Loan Modification

Loan modification is another strategy for managing homeownership during a recession. Loan modification involves negotiating with lenders to modify the terms of a mortgage to make it more affordable. This may involve reducing the interest rate, extending the loan term, or forgiving past-due payments.

Short Sale

A short sale is another option for homeowners facing financial difficulties during a recession. A short sale involves selling a home for less than the amount owed on the mortgage, with the lender accepting the proceeds as payment in full. While a short sale can have a negative impact on a homeowner's credit score, it may be preferable to foreclosure.

Renting Out a Property

During a recession, homeowners may consider renting out their property as a way to generate additional income. Renting out a property can help offset mortgage payments and provide a source of income during difficult economic times. However, homeowners must be aware of the risks associated with being a landlord, including property damage and late rent payments.

Seeking Financial Assistance

Homeowners facing financial difficulties during a recession may be eligible for financial assistance through government programs or nonprofit organizations. These programs may provide assistance with mortgage payments, foreclosure prevention, or home repairs.

Recessions can have a significant impact on homeownership, with changes in economic conditions leading to challenges in paying mortgages and fluctuations in home values. Strategies for managing homeownership during a recession include refinancing, loan modification, short sale, renting out a property, and seeking financial assistance. By recognizing the impact of recessions on homeownership and implementing strategies to manage these challenges, homeowners can maintain their investment in their homes and navigate the challenges of economic downturns.

The Impact of Recessions on Small Businesses

Recessions have a significant impact on small businesses, with changes in consumer demand, financing options, and economic conditions leading to fluctuations in sales and profitability. Below we will explore the impact of recessions on small businesses and the factors that contribute to this impact.

Decrease in Sales

One of the most significant impacts of recessions on small businesses is a decrease in sales. During an economic downturn, consumer demand for goods and services typically declines, leading to a decrease in sales for small businesses. Small businesses may be forced to reduce prices or offer discounts to attract customers, leading to reduced profitability.

Difficulty in Obtaining Financing

During a recession, lenders may become more risk-averse, leading to tighter credit standards and difficulty in obtaining financing. This can make it more challenging for small businesses to obtain loans or lines of credit, which can limit their ability to invest in their businesses and meet their financial obligations.

Increase in Competition

During a recession, larger businesses may offer lower prices or discounts to attract customers, leading to increased competition for small businesses. Small businesses may be unable to match these prices, leading to a decline in sales and profitability.

Reduction in Workforce

During a recession, small businesses may be forced to reduce their workforce to cut costs. This can lead to increased workload for remaining employees and decreased morale, which can further impact the business's ability to remain profitable.

Difficulty in Paying Debts

Small businesses may also face challenges in paying their debts during a recession. As sales decline and profitability decreases, small businesses may be unable to meet their financial obligations, leading to late payments and potentially damaging their credit score.

Recessions have a significant impact on small businesses, with decreasing sales, difficulty in obtaining financing, increased competition, reduction in workforce, and difficulty in paying debts leading to decreased profitability and potentially damaging the business's credit score. Governments and policymakers have a significant role to play in mitigating the impact of recessions on small businesses, including implementing fiscal stimulus programs, monetary policy measures, and targeted support for small businesses facing financial difficulties. By recognizing the impact of recessions on small businesses and implementing strategies to manage these challenges, small businesses can navigate the challenges of economic downturns and maintain their viability in the long term.

The unique challenges faced by small businesses during a recession

Small businesses face unique challenges during a recession due to their limited resources and ability to withstand economic downturns. Below we will explore the unique challenges faced by small businesses during a recession and the factors that contribute to these challenges.

Limited Financial Resources

One of the most significant challenges faced by small businesses during a recession is their limited financial resources. Small businesses may have limited cash reserves or access to credit, which can make it difficult to weather the economic challenges of a recession. Small businesses may need to cut costs and reduce their workforce, which can impact their ability to operate effectively.

Increased Competition

During a recession, larger businesses may be able to offer lower prices or discounts to attract customers, leading to increased competition for small businesses. Small businesses may be unable to match these prices, leading to a decline in sales and profitability. Small businesses may also face increased competition from online retailers, which can further impact their ability to attract customers.

Reduced Consumer Confidence

During a recession, consumer confidence may decline, leading to a decrease in consumer spending. Small businesses that rely on consumer spending may be particularly vulnerable to this decline, as they may not have the resources to weather prolonged periods of reduced sales.

Supply Chain Disruptions

During a recession, supply chain disruptions may occur, leading to delays in receiving necessary goods or materials. This can impact small businesses that rely on timely delivery of goods or materials to operate effectively. Small businesses may need to find alternative suppliers or adjust their operations to accommodate the disruptions, which can lead to increased costs and reduced profitability.

Difficulty in Obtaining Financing

During a recession, lenders may become more risk-averse, leading to tighter credit standards and difficulty in obtaining financing. This can make it more challenging for small businesses to obtain loans or lines of credit, which can limit their ability to invest in their businesses and meet their financial obligations.

Small businesses face unique challenges during a recession due to their limited resources and ability to withstand economic downturns. Limited financial resources, increased competition, reduced consumer confidence, supply chain disruptions, and difficulty in obtaining financing are just a few of the challenges small businesses may face during a recession. Governments and policymakers have a significant role to play in mitigating the impact of recessions on small businesses, including implementing fiscal stimulus programs, monetary policy measures, and targeted support for small businesses facing financial difficulties. By recognizing the unique challenges faced by small businesses during a recession and implementing strategies to manage these challenges, small businesses can navigate the challenges of economic downturns and maintain their viability in the long term.

Strategies for managing a small business during a recession

Managing a small business during a recession can be a significant challenge, with limited financial resources and decreased consumer spending impacting the business's profitability. Below we will explore strategies for managing a small business during a recession and the factors that contribute to the success of these strategies.

Develop a Contingency Plan

One strategy for managing a small business during a recession is to develop a contingency plan. This plan should outline the steps the business will take in the event of reduced sales or profitability, including cost-cutting measures, changes to the business's products or services, and adjustments to the business's marketing strategy.

Focus on Customer Retention

During a recession, it may be more challenging to attract new customers, making customer retention a critical strategy for managing a small business. The business should focus on providing exceptional customer service, offering discounts or promotions to existing customers, and engaging with customers through social media and email marketing.

Reduce Operating Costs

During a recession, it may be necessary to reduce operating costs to maintain profitability. The business should evaluate its expenses and look for areas to cut costs, such as reducing inventory levels, renegotiating supplier contracts, and reducing employee hours or salaries.

Diversify Revenue Streams

Diversifying revenue streams can be a useful strategy for managing a small business during a recession. The business should consider expanding its product or service offerings or entering new markets to increase revenue and reduce dependence on a single revenue stream.

Seek Financial Assistance

Small businesses facing financial difficulties during a recession may be eligible for financial assistance through government programs or nonprofit organizations. These programs may provide assistance with business loans, debt relief, or other financial support to help small businesses weather the economic challenges of a recession.

Managing a small business during a recession can be a significant challenge, but strategies such as developing a contingency plan, focusing on customer retention, reducing operating costs, diversifying revenue streams, and seeking financial assistance can help businesses maintain their profitability and viability. By recognizing the unique challenges faced by small businesses during a recession and implementing strategies to manage these challenges, small businesses can navigate the challenges of economic downturns and maintain their viability in the long term.

Government programs and assistance for small businesses during a recession

Small businesses are often the hardest hit during a recession, as decreased consumer spending and limited access to credit can impact their ability to maintain profitability and viability. In response, governments may implement programs and assistance for small businesses during a recession to support their operations and help them weather the economic challenges. Below we will explore government programs and assistance for small businesses during a recession and the factors that contribute to the success of these programs.

Small Business Administration (SBA)

The Small Business Administration (SBA) is a government agency that provides assistance to small businesses, including loans, grants, and other financial support. During a recession, the SBA may increase its lending programs to support small businesses facing financial difficulties. The SBA may also provide guidance on managing cash flow, reducing expenses, and accessing government assistance programs.

Tax Relief Programs

Governments may implement tax relief programs to support small businesses during a recession. These programs may include tax credits, deferred tax payments, or other tax relief measures to help small businesses manage their cash flow and reduce their operating costs.

Access to Credit

During a recession, access to credit may be limited, making it more challenging for small businesses to obtain financing. Governments may implement programs to increase access to credit for small businesses, such as loan guarantees, interest rate subsidies, or other financial support programs.

Job Training and Employment Assistance

Small businesses may face challenges in retaining their employees during a recession, as reduced sales and profitability may require workforce reductions. Governments may provide job training and employment assistance programs to help displaced workers find new jobs or retrain for new industries.

Economic Development Programs

Governments may implement economic development programs to support small businesses during a recession. These programs may include grants or low-interest loans to support business expansion or other economic development initiatives.

Small businesses are often the hardest hit during a recession, but government programs and assistance can provide critical support to help these businesses maintain their viability and weather the economic challenges. The Small Business Administration (SBA), tax relief programs, access to credit, job training and employment assistance, and economic development programs are just a few of the programs and assistance available to small businesses during a recession. By recognizing the importance of small businesses to the economy and implementing strategies to support their operations, governments can help small businesses navigate the challenges of economic downturns and maintain their viability in the long term.

The Role of Government in Managing Recessions

Recessions can have a significant impact on the economy, with decreased consumer spending, increased unemployment rates, and reduced economic growth. Governments have a critical role to play in managing recessions, implementing policies and programs to support the economy and mitigate the impact of economic downturns. Below we will explore the role of the government in managing recessions and the factors that contribute to the success of government intervention.

Fiscal Policy

Fiscal policy refers to government spending and taxation policies. During a recession, governments may implement fiscal policies to stimulate economic growth and support the economy. This may include increased government spending on infrastructure projects or social programs, as well as tax cuts to provide additional resources to consumers and businesses.

Monetary Policy

Monetary policy refers to policies related to the supply and demand of money and credit in the economy. During a recession, governments may implement monetary policies to support the economy, such as lowering interest rates or increasing the money supply to encourage borrowing and investment.

Social Safety Net Programs

During a recession, unemployment rates may increase, leading to financial difficulties for individuals and families. Governments may implement social safety net programs, such as unemployment insurance, food assistance programs, and housing assistance programs, to provide support to individuals and families facing financial difficulties.

Small Business Support

Small businesses may be particularly vulnerable during a recession, with limited financial resources and decreased consumer spending impacting their profitability. Governments may implement programs to support small businesses during a recession, such as access to credit, tax relief programs, and other financial assistance programs.

International Cooperation

Recessions can have a global impact, with economic downturns in one country potentially impacting the economies of other countries. Governments may work together through international organizations such as the International Monetary Fund (IMF) to coordinate policies and programs to support the global economy during a recession.

Governments have a critical role to play in managing recessions, implementing policies and programs to support the economy and mitigate the impact of economic downturns. Fiscal policy, monetary policy, social safety net programs, small business support, and international cooperation are just a few of the strategies available to governments to manage recessions. By recognizing the importance of government intervention in managing recessions and implementing effective policies and programs, governments can support the economy and maintain economic stability in the long term.

Fiscal policy during a recession

Fiscal policy is a critical tool for governments to manage the economy during a recession. Fiscal policy refers to government spending and taxation policies, and during a recession, governments may implement fiscal policies to stimulate economic growth and support the economy. Below we will explore fiscal policy during a recession and the factors that contribute to the success of fiscal policy intervention.

Increased Government Spending

During a recession, consumer spending may decrease, leading to decreased economic activity. Governments may implement fiscal policies to increase government spending on infrastructure projects or social programs to stimulate economic growth and support the economy. This may include investments in transportation infrastructure, public education, or other areas that promote economic growth and job creation.

Tax Cuts

Governments may implement tax cuts during a recession to provide additional resources to consumers and businesses. Tax cuts may increase disposable income for consumers, encouraging increased spending and economic activity. For businesses, tax cuts may provide additional resources to invest in operations and hire new employees, promoting economic growth and job creation.

Automatic Stabilizers

Automatic stabilizers refer to government programs that automatically provide support during a recession, such as unemployment insurance and food assistance programs. These programs can help support individuals and families facing financial difficulties during a recession, reducing the impact of economic downturns on vulnerable populations.

Debt Relief

During a recession, individuals and businesses may face challenges in managing their debt obligations. Governments may implement policies to provide debt relief, such as mortgage forbearance programs or loan forgiveness programs, to reduce the financial burden on individuals and businesses and promote economic stability.

Balanced Budgets

Governments may strive to maintain balanced budgets during a recession, balancing the need for fiscal stimulus with the need to maintain long-term fiscal stability. This may involve prioritizing spending on critical areas such as infrastructure and social programs while reducing spending in other areas to maintain overall fiscal balance.

Fiscal policy is a critical tool for governments to manage the economy during a recession. Increased government spending, tax cuts, automatic stabilizers, debt relief, and balanced budgets are just a few of the strategies available to governments to implement fiscal policy during a recession. By recognizing the importance of fiscal policy in managing economic downturns and implementing effective policies and programs, governments can support the economy and maintain economic stability in the long term. However, the success of fiscal policy intervention during a recession relies on careful planning, effective implementation, and ongoing evaluation to ensure that policies and programs are achieving their intended goals.

Monetary policy during a recession

Monetary policy is another critical tool for governments to manage the economy during a recession. Monetary policy refers to policies related to the supply and demand of money and credit in the economy. During a recession, governments may implement monetary policies to support the economy, such as lowering interest rates or increasing the money supply to encourage borrowing and investment. Below we will explore monetary policy during a recession and the factors that contribute to the success of monetary policy intervention.

Lowering Interest Rates

Lowering interest rates is a common monetary policy tool used during a recession. Lower interest rates can make it cheaper for businesses and consumers to borrow money, increasing economic activity and promoting job creation. Additionally, lower interest rates may encourage increased consumer spending and investment in the stock market, further stimulating economic growth.

Quantitative Easing

Quantitative easing is a monetary policy tool that involves purchasing government bonds or other securities to increase the money supply and encourage lending and investment. During a recession, governments may implement quantitative easing to increase the money supply and stimulate economic activity.

Open Market Operations

Open market operations refer to the buying and selling of government securities by central banks to manage the money supply and interest rates. During a recession, governments may implement open market operations to stimulate economic growth by increasing the money supply and lowering interest rates.

Discount Window Lending

Discount window lending is a monetary policy tool that involves providing loans to banks and other financial institutions at a discount rate. During a recession, governments may implement discount window lending to encourage banks to lend money to businesses and consumers, promoting economic growth and job creation.

Reserve Requirements

Reserve requirements refer to the amount of money that banks must hold in reserve to meet potential withdrawal requests from customers. During a recession, governments may decrease reserve requirements to encourage banks to lend more money to businesses and consumers, promoting economic growth and job creation.

Monetary policy is a critical tool for governments to manage the economy during a recession. Lowering interest rates, quantitative easing, open market operations, discount window lending, and reserve requirements are just a few of the strategies available to governments to implement monetary policy during a recession. By recognizing the importance of monetary policy in managing economic downturns and implementing effective policies and programs, governments can support the economy and maintain economic stability in the long term. However, the success of monetary policy intervention during a recession relies on careful planning, effective implementation, and ongoing evaluation to ensure that policies and programs are achieving their intended goals.

The effectiveness of government intervention during a recession

The effectiveness of government intervention during a recession can have a significant impact on the economy and the well-being of individuals and businesses. Governments have a critical role to play in managing recessions, implementing policies and programs to support the economy and mitigate the impact of economic downturns. Below we will explore the effectiveness of government intervention during a recession and the factors that contribute to successful intervention.

Timeliness of Intervention

The timeliness of government intervention is critical in managing a recession. Early and decisive action can help mitigate the impact of economic downturns and prevent a more severe economic crisis. Effective government intervention during a recession requires a quick and coordinated response, with policies and programs implemented in a timely manner.

Effectiveness of Policy

The effectiveness of government policy is another critical factor in managing a recession. Policies and programs must be carefully designed and targeted to address the specific economic challenges faced during a recession. Effective policies and programs can help stimulate economic growth, create jobs, and support vulnerable populations during a recession.

Political Will and Cooperation

Political will and cooperation are essential for effective government intervention during a recession. Governments must be willing to take bold action to support the economy, even if it involves difficult political decisions. Additionally, international cooperation can help ensure that policies and programs are coordinated and effective on a global scale.

Public Trust and Confidence

Public trust and confidence are critical for successful government intervention during a recession. Governments must communicate clearly and effectively with the public about their policies and programs, providing transparency and accountability. Additionally, governments must work to build public trust and confidence in the economy, promoting consumer spending and investment.

Long-Term Planning

Effective government intervention during a recession requires a long-term planning perspective. Governments must plan for economic stability and growth beyond the immediate challenges of a recession, implementing policies and programs that promote long-term economic stability.

The effectiveness of government intervention during a recession is critical in managing the impact of economic downturns on individuals and businesses. Timeliness of intervention, effectiveness of policy, political will and cooperation, public trust and confidence, and long-term planning are just a few of the factors that contribute to successful government intervention during a recession. By recognizing the importance of government intervention in managing recessions and implementing effective policies and programs, governments can support the economy and maintain economic stability in the long term. However, the success of government intervention during a recession relies on careful planning, effective implementation, and ongoing evaluation to ensure that policies and programs are achieving their intended goals.

International Recessions and Globalization

International recessions and globalization are deeply interconnected, with economic downturns in one part of the world often having significant ripple effects on global markets and economies. The interconnectedness of the global economy means that economic challenges in one region can quickly spread to other regions, with economic policies and programs implemented on a global scale. Below we will explore the relationship between international recessions and globalization and the factors that contribute to successful global management of economic downturns.

Global Economic Integration

The increasing interconnectedness of the global economy has contributed to the spread of economic challenges during a recession. Global trade, investment, and finance have all contributed to the growth of a global economy, with economic challenges in one part of the world having significant impacts on other regions. Effective management of international recessions requires coordinated global policies and programs to address economic challenges on a global scale.

International Cooperation

International cooperation is essential for effective management of international recessions. Governments must work together to coordinate policies and programs to address global economic challenges, such as implementing coordinated fiscal and monetary policies. Additionally, international organizations such as the International Monetary Fund (IMF) and the World Bank play a critical role in supporting global economic stability during a recession.

Economic Imbalances

Economic imbalances between regions can contribute to the spread of international recessions. For example, if one region of the world is heavily reliant on exports to another region, a recession in the importing region can have significant impacts on the exporting region's economy. Addressing economic imbalances requires coordinated global policies and programs to support economic growth and stability across regions.

Financial Market Integration

Financial market integration has contributed to the spread of international recessions, with economic challenges in one region quickly spreading to global financial markets. Global financial markets are deeply interconnected, with investments and transactions occurring across borders and regions. Effective management of international recessions requires coordinated global policies and programs to address financial market challenges and promote economic stability.

Global Economic Leadership

Global economic leadership is essential for effective management of international recessions. Governments and international organizations must provide leadership and guidance during a recession, coordinating policies and programs to address economic challenges on a global scale. Additionally, global economic leadership can promote public trust and confidence in the economy, promoting consumer spending and investment.

International recessions and globalization are deeply interconnected, with economic challenges in one part of the world quickly spreading to other regions. The increasing interconnectedness of the global economy has contributed to the need for coordinated global policies and programs to address economic challenges on a global scale. Global economic integration, international cooperation, economic imbalances, financial market integration, and global economic leadership are just a few of the factors that contribute to successful global management of international recessions. By recognizing the importance of global cooperation and coordination during a recession and implementing effective policies and programs, governments and international organizations can support the global economy and maintain economic stability in the long term.

The impact of recessions on international trade

Recessions can have a significant impact on international trade, with economic downturns leading to a decrease in global demand for goods and services. Additionally, recessions can lead to the implementation of protectionist trade policies, such as tariffs and quotas, which can further impact international trade. Below we will explore the impact of recessions on international trade and the factors that contribute to successful management of trade during a recession.

Decreased Global Demand

During a recession, decreased global demand for goods and services can significantly impact international trade. As consumers and businesses cut back on spending, demand for imported goods and services decreases. Additionally, recessions can lead to a decrease in global investment, further impacting international trade.

Protectionist Trade Policies

Recessions can lead to the implementation of protectionist trade policies, such as tariffs and quotas, which can further impact international trade. Protectionist trade policies are intended to protect domestic industries from foreign competition, but they can also lead to retaliatory measures by other countries, creating a trade war that can have significant impacts on the global economy.

Impact on Developing Countries

Developing countries can be particularly vulnerable to the impacts of recessions on international trade. Many developing countries rely heavily on exports to support their economies, making them vulnerable to changes in global demand. Additionally, developing countries may have limited resources to implement policies and programs to support their economies during a recession.

International Cooperation

International cooperation is critical for managing the impact of recessions on international trade. Governments and international organizations must work together to coordinate policies and programs to support economic growth and stability on a global scale. Additionally, international organizations such as the World Trade Organization (WTO) play a critical role in promoting free and fair trade during a recession.

Long-Term Planning

Effective management of the impact of recessions on international trade requires a long-term planning perspective. Governments and international organizations must plan for economic stability and growth beyond the immediate challenges of a recession, implementing policies and programs that promote long-term economic stability and growth.

Recessions can have a significant impact on international trade, with decreased global demand and protectionist trade policies impacting the global economy. The impact of recessions on international trade can be particularly significant for developing countries, which may have limited resources to support their economies during a recession. Effective management of the impact of recessions on international trade requires international cooperation, long-term planning, and policies and programs that promote economic stability and growth on a global scale. By recognizing the importance of international trade and implementing effective policies and programs, governments and international organizations can support the global economy and maintain economic stability in the long term.

The role of globalization in the spread of recessions

Globalization has played a significant role in the spread of recessions across the world. As economies have become increasingly interconnected, economic challenges in one region can quickly spread to other regions, leading to global economic downturns. Below we will explore the role of globalization in the spread of recessions and the factors that contribute to the spread of economic challenges on a global scale.

Global Trade

Global trade has played a significant role in the spread of recessions, with economic challenges in one region quickly impacting global demand for goods and services. As economies have become increasingly reliant on global trade, economic challenges in one part of the world can quickly spread to other regions, leading to decreased global demand and economic downturns.

Financial Integration

Financial market integration has contributed to the spread of recessions, with economic challenges in one part of the world quickly impacting global financial markets. As financial markets have become increasingly integrated, investments and transactions occurring across borders and regions can quickly spread economic challenges, leading to increased volatility in global financial markets.

Economic Interdependence

The increasing economic interdependence of the world's economies has also contributed to the spread of recessions. As economies have become more interconnected, economic challenges in one region can quickly impact other regions, leading to a global economic downturn. Additionally, the spread of economic challenges can lead to increased protectionist trade policies, further impacting global economic stability.

Globalization of Production

The globalization of production has contributed to the spread of recessions, with economic challenges in one part of the world quickly impacting global supply chains. As production has become increasingly globalized, economic challenges in one region can quickly impact production in other regions, leading to decreased global supply and demand for goods and services.

Globalization of Labor

The globalization of labor has also contributed to the spread of recessions, with economic challenges in one part of the world leading to decreased demand for labor on a global scale. As labor has become increasingly mobile, economic challenges in one region can quickly lead to decreased demand for labor in other regions, leading to increased unemployment and economic challenges.

Globalization has played a significant role in the spread of recessions on a global scale, with economic challenges in one region quickly impacting other regions. The increasing interconnectedness of the world's economies has contributed to decreased global demand for goods and services, increased volatility in global financial markets, and decreased demand for labor on a global scale. Effective management of the impact of recessions on a global scale requires international cooperation, long-term planning, and policies and programs that promote economic stability and growth on a global scale. By recognizing the role of globalization in the spread of recessions and implementing effective policies and programs, governments and international organizations can support the global economy and maintain economic stability in the long term.

Strategies for managing the impact of international recessions

International recessions can have significant impacts on economies around the world, leading to decreased global demand for goods and services, increased unemployment, and decreased economic growth. Effective management of the impact of international recessions requires a range of strategies and policies that promote economic stability and growth on a global scale. Below we will explore strategies for managing the impact of international recessions and the factors that contribute to successful management of economic challenges on a global scale.

International Cooperation

International cooperation is critical for managing the impact of international recessions. Governments and international organizations must work together to coordinate policies and programs to support economic growth and stability on a global scale. Additionally, international organizations such as the World Trade Organization (WTO) play a critical role in promoting free and fair trade during an economic downturn.

Fiscal and Monetary Policies

Fiscal and monetary policies can be effective strategies for managing the impact of international recessions. Governments can implement fiscal policies, such as increased government spending, to stimulate economic growth and support businesses and individuals during an economic downturn. Central banks can implement monetary policies, such as interest rate adjustments, to support economic stability and promote growth.

Infrastructure Investment

Infrastructure investment can be a powerful tool for managing the impact of international recessions. Investments in infrastructure can create jobs and stimulate economic growth, providing a long-term solution to economic challenges. Additionally, investments in infrastructure can increase the efficiency of transportation and communication networks, improving economic competitiveness on a global scale.

Job Training and Education

Job training and education can be effective strategies for managing the impact of international recessions. Investing in job training and education can provide individuals with the skills and knowledge needed to compete in the global economy, increasing the competitiveness of economies on a global scale. Additionally, job training and education can support individuals who have lost jobs during an economic downturn, helping them to transition into new careers and industries.

Diversification of Economies

Diversification of economies can be an effective strategy for managing the impact of international recessions. Economies that are overly reliant on one industry or sector are particularly vulnerable to economic downturns. Diversification can help to spread economic risks across a range of industries and sectors, reducing the impact of economic challenges on a global scale.

Effective management of the impact of international recessions requires a range of strategies and policies that promote economic stability and growth on a global scale. International cooperation, fiscal and monetary policies, infrastructure investment, job training and education, and diversification of economies are all effective strategies for managing the impact of economic challenges on a global scale. By recognizing the importance of international cooperation and implementing effective policies and programs, governments and international organizations can support the global economy and maintain economic stability in the long term.

The Psychology of Recessions

Recessions can have a significant impact on individuals and society as a whole, leading to decreased economic opportunities, increased stress and anxiety, and decreased overall well-being. The psychology of recessions plays a critical role in how individuals and society respond to economic challenges and can impact the effectiveness of policies and programs aimed at promoting economic stability and growth. Below we will explore the psychology of recessions and the factors that contribute to effective management of economic challenges from a psychological perspective.

Economic Anxiety and Stress

Economic anxiety and stress are common psychological responses to recessions. Economic anxiety and stress can impact individuals' ability to make rational decisions, leading to decreased economic activity and decreased economic growth. Effective management of economic anxiety and stress requires policies and programs that promote economic stability and support individuals and businesses during an economic downturn.

Social Support and Community Resilience

Social support and community resilience can play a critical role in managing the psychological impact of recessions. Strong social support networks and community resilience can help individuals and communities to cope with economic challenges and can promote economic stability and growth. Policies and programs aimed at promoting social support and community resilience can be effective strategies for managing the psychological impact of recessions.

Perception of Economic Inequality

The perception of economic inequality can have a significant impact on the psychological response to recessions. The perception of economic inequality can lead to decreased trust in economic systems and institutions, decreased economic activity, and decreased economic growth. Effective management of the psychological impact of economic inequality requires policies and programs that promote economic equality and support individuals and communities impacted by economic challenges.

Economic Optimism

Economic optimism can be an effective strategy for managing the psychological impact of recessions. Economic optimism can promote economic activity and growth, leading to increased economic opportunities and improved well-being. Policies and programs that promote economic optimism, such as investments in infrastructure and education, can be effective strategies for managing the psychological impact of recessions.

Perception of Economic Control

The perception of economic control can impact the psychological response to recessions. Individuals who perceive themselves as having control over their economic circumstances may be more likely to make rational economic decisions and may be less impacted by economic challenges. Policies and programs that promote economic control, such as job training and education, can be effective strategies for managing the psychological impact of recessions.

The psychology of recessions plays a critical role in how individuals and society respond to economic challenges. Economic anxiety and stress, social support and community resilience, perception of economic inequality, economic optimism, and perception of economic control are all factors that impact the psychological response to recessions. Effective management of the psychological impact of recessions requires policies and programs that promote economic stability and support individuals and communities impacted by economic challenges. By recognizing the importance of the psychological response to recessions and implementing effective policies and programs, governments and organizations can promote economic stability and growth and improve overall well-being.

The impact of fear and uncertainty during a recession

Recessions can cause fear and uncertainty for individuals, businesses, and society as a whole. The fear and uncertainty can be fueled by job loss, decreased economic activity, and a lack of confidence in economic systems and institutions. The impact of fear and uncertainty during a recession can have significant implications for the economy, the workforce, and overall well-being. Below we will explore the impact of fear and uncertainty during a recession and the strategies that can be employed to manage these emotions.

Reduced Consumer Confidence

Fear and uncertainty can lead to reduced consumer confidence. Consumers may cut back on spending, leading to decreased economic activity and decreased economic growth. Effective management of fear and uncertainty requires policies and programs that promote consumer confidence, such as investments in infrastructure and education.

Business Closures and Layoffs

Fear and uncertainty can also lead to business closures and layoffs. Businesses may struggle to stay afloat during an economic downturn, leading to layoffs and closures. Effective management of fear and uncertainty requires policies and programs that support businesses and promote economic stability, such as tax incentives and access to credit.

Mental Health

Fear and uncertainty can also impact mental health. Individuals may experience stress, anxiety, and depression during an economic downturn, leading to decreased well-being and increased healthcare costs. Effective management of fear and uncertainty requires policies and programs that support mental health and well-being, such as access to mental health services and support for individuals impacted by economic challenges.

Social Cohesion

Fear and uncertainty can impact social cohesion. Individuals may become distrustful of economic systems and institutions, leading to decreased social cohesion and increased political polarization. Effective management of fear and uncertainty requires policies and programs that promote social cohesion and trust in economic systems and institutions.

Economic Recovery

Fear and uncertainty can impact the pace and effectiveness of economic recovery. Individuals and businesses may be hesitant to invest in the economy during an economic downturn, leading to a slow recovery. Effective management of fear and uncertainty requires policies and programs that promote economic recovery, such as investments in infrastructure and education and access to credit for businesses and individuals.

The impact of fear and uncertainty during a recession can have significant implications for the economy, the workforce, and overall well-being. Reduced consumer confidence, business closures and layoffs, mental health, social cohesion, and economic recovery are all factors impacted by fear and uncertainty during an economic downturn. Effective management of fear and uncertainty requires policies and programs that promote economic stability, support businesses and individuals impacted by economic challenges, and promote social cohesion and trust in economic systems and institutions. By recognizing the importance of managing fear and uncertainty during a recession and implementing effective policies and programs, governments and organizations can support the global economy and maintain economic stability in the long term.

Strategies for managing anxiety during a recession

Recessions can cause significant anxiety and stress for individuals and society as a whole. The fear of job loss, financial instability, and economic uncertainty can all contribute to increased anxiety and decreased well-being. Managing anxiety during a recession is essential for maintaining mental health and overall well-being. Below we will explore strategies for managing anxiety during a recession.

Focus on What You Can Control

During a recession, there may be many factors outside of your control that contribute to anxiety and stress. One strategy for managing anxiety is to focus on what you can control. You can control your spending habits, your savings, and your investment choices. Focusing on these areas can give you a sense of control and can help alleviate anxiety.

Practice Self-Care

Practicing self-care is another effective strategy for managing anxiety during a recession. Self-care can include activities such as exercise, meditation, and spending time with loved ones. Practicing self-care can help alleviate stress and promote well-being.

Seek Support

During a recession, it is essential to seek support from friends, family, or a mental health professional. Seeking support can provide a sense of connection and can help manage anxiety and stress.

Stay Informed

Staying informed about economic trends and government policies can also help manage anxiety during a recession. Understanding the economic situation can provide a sense of control and can help you make informed decisions about your finances and investments.

Create a Budget

Creating a budget is another effective strategy for managing anxiety during a recession. A budget can help you track your spending, identify areas where you can cut costs, and plan for the future. Having a plan in place can alleviate anxiety and promote financial stability.

Focus on the Long-Term

During a recession, it is essential to focus on the long-term. The economy will eventually recover, and there will be opportunities for growth and success. Focusing on the long-term can provide hope and can help manage anxiety during difficult times.

Managing anxiety during a recession is essential for maintaining mental health and overall well-being. Strategies for managing anxiety during a recession include focusing on what you can control, practicing self-care, seeking support, staying informed, creating a budget, and focusing on the long-term. By implementing these strategies, individuals can manage anxiety and stress during a recession and maintain financial stability and overall well-being.

The role of optimism and hope in recovering from a recession

Recessions can be challenging times for individuals and society as a whole. The fear of job loss, financial instability, and economic uncertainty can all contribute to increased anxiety and decreased well-being. During these difficult times, optimism and hope can play a vital role in recovering from a recession. Below we will explore the role of optimism and hope in recovering from a recession.

Promoting Resilience

Optimism and hope can promote resilience during a recession. Resilience is the ability to adapt and bounce back from difficult times. Optimistic and hopeful individuals are more likely to have the resilience needed to weather the storm during a recession.

Encouraging Innovation

Optimism and hope can also encourage innovation during a recession. When individuals are optimistic and hopeful, they are more likely to take risks and try new things. These actions can lead to new innovations and opportunities that can help in the recovery from a recession.

Building Confidence

Optimism and hope can also build confidence during a recession. When individuals are optimistic and hopeful, they are more likely to have confidence in themselves and their abilities. This confidence can help individuals take action to improve their situation and promote economic recovery.

Inspiring Action

Optimism and hope can inspire action during a recession. When individuals are optimistic and hopeful, they are more likely to take action to improve their situation. This action can lead to a sense of empowerment and can promote economic recovery.

Promoting Cooperation

Optimism and hope can also promote cooperation during a recession. When individuals are optimistic and hopeful, they are more likely to work together to find solutions to economic challenges. This cooperation can promote economic recovery and build a sense of community.

Optimism and hope can play a vital role in recovering from a recession. Promoting resilience, encouraging innovation, building confidence, inspiring action, and promoting cooperation are all benefits of optimism and hope during difficult economic times. By fostering optimism and hope, individuals can promote their own well-being and contribute to the recovery of society as a whole. While it may be challenging to remain optimistic and hopeful during a recession, these qualities are essential for promoting economic recovery and maintaining well-being.

Surviving a Recession:

Recessions can be challenging times for individuals, families, and businesses. The fear of job loss, financial instability, and economic uncertainty can all contribute to increased stress and decreased well-being. Surviving a recession requires a combination of financial planning, resilience, and adaptability. Below we will explore strategies for surviving a recession.

Build an Emergency Fund

Building an emergency fund is one of the most important strategies for surviving a recession. An emergency fund can provide a financial cushion in case of job loss, unexpected expenses, or other financial challenges. Experts recommend having three to six months' worth of expenses in an emergency fund.

Reduce Expenses

Reducing expenses is another important strategy for surviving a recession. Cutting back on discretionary spending, negotiating bills, and finding ways to save on everyday expenses can help stretch your budget during difficult economic times.

Diversify Income

Diversifying income is another important strategy for surviving a recession. Having multiple streams of income can provide a financial cushion in case of job loss or other financial challenges. Consider starting a side business or taking on freelance work to diversify your income.

Maintain Health Insurance

Maintaining health insurance is another essential strategy for surviving a recession. A major illness or injury can quickly drain your finances without proper health coverage. Consider maintaining health insurance through COBRA or other options if you lose your job.

Seek Professional Advice

Seeking professional advice is another important strategy for surviving a recession. Financial planners, accountants, and other professionals can provide valuable guidance and advice on how to manage your finances during difficult economic times.

Stay Positive

Staying positive and maintaining a resilient attitude is another important strategy for surviving a recession. While it may be challenging to stay positive during difficult times, a positive attitude can help you stay motivated and focused on your goals.

Look for New Opportunities

Looking for new opportunities is another important strategy for surviving a recession. While some industries may be struggling during a recession, others may be thriving. Look for new job opportunities or consider starting your own business if you have an entrepreneurial spirit.

Pay Down Debt

Paying down debt is another important strategy for surviving a recession. High levels of debt can make it difficult to weather financial challenges during a recession. Consider paying down high-interest debt first and making extra payments on your loans to reduce your overall debt load.

Stay Educated

Staying educated about economic trends, government policies, and other financial news is another important strategy for surviving a recession. Understanding the economic situation can provide a sense of control and can help you make informed decisions about your finances and investments.

Build Your Network

Building your network is another important strategy for surviving a recession. Networking with colleagues, friends, and acquaintances can provide new job opportunities, business connections, and other valuable resources during difficult economic times.

Surviving a recession requires a combination of financial planning, resilience, and adaptability. Building an emergency fund, reducing expenses, diversifying income, maintaining health insurance, seeking professional advice, and staying positive are all important strategies for surviving a recession. By implementing these strategies, individuals and families can weather the storm during difficult economic times and maintain financial stability and overall well-being.

Maintaining a budget and reducing expenses

Maintaining a budget and reducing expenses are critical skills for individuals and families, especially during difficult economic times like recessions. A budget is a financial plan that helps you track your income and expenses, while reducing expenses involves finding ways to cut back on your spending. Below we will discuss the importance of maintaining a budget and reducing expenses, as well as strategies for implementing these practices.

Importance of Maintaining a Budget

Maintaining a budget is essential for several reasons. First, it helps you track your income and expenses, allowing you to see where your money is going and identify areas where you can cut back. This can be especially important during a recession when income may be lower or less stable. A budget can also help you plan for future expenses, such as emergency funds, retirement, or saving for a home or college tuition.

Additionally, maintaining a budget can help you avoid overspending and accruing debt. It can help you stay on track with your financial goals and avoid impulse purchases that can quickly add up over time. It can also help you maintain a sense of control over your finances, reducing stress and improving overall well-being.

Strategies for Maintaining a Budget

There are several strategies for maintaining a budget. First, start by creating a realistic budget that reflects your income and expenses. This should include all sources of income, such as wages, investments, and other sources, as well as all expenses, including rent or mortgage, utilities, groceries, transportation, entertainment, and other expenses.

Next, track your spending to see how closely your actual expenses align with your budget. This can help you identify areas where you need to cut back and adjust your budget accordingly. Consider using a budgeting app or spreadsheet to track your expenses and keep your budget up-to-date.

Finally, review your budget regularly and make adjustments as needed. For example, if you receive a raise or have a change in income, adjust your budget to reflect the new income. Similarly, if you have a major expense, such as a medical bill or home repair, adjust your budget to reflect the new expense.

Importance of Reducing Expenses

Reducing expenses is also critical, especially during a recession when income may be lower or less stable. Reducing expenses involves finding ways to cut back on your spending without sacrificing your quality of life. This can be challenging, but it is essential for maintaining financial stability and avoiding debt.

Strategies for Reducing Expenses

There are several strategies for reducing expenses. First, focus on the big-ticket items, such as housing, transportation, and food. Consider downsizing to a smaller home or apartment, carpooling or using public transportation instead of driving, and cooking at home instead of eating out. These changes can have a significant impact on your budget and can help you save money over time.

Next, consider cutting back on discretionary spending, such as entertainment, clothing, and hobbies. Look for free or low-cost alternatives to expensive activities, such as hiking or visiting local museums. Consider buying second-hand clothing or borrowing items from friends instead of purchasing new items.

Finally, negotiate bills and shop around for better deals on services like internet, cable, and phone bills. Call your service provider and ask if there are any promotions or discounts available, or consider switching to a different provider that offers better rates.

Maintaining a budget and reducing expenses are critical skills for individuals and families, especially during difficult economic times like recessions. By creating a realistic budget, tracking your spending, and making adjustments as needed, you can maintain financial stability and avoid overspending. Similarly, by cutting back on discretionary spending and finding ways to save on major expenses like housing and transportation, you can reduce expenses and maintain a higher level of financial security. By implementing these strategies, you can weather the storm during difficult economic times

Finding alternate sources of income

During recessions, finding alternate sources of income can be critical for maintaining financial stability. When jobs are scarce and wages are low, supplementing your income with additional sources of revenue can make all the difference. Below we will discuss the importance of finding alternate sources of income during recessions, as well as strategies for identifying and pursuing these opportunities.

Importance of Finding Alternate Sources of Income

Finding alternate sources of income is critical during recessions for several reasons. First, it can help you maintain financial stability and avoid falling into debt. When job prospects are limited, having additional sources of revenue can help you make ends meet and cover your basic expenses. This can reduce financial stress and improve overall well-being.

Additionally, finding alternate sources of income can help you build resilience and adaptability. By developing new skills and pursuing different opportunities, you can expand your professional network and open up new possibilities for your career. This can help you weather the storm during recessions and emerge stronger and more prepared for future challenges.

Strategies for Finding Alternate Sources of Income

There are several strategies for finding alternate sources of income during recessions. First, consider taking on part-time or freelance work in your current field. This can be an excellent way to supplement your income while leveraging your existing skills and experience. Look for opportunities on job boards, social media platforms, or through professional networks.

Another strategy is to explore new industries or opportunities that align with your interests and skills. Consider taking on a side hustle, such as starting a small business or offering consulting services. Look for ways to leverage your hobbies or passions, such as selling handmade crafts or offering tutoring services.

You can also consider pursuing additional education or training to develop new skills and open up new opportunities. This can include online courses, certifications, or even pursuing a degree in a related field. Look for scholarships or financial aid programs to help cover the costs of education.

Finally, consider leveraging the gig economy by driving for ride-sharing services, delivering food or packages, or participating in online surveys or research studies. While these opportunities may not provide a significant source of income, they can be a great way to supplement your earnings and add flexibility to your schedule.

Finding alternate sources of income during recessions can be critical for maintaining financial stability and building resilience. By taking on part-time or freelance work, exploring new industries or opportunities, pursuing additional education or training, or leveraging the gig economy, you can supplement your income and reduce financial stress. While these strategies may require some additional effort and time, they can pay off in the long run by providing new opportunities for your career and improving your overall financial well-being.

Protecting assets and investments

During recessions, protecting your assets and investments becomes even more important. Economic downturns can cause significant losses in the stock market and other investment vehicles, and may also lead to job losses and reduced income. Below we will discuss the importance of protecting assets and investments during recessions, as well as strategies for safeguarding your financial future.

Importance of Protecting Assets and Investments

Protecting assets and investments is critical during recessions for several reasons. First, it can help you preserve your wealth and minimize losses during market downturns. By taking steps to protect your investments, you can reduce the impact of economic uncertainty and improve your long-term financial stability.

Additionally, protecting your assets can help you maintain liquidity and access to cash during a recession. This can be important for covering basic expenses and maintaining financial stability, especially in the event of job loss or reduced income.

Strategies for Protecting Assets and Investments

There are several strategies for protecting assets and investments during recessions. First, consider diversifying your portfolio to reduce risk. This can include investing in a mix of stocks, bonds, and other investment vehicles, as well as diversifying within each asset class. By spreading your investments across multiple sectors and industries, you can reduce the impact of economic uncertainty and minimize losses.

Another strategy is to maintain a cash reserve to cover basic expenses and emergencies. This can include setting aside 3-6 months of living expenses in a high-yield savings account or other liquid asset. Having a cash reserve can help you weather the storm during recessions and reduce the impact of job loss or reduced income.

You can also consider investing in defensive stocks or other low-risk assets. Defensive stocks are those that tend to perform well during economic downturns, such as consumer staples, utilities, and healthcare. By investing in defensive stocks, you can protect your portfolio and minimize losses during recessions.

Finally, consider seeking the advice of a financial advisor to help you develop a recession-proof investment strategy. A financial advisor can help you identify opportunities for growth and diversification, as well as provide guidance on risk management and asset protection.

Protecting assets and investments during recessions is critical for maintaining financial stability and building resilience. By diversifying your portfolio, maintaining a cash reserve, investing in defensive stocks, and seeking the advice of a financial advisor, you can safeguard your financial future and minimize losses during economic downturns. While these strategies may require some additional effort and attention, they can pay off in the long run by improving your financial well-being and protecting your assets and investments.

Coping with the emotional impact of a recession

Recessions can have a significant emotional impact on individuals and families. Economic uncertainty, job loss, and financial stress can lead to feelings of anxiety, depression, and hopelessness. Coping with the emotional impact of a recession is critical for maintaining mental health and well-being during challenging times. Below we will discuss the emotional impact of a recession and strategies for coping with these challenges.

Emotional Impact of a Recession

The emotional impact of a recession can be significant and varied. For some, job loss or reduced income can lead to feelings of shame, guilt, or inadequacy. Others may experience anxiety or depression due to financial stress, uncertainty, or the loss of a sense of control over their lives. Additionally, the stress of a recession can strain relationships and lead to feelings of isolation or loneliness.

Strategies for Coping with the Emotional Impact of a Recession

There are several strategies for coping with the emotional impact of a recession. First, it is important to prioritize self-care and mental health. This can include maintaining a healthy routine, such as eating well, exercising, and getting enough sleep. Practicing mindfulness or meditation can also help manage stress and anxiety.

Additionally, seeking support from friends, family, or a mental health professional can be helpful. Talking about your feelings and concerns with a trusted person can help alleviate stress and provide perspective. A mental health professional can also provide guidance on coping strategies and help you develop a plan for managing stress and anxiety.

Another strategy is to focus on areas of your life that are within your control. This can include setting goals, developing new skills, or pursuing hobbies or interests. By focusing on areas of your life that bring you joy and fulfillment, you can maintain a sense of purpose and resilience during challenging times.

Finally, it can be helpful to reframe your mindset around financial stress and uncertainty. Instead of focusing on what you can't control, try to focus on what you can do to improve your situation. This can include developing a budget, looking for ways to reduce expenses, or pursuing alternate sources of income. By taking action and focusing on what is within your control, you can regain a sense of agency and reduce feelings of helplessness.

Coping with the emotional impact of a recession can be challenging, but it is important for maintaining mental health and well-being. By prioritizing self-care, seeking support from friends or professionals, focusing on areas of your life within your control, and reframing your mindset around financial stress, you can build resilience and navigate challenging times with greater ease. While these strategies may require effort and practice, they can pay off in the long run by improving your overall well-being and helping you weather the storm of a recession.

Job Loss and Unemployment:

Job loss and unemployment are among the most significant impacts of recessions on individuals and families. Economic downturns can lead to layoffs, reduced work hours, and increased competition for jobs, making it difficult for many people to find employment. Coping with job loss and unemployment during a recession can be challenging, but there are strategies and resources available to help navigate these challenges. Below we will discuss the impact of job loss and unemployment during recessions, as well as strategies for coping with these challenges.

Impact of Job Loss and Unemployment During Recessions

Job loss and unemployment can have significant financial and emotional impacts on individuals and families. In addition to the loss of income, job loss can lead to feelings of stress, anxiety, and depression. Unemployment can also lead to social isolation and a loss of sense of purpose or identity. Furthermore, job loss and unemployment can impact long-term career prospects and earning potential.

During recessions, the impact of job loss and unemployment can be even more severe. High levels of competition for jobs can make it difficult for individuals to find work, even for those with significant skills and experience. This can lead to increased financial strain, as well as feelings of frustration and hopelessness.

Strategies for Coping with Job Loss and Unemployment During Recessions

There are several strategies for coping with job loss and unemployment during recessions. First, it is important to prioritize self-care and mental health. Coping with job loss and unemployment can be stressful and emotionally challenging, so it is important to prioritize self-care and seek support from friends, family, or mental health professionals.

Another strategy is to take action to improve job prospects and develop new skills. This can include pursuing additional education or training, volunteering or pursuing internships, or networking with other professionals in your field. By actively seeking new opportunities and developing new skills, you can improve your chances of finding employment and build resilience during challenging times.

It can also be helpful to seek out government resources and support programs for job loss and unemployment. This can include unemployment insurance, job training programs, and job placement services. These resources can provide financial assistance and help you navigate the job market during difficult times.

Finally, it can be helpful to pursue alternate sources of income or start a small business. This can include freelancing or consulting work, selling goods or services online, or starting a small business. By diversifying your income sources, you can reduce the impact of job loss or unemployment and improve your financial stability.

Job loss and unemployment are significant challenges during recessions, but there are strategies and resources available to help cope with these challenges. By prioritizing self-care, developing new skills and pursuing new opportunities, seeking government resources and support, and pursuing alternate sources of income, individuals can build resilience and improve their long-term financial prospects. While these strategies may require effort and perseverance, they can pay off in the long run by providing financial stability and improving career prospects during and after a recession.

Overview of job loss and unemployment during a recession

Job loss and unemployment are among the most significant impacts of recessions on individuals and families. During an economic downturn, companies may lay off employees or reduce work hours, making it difficult for many people to find employment. Coping with job loss and unemployment during a recession can be challenging, but there are strategies and resources available to help navigate these challenges. Below we will provide an overview of job loss and unemployment during a recession.

Job Loss During a Recession

Job loss during a recession can be sudden and unexpected. Companies may need to cut costs to stay afloat, leading to layoffs or reduced work hours for employees. These job losses can impact workers in a wide range of industries, including manufacturing, finance, and retail.

During a recession, job loss can be particularly challenging due to increased competition for jobs. Many companies may be hesitant to hire new employees, making it difficult for those who have been laid off to find work. This can lead to increased financial strain, as well as feelings of frustration and hopelessness.

Unemployment During a Recession

Unemployment during a recession is a significant challenge for many individuals and families. Unemployment rates may increase during a recession as companies reduce staff or close their doors altogether. This can lead to a reduced number of job opportunities and increased competition for available jobs.

Unemployment during a recession can have significant financial and emotional impacts. In addition to the loss of income, unemployment can lead to feelings of stress, anxiety, and depression. Unemployment can also lead to social isolation and a loss of sense of purpose or identity.

Strategies for Coping with Job Loss and Unemployment During a Recession

There are several strategies for coping with job loss and unemployment during a recession. First, it is important to prioritize self-care and mental health. Coping with job loss and unemployment can be stressful and emotionally challenging, so it is important to prioritize self-care and seek support from friends, family, or mental health professionals.

Another strategy is to take action to improve job prospects and develop new skills. This can include pursuing additional education or training, volunteering or pursuing internships, or networking with other professionals in your field. By actively seeking new opportunities and developing new skills, you can improve your chances of finding employment and build resilience during challenging times.

It can also be helpful to seek out government resources and support programs for job loss and unemployment. This can include unemployment insurance, job training programs, and job placement services. These resources can provide financial assistance and help you navigate the job market during difficult times.

Finally, it can be helpful to pursue alternate sources of income or start a small business. This can include freelancing or consulting work, selling goods or services online, or starting a small business. By diversifying your income sources, you can reduce the impact of job loss or unemployment and improve your financial stability.

Job loss and unemployment are significant challenges during recessions, but there are strategies and resources available to help cope with these challenges. By prioritizing self-care, developing new skills and pursuing new opportunities, seeking government resources and support, and pursuing alternate sources of income, individuals can build resilience and improve their long-term financial prospects. While these strategies may require effort and perseverance, they can pay off in the long run by providing financial stability and improving career prospects during and after a recession.

Strategies for coping with job loss and unemployment

Job loss and unemployment are among the most significant challenges individuals face during a recession. The sudden loss of a job can be emotionally and financially challenging, and it can be difficult to know where to turn for support. However, there are strategies and resources available to help individuals cope with job loss and unemployment during a recession. Below we will discuss some of the strategies for coping with job loss and unemployment during a recession.

Prioritize Self-Care and Mental Health

Coping with job loss and unemployment can be stressful and emotionally challenging, so it is important to prioritize self-care and seek support from friends, family, or mental health professionals. This can include activities such as exercise, meditation, or spending time in nature, as well as seeking out support from friends or family members who can provide emotional support and encouragement.

In addition, it is important to seek professional support if you are struggling with your mental health. Many mental health professionals offer services on a sliding scale, so even if you do not have health insurance, you may be able to find affordable support. Seeking support from a mental health professional can help you process your feelings and develop coping strategies to manage the stress and anxiety of job loss or unemployment.

Develop New Skills and Pursue New Opportunities

During a recession, it can be challenging to find employment due to increased competition for jobs. However, by actively seeking new opportunities and developing new skills, you can improve your chances of finding employment and build resilience during challenging times.

This can include pursuing additional education or training, volunteering or pursuing internships, or networking with other professionals in your field. By developing new skills and pursuing new opportunities, you can expand your professional network and improve your chances of finding employment, even in a challenging job market.

Seek Out Government Resources and Support Programs

There are several government resources and support programs available to help individuals cope with job loss and unemployment during a recession. This can include unemployment insurance, job training programs, and job placement services.

Unemployment insurance provides financial assistance to individuals who have lost their jobs due to no fault of their own. This can help individuals meet their basic needs while they look for new employment opportunities. Additionally, job training programs can provide individuals with the skills and knowledge necessary to succeed in new industries or job roles, while job placement services can help connect individuals with job opportunities in their field.

Pursue Alternate Sources of Income

In addition to seeking government resources and support programs, it can be helpful to pursue alternate sources of income or start a small business. This can include freelancing or consulting work, selling goods or services online, or starting a small business.

By diversifying your income sources, you can reduce the impact of job loss or unemployment and improve your financial stability. Additionally, pursuing alternate sources of income can provide you with new opportunities to develop skills and build your professional network, which can help you find new employment opportunities in the future.

Job loss and unemployment can be challenging during a recession, but there are strategies and resources available to help individuals cope with these challenges. By prioritizing self-care, developing new skills and pursuing new opportunities, seeking government resources and support, and pursuing alternate sources of income, individuals can build resilience and improve their long-term financial prospects. While these strategies may require effort and perseverance, they can pay off in the long run by providing financial stability and improving career prospects during and after a recession.

Finding new employment opportunities

During a recession, the job market becomes highly competitive and finding new employment opportunities can be challenging. However, there are strategies and resources available to help individuals navigate the job market and find new employment opportunities. Below we will discuss some of the strategies for finding new employment opportunities during a recession.

Expand Your Job Search

During a recession, it may be necessary to expand your job search beyond your current industry or geographic location. This can include searching for jobs in related industries or exploring remote work opportunities. By expanding your job search, you can increase your chances of finding new employment opportunities and reduce the impact of the recession on your career prospects.

Develop a Targeted Resume and Cover Letter

When applying for new jobs during a recession, it is important to develop a targeted resume and cover letter that highlight your skills and experience relevant to the job. This can help you stand out in a highly competitive job market and increase your chances of getting an interview.

In addition, tailoring your resume and cover letter to each job you apply for can show that you have put in the effort to understand the job requirements and can meet the employer's needs.

Network and Seek Referrals

Networking and seeking referrals from friends, family, or professional contacts can be a powerful way to find new employment opportunities. Many job openings are never publicly advertised, and networking can help you tap into these hidden job opportunities.

In addition, seeking referrals from professional contacts can provide you with an advantage in the job market, as employers are often more likely to hire someone who has been recommended by someone they trust.

Use Job Search Engines and Online Resources

There are several job search engines and online resources available to help individuals find new employment opportunities. These can include websites such as Indeed, Glassdoor, and LinkedIn, as well as professional organizations and industry-specific job boards.

By using these online resources, you can expand your job search and access a broader range of job opportunities. Additionally, many of these resources provide tools and resources to help you develop your resume and cover letter, prepare for interviews, and negotiate job offers.

Consider Freelancing or Consulting Work

During a recession, many employers may be hesitant to hire full-time employees due to financial uncertainty. However, freelancing or consulting work can provide an alternative way to earn income and develop your skills and experience.

By offering your services as a freelancer or consultant, you can access a broader range of job opportunities and gain experience in new industries or job roles. Additionally, freelancing or consulting work can provide you with more flexibility and control over your schedule, which can be valuable during a recession.

Finding new employment opportunities during a recession can be challenging, but by expanding your job search, developing targeted resumes and cover letters, networking and seeking referrals, using job search engines and online resources, and considering freelancing or consulting work, you can improve your chances of finding new employment opportunities and build resilience during challenging times.

While the job market during a recession may be highly competitive, by being proactive and persistent in your job search, you can find new employment opportunities and improve your long-term career prospects. By using the strategies outlined Below individuals can adapt to the changing job market and successfully navigate the challenges of a recession.

Managing finances during unemployment

During a recession, job loss and unemployment rates tend to increase, making it crucial to manage finances effectively during this challenging time. With no steady income, it can be difficult to maintain a standard of living and meet financial obligations. Below we will discuss some strategies for managing finances during unemployment.

Create a Budget

Creating a budget is essential during unemployment as it helps to track expenses and identify areas where you can cut back. Start by analyzing your income and expenses, and allocate your funds accordingly. Prioritize essential expenses such as rent, utilities, food, and healthcare costs. Cut back on discretionary expenses such as entertainment, dining out, and travel.

By creating a budget and sticking to it, you can manage your finances effectively and avoid falling into debt.

Evaluate Available Resources

During unemployment, it is important to evaluate available resources such as unemployment benefits, severance packages, and emergency funds. Unemployment benefits are designed to provide temporary financial support to individuals who have lost their job. Severance packages may include a lump sum payment, health insurance, or other benefits.

Emergency funds are also essential during unemployment. These funds can help cover unexpected expenses such as medical bills, car repairs, or home repairs. It is recommended to have at least six months' worth of living expenses saved in an emergency fund.

By utilizing available resources, you can ease financial stress and manage your finances effectively during unemployment.

Reduce Expenses

Reducing expenses is a key strategy for managing finances during unemployment. Start by cutting back on non-essential expenses such as entertainment, dining out, and travel. Consider downsizing to a smaller home or car to reduce monthly expenses. Shop around for lower rates on utilities, insurance, and other expenses.

By reducing expenses, you can stretch your finances further and avoid falling into debt.

Generate Income through Freelancing or Part-Time Work

Generating income through freelancing or part-time work is another strategy for managing finances during unemployment. Freelancing or part-time work can provide a source of income while you search for full-time employment.

Consider using your skills and expertise to offer freelance services such as writing, graphic design, or consulting. Look for part-time work in industries that interest you, or consider taking on temporary work to generate income.

By generating income through freelancing or part-time work, you can reduce financial stress and maintain your standard of living during unemployment.

Seek Financial Counseling

Seeking financial counseling can provide valuable guidance and support during unemployment. Financial counselors can help you create a budget, evaluate available resources, and develop a plan for managing your finances during unemployment.

Financial counselors can also provide guidance on debt management, credit counseling, and other financial topics. By seeking financial counseling, you can develop the skills and knowledge needed to manage your finances effectively during unemployment and beyond.

Managing finances during unemployment can be challenging, but by creating a budget, evaluating available resources, reducing expenses, generating income through freelancing or part-time work, and seeking financial counseling, individuals can manage their finances effectively and avoid falling into debt.

During a recession, it is essential to be proactive and develop a plan for managing finances during unemployment. By utilizing the strategies outlined Below individuals can build resilience and maintain financial stability during challenging times.

Practical tips / strategies to reduce debt

Create a budget: Track your income and expenses to understand where your money is going. Use this information to create a realistic budget that allocates funds for debt repayment.

Prioritize high-interest debt: Focus on paying off high-interest debts first, such as credit card balances, as they can accumulate interest quickly and prolong your repayment period.

Consolidate debts: If you have multiple debts, consider consolidating them into a single loan with a lower interest rate. This can help simplify your payments and potentially reduce the overall amount you pay in interest.

Cut unnecessary expenses: Review your spending habits and eliminate any non-essential expenses, such as dining out, subscription services, or impulse purchases. Redirect these savings towards debt repayment.

Increase your income: Look for opportunities to earn extra money, such as taking on a part-time job, freelancing, or selling items you no longer need. Use the additional income to pay off your debt faster.

Make bi-weekly payments: If possible, switch to making payments every two weeks instead of monthly. This can help you pay off your debt faster and reduce the amount of interest you pay over time.

Negotiate with creditors: Contact your creditors to discuss your financial situation and ask for a reduced interest rate or a more manageable repayment plan.

Set up automatic payments: Automate your debt payments to ensure you never miss a payment, which can help you avoid late fees and improve your credit score.

Create an emergency fund: Set aside money in a separate account for emergencies to avoid relying on credit cards or loans in times of need.

Stay disciplined and focused: Reducing debt takes time and dedication. Stay committed to your repayment plan and avoid taking on new debt until you've successfully reduced your existing obligations.

Business and Entrepreneurship During a Recession:

During a recession, businesses and entrepreneurs face unique challenges as consumer spending decreases, unemployment rates rise, and economic uncertainty increases. However, with careful planning and strategic decision-making, businesses and entrepreneurs can not only survive but thrive during a recession. Below we will discuss some strategies for succeeding in business and entrepreneurship during a recession.

Re-evaluate Business Models

During a recession, it is essential to re-evaluate business models and make necessary adjustments to align with the changing economic landscape. This may involve reducing costs, exploring new revenue streams, or pivoting to new business models.

For example, businesses can reduce costs by renegotiating contracts with suppliers or switching to more cost-effective production methods. They can also explore new revenue streams by developing new products or services that meet changing consumer needs.

By re-evaluating business models and making necessary adjustments, businesses can adapt to changing market conditions and position themselves for success during a recession.

Diversify Revenue Streams

Diversifying revenue streams is another strategy for succeeding in business and entrepreneurship during a recession. By offering a range of products or services, businesses can reduce their reliance on a single revenue stream and mitigate the risk of revenue loss.

For example, a restaurant can diversify its revenue streams by offering catering services or launching a food delivery service. A clothing retailer can diversify its revenue streams by selling merchandise online or launching a subscription box service.

By diversifying revenue streams, businesses can expand their customer base, increase revenue, and reduce the impact of economic downturns.

Focus on Customer Retention

During a recession, it is essential to focus on customer retention. Retaining existing customers is often less expensive than acquiring new ones, and satisfied customers are more likely to refer new customers to the business.

Businesses can focus on customer retention by offering exceptional customer service, personalized experiences, and loyalty programs. They can also leverage customer feedback to improve products or services and increase customer satisfaction.

By focusing on customer retention, businesses can maintain revenue and build a loyal customer base, even during a recession.

Embrace Innovation and Creativity

During a recession, businesses and entrepreneurs must embrace innovation and creativity to stand out in a crowded market. This may involve developing new products or services, adopting new technologies, or finding new ways to market products or services.

For example, a marketing agency can embrace innovation and creativity by developing new marketing strategies or offering social media management services. A retail store can embrace innovation and creativity by launching an online store or offering curbside pickup services.

By embracing innovation and creativity, businesses and entrepreneurs can differentiate themselves from competitors and position themselves for success during a recession.

Seek Support and Resources

During a recession, it is essential to seek support and resources to help navigate the challenging economic landscape. This may involve seeking financial assistance, mentorship, or networking opportunities.

For example, businesses can seek financial assistance from government programs, grants, or loans. Entrepreneurs can seek mentorship from experienced professionals or join networking groups to connect with other entrepreneurs and share knowledge and resources.

By seeking support and resources, businesses and entrepreneurs can build resilience and overcome the challenges of a recession.

Succeeding in business and entrepreneurship during a recession requires careful planning, strategic decision-making, and a willingness to adapt to changing market conditions. By re-evaluating business models, diversifying revenue streams, focusing on customer retention, embracing innovation and creativity, and seeking support and resources, businesses and entrepreneurs can not only survive but thrive during a recession.

Overview of strategies for business survival during a recession

A recession can be a challenging time for businesses, as decreased consumer spending, rising unemployment rates, and economic uncertainty can all lead to decreased revenue and profitability. However, with the right strategies in place, businesses can not only survive but even thrive during a recession. Below we will discuss some strategies for business survival during a recession.

Cash Flow Management

Cash flow management is critical during a recession. By carefully managing cash flow, businesses can ensure that they have enough cash on hand to pay bills and meet financial obligations. This may involve reducing expenses, negotiating with suppliers for extended payment terms, or offering discounts to customers for early payment.

In addition, businesses can explore ways to improve cash flow, such as accelerating accounts receivable collection or taking advantage of low-interest loans or credit lines. By managing cash flow effectively, businesses can weather the recession and position themselves for growth when the economy improves.

Marketing and Sales Strategies

During a recession, it is essential to maintain a robust marketing and sales strategy. This may involve identifying new markets, launching new products or services, or offering promotions or discounts to attract new customers.

Businesses can also explore alternative sales channels, such as e-commerce or social media, to reach customers who may be more hesitant to visit physical stores during a recession.

By maintaining a robust marketing and sales strategy, businesses can continue to attract customers and maintain revenue, even during a recession.

Strategic Cost Reduction

Cost reduction is an important strategy for business survival during a recession. However, it is essential to make strategic cost reductions that will not compromise the quality of products or services or harm employee morale.

Businesses can explore ways to reduce costs, such as renegotiating contracts with suppliers, outsourcing non-core functions, or implementing energy-saving measures to reduce utility costs.

By making strategic cost reductions, businesses can maintain profitability and position themselves for growth when the economy improves.

Productivity and Efficiency Improvement

Improving productivity and efficiency is another important strategy for business survival during a recession. By optimizing operations, businesses can reduce costs, improve customer service, and increase profitability.

Businesses can explore ways to improve productivity and efficiency, such as streamlining processes, investing in automation or technology, or implementing lean manufacturing or Six Sigma methodologies.

By improving productivity and efficiency, businesses can reduce costs, increase profitability, and remain competitive even during a recession.

Flexibility and Adaptability

During a recession, it is essential to remain flexible and adaptable to changing market conditions. Businesses can explore ways to pivot their operations or offerings to align with the changing economic landscape.

For example, a restaurant can offer take-out or delivery services to cater to customers who may be hesitant to dine in. A retail store can offer e-commerce or curbside pickup services to reach customers who may be avoiding physical stores.

By remaining flexible and adaptable, businesses can respond to changing market conditions and position themselves for success during a recession.

Surviving a recession requires careful planning, strategic decision-making, and a willingness to adapt to changing market conditions. By implementing strategies for cash flow management, marketing and sales, strategic cost reduction, productivity and efficiency improvement, and flexibility and adaptability, businesses can not only survive but thrive during a recession. With these strategies in place, businesses can weather the recession and emerge stronger and more competitive when the economy improves.

Pivoting business models to adapt to a recession

A recession can be a challenging time for businesses, as decreased consumer spending, rising unemployment rates, and economic uncertainty can all lead to decreased revenue and profitability. However, businesses that are able to pivot their business models to adapt to changing market conditions can position themselves for success even during a recession. Below we will discuss strategies for pivoting business models to adapt to a recession.

Identify New Markets

During a recession, it is essential to identify new markets that may be more resilient to economic downturns. Businesses can explore ways to pivot their offerings to align with these new markets.

For example, a company that produces luxury goods may shift its focus to offering more affordable products that appeal to budget-conscious consumers. Alternatively, a company that primarily sells to businesses may explore opportunities to sell directly to consumers who may be more hesitant to purchase from traditional channels during a recession.

By identifying new markets and adjusting business models accordingly, businesses can maintain revenue and profitability even during a recession.

Offer New Products or Services

During a recession, businesses can explore opportunities to launch new products or services that are better suited to changing market conditions.

For example, a company that produces office furniture may pivot its offerings to focus on home office furniture as more people work from home during a recession. Alternatively, a restaurant may shift its menu to focus on take-out or delivery options that cater to customers who may be hesitant to dine in.

By offering new products or services that are better suited to changing market conditions, businesses can attract new customers and maintain revenue during a recession.

Explore New Sales Channels

During a recession, businesses can explore opportunities to sell through new channels that may be more resilient to economic downturns.

For example, a retail store may shift its focus to e-commerce to reach customers who may be avoiding physical stores during a recession. Alternatively, a business-to-business company may explore opportunities to sell through online marketplaces that cater to small businesses.

By exploring new sales channels, businesses can reach new customers and maintain revenue during a recession.

Diversify Revenue Streams

During a recession, businesses can explore opportunities to diversify their revenue streams to reduce dependence on any one source of revenue.

For example, a company that primarily sells products may explore opportunities to offer services that complement its existing offerings. Alternatively, a company that primarily sells to businesses may explore opportunities to sell directly to consumers through new channels.

By diversifying revenue streams, businesses can reduce dependence on any one source of revenue and maintain profitability even during a recession.

Embrace Technology

During a recession, businesses can explore opportunities to embrace technology to increase efficiency, reduce costs, and reach new customers.

For example, a restaurant may implement an online ordering system to streamline its operations and attract customers who may be hesitant to dine in. Alternatively, a manufacturing company may invest in automation to increase efficiency and reduce labor costs.

By embracing technology, businesses can position themselves for success even during a recession.

Adapting to a recession requires careful planning, strategic decision-making, and a willingness to pivot business models to align with changing market conditions. By identifying new markets, offering new products or services, exploring new sales channels, diversifying revenue streams, and embracing technology, businesses can not only survive but thrive during a recession. With these strategies in place, businesses can position themselves for success and emerge stronger and more competitive when the economy improves.

Finding opportunities for growth during a recession

A recession can be a challenging time for businesses, but it can also present opportunities for growth and innovation. Below we will discuss strategies for finding opportunities for growth during a recession.

Research and Analyze Market Trends

During a recession, market trends may shift and change in unexpected ways. It is important for businesses to research and analyze these trends to identify new opportunities for growth.

For example, a company that produces luxury goods may identify an opportunity to produce affordable products that appeal to budget-conscious consumers during a recession. Alternatively, a business may identify a new market or customer segment that is more resilient to economic downturns and pivot their offerings accordingly.

By researching and analyzing market trends, businesses can identify opportunities for growth and adapt their strategies accordingly.

Focus on Customer Needs

During a recession, customers may have different needs and priorities. Businesses that are able to identify and meet these needs can position themselves for growth even during a challenging economic environment.

For example, a company that produces cleaning products may identify an opportunity to develop new products that address increased demand for sanitization during a pandemic. Alternatively, a retailer may identify an opportunity to offer financing options that cater to budget-conscious customers during a recession.

By focusing on customer needs, businesses can attract new customers and retain existing ones, positioning themselves for growth even during a recession.

Innovate and Improve Processes

During a recession, businesses may be forced to operate with reduced resources and tighter budgets. This can present an opportunity for businesses to innovate and improve their processes to operate more efficiently and effectively.

For example, a manufacturing company may invest in automation to increase efficiency and reduce labor costs. Alternatively, a retailer may implement new inventory management systems to reduce waste and improve margins.

By innovating and improving processes, businesses can reduce costs and position themselves for growth even during a recession.

Collaborate and Build Partnerships

During a recession, businesses may need to collaborate and build partnerships to share resources and reduce costs. This can present an opportunity for businesses to expand their networks and create new opportunities for growth.

For example, a small business may partner with a larger company to share resources and reach new customers. Alternatively, businesses in similar industries may collaborate to develop new products or services that cater to changing market needs.

By collaborating and building partnerships, businesses can share resources, reduce costs, and position themselves for growth even during a recession.

Invest in Marketing and Branding

During a recession, businesses may be tempted to cut back on marketing and branding efforts to save costs. However, this can be a missed opportunity for growth.

By investing in marketing and branding efforts, businesses can attract new customers and increase their visibility in a crowded marketplace. This can help businesses to position themselves for growth even during a recession.

While a recession can be a challenging time for businesses, it can also present opportunities for growth and innovation. By researching and analyzing market trends, focusing on customer needs, innovating and improving processes, collaborating and building partnerships, and investing in marketing and branding efforts, businesses can position themselves for growth even during a challenging economic environment. With these strategies in place, businesses can not only survive a recession but emerge stronger and more competitive than before.

Starting a business during a recession

Starting a business is always a risk, but starting a business during a recession can be even more challenging. Below we will discuss some of the key factors to consider when starting a business during a recession and strategies for success.

Identify a Resilient Market

During a recession, certain industries may be more resilient than others. For example, industries such as healthcare, technology, and e-commerce have shown resilience during recent recessions. It is important to identify a market that is less likely to be impacted by an economic downturn and that has the potential for growth.

Develop a Solid Business Plan

A solid business plan is essential for any new business, but it is especially important during a recession. The plan should include a detailed analysis of the market, the competition, the target audience, and the financial projections. It should also outline a strategy for adapting to changing market conditions.

Keep Costs Low

During a recession, cash flow is critical. To maximize cash flow, it is important to keep costs as low as possible. This means finding ways to operate efficiently, such as by outsourcing, using technology to streamline processes, and minimizing unnecessary expenses.

Be Creative with Financing

Access to financing can be more challenging during a recession, but there are still options available. Consider alternative sources of funding, such as crowdfunding, angel investors, or government grants. It is also important to maintain a good credit score and develop strong relationships with lenders.

Build a Strong Network

Networking is important for any new business, but it is especially important during a recession. Build relationships with other entrepreneurs, industry experts, and potential customers. Attend industry events, join professional organizations, and participate in online forums and communities.

Focus on Marketing

Marketing is critical for any business, but it is especially important during a recession. To be successful, a business must have a clear and compelling message that resonates with its target audience. This means developing a strong brand, creating a website and social media presence, and investing in advertising and public relations.

Remain Flexible and Adaptable

During a recession, the market can change rapidly. A successful business must be able to adapt quickly to changing market conditions. This means being open to new ideas, being willing to pivot the business model if necessary, and remaining flexible in terms of operations and financing.

Starting a business during a recession can be challenging, but it can also be an opportunity for success. By identifying a resilient market, developing a solid business plan, keeping costs low, being creative with financing, building a strong network, focusing on marketing, and remaining flexible and adaptable, a new business can position itself for success even in a challenging economic environment. With the right strategies in place, a new business can not only survive a recession but emerge stronger and more competitive than before.

Successful Businesses Started During Past Recessions

Microsoft - Microsoft was founded in 1975 during the Recession of 1973-1975. The company became a dominant player in the technology industry and has had a lasting impact on the global economy.

Hewlett-Packard - Hewlett-Packard was founded in 1939 during the Great Depression. The technology company became a leading manufacturer of computers and other electronic devices.

General Electric - General Electric was founded in 1892 during the Panic of 1890. The company became a leading manufacturer of a wide range of products, including appliances, aircraft engines, and medical equipment.

Burger King - Burger King was founded in 1953 during the Recession of 1953-1954. The fast-food chain became a popular alternative to traditional sit-down restaurants.

FedEx - FedEx was founded in 1971 during a period of economic uncertainty. The shipping company became a popular option for businesses and consumers looking for fast and reliable shipping services.

Trader Joe's - Trader Joe's was founded in 1958 during the Recession of 1958. The grocery store chain became popular for its unique and affordable products.

Electronic Arts - Electronic Arts was founded in 1982 during a period of economic uncertainty. The video game company became a leading player in the industry and has produced many popular games.

Procter & Gamble - Procter & Gamble was founded in 1837 during a period of economic uncertainty. The consumer goods company became a leading manufacturer of a wide range of products, including household cleaning products and personal care items.

LinkedIn - LinkedIn was founded in 2002 during the aftermath of the dot-com bubble. The professional networking site became popular as individuals and businesses looked for ways to connect and network during difficult economic times.

Salesforce - Salesforce was founded in 1999 during the dot-com bubble. The cloud-based software company became a leading player in the industry and has had a significant impact on the way businesses operate.

Uber - Uber was founded in 2009 during the Great Recession. The ride-hailing company experienced rapid growth and became a popular alternative to traditional taxi services.

Airbnb - Airbnb was founded in 2008 during the Great Recession. The home-sharing platform became a popular option for travelers seeking affordable accommodations.

WhatsApp - WhatsApp was founded in 2009 during the Great Recession. The messaging app experienced rapid growth and was eventually acquired by Facebook.

Groupon - Groupon was founded in 2008 during the Great Recession. The online coupon company became popular as consumers looked for ways to save money during difficult economic times.

Venmo - Venmo was founded in 2009 during the Great Recession. The mobile payment app became popular as consumers looked for convenient and affordable payment options.

Square - Square was founded in 2009 during the Great Recession. The mobile payment company became popular as small businesses looked for affordable and convenient payment options.

Instagram - Instagram was founded in 2010 during the aftermath of the Great Recession. The photo-sharing app became popular as consumers looked for ways to connect and share during difficult economic times.

Slack - Slack was founded in 2009 during the Great Recession. The workplace messaging platform became popular as businesses looked for affordable and efficient ways to communicate.

Pinterest - Pinterest was founded in 2009 during the Great Recession. The social media platform became popular as consumers looked for ways to explore and share ideas during difficult economic times.

Dropbox - Dropbox was founded in 2007, just before the Great Recession. The cloud storage company experienced rapid growth as consumers and businesses looked for affordable and efficient ways to store and share data.

Community and Government Response to a Recession:

A recession can have a significant impact on a community, causing job losses, business closures, and financial hardships for many individuals and families. Below we will discuss the role of the community and government in responding to a recession and strategies for supporting those impacted by economic downturns.

Community Support

Communities can play an important role in supporting individuals and families impacted by a recession. This can include the creation of local support networks, such as food banks, job placement services, and financial assistance programs. In addition, community leaders can work together to support local businesses, such as by encouraging residents to shop locally or by promoting tourism to the area.

Government Response

Governments can also play a significant role in responding to a recession. This can include fiscal policies, such as tax cuts or stimulus spending, as well as monetary policies, such as interest rate reductions or quantitative easing. In addition, governments can create programs and initiatives to support businesses and workers, such as job training programs, small business loans, and unemployment benefits.

Public-Private Partnerships

Public-private partnerships can also be effective in responding to a recession. These partnerships can bring together government entities, businesses, and community organizations to coordinate efforts and maximize resources. For example, a local government might work with a chamber of commerce to create a job placement program for unemployed residents.

Economic Development Strategies

During a recession, economic development strategies can be particularly important. These strategies can include efforts to attract new businesses to the area, as well as initiatives to support existing businesses. For example, a local government might offer tax incentives or other benefits to businesses that relocate to the area or expand their operations.

Education and Training

Education and training programs can also be important in responding to a recession. For example, a local community college might offer job training programs to help workers gain the skills they need to succeed in a changing job market. In addition, educational programs can help entrepreneurs develop the skills and knowledge they need to start and grow successful businesses.

Social Safety Net Programs

Social safety net programs, such as food stamps and Medicaid, can be a critical source of support for individuals and families impacted by a recession. These programs can help to ensure that those who are struggling financially have access to basic needs, such as food, healthcare, and housing.

The role of international organizations in

responding to global recessions

In today's globalized world, economic crises and recessions can have far-reaching consequences, impacting people and businesses in every corner of the planet. As a result, international organizations play a critical role in responding to global recessions, working to mitigate the negative effects and promote recovery. Below we will explore the role of international organizations in responding to global recessions, highlighting their efforts to stabilize markets, promote growth, and support those most affected by economic downturns.

First, let's define what we mean by a "global recession." Typically, a global recession is characterized by a significant and widespread decline in economic activity across multiple countries or regions. This can be triggered by a variety of factors, including financial crises, natural disasters, geopolitical tensions, or other external shocks. When a recession hits, the effects can be felt by individuals, families, and businesses alike. High unemployment, decreased consumer spending, and reduced investment can all contribute to a downward spiral of economic activity, which can be difficult to reverse without intervention.

International organizations such as the International Monetary Fund (IMF) and the World Bank have a crucial role to play in responding to global recessions. These organizations work to promote economic stability and growth around the world, providing technical assistance, financial support, and policy advice to member countries. In times of crisis, the IMF can provide emergency financing to countries experiencing balance of payment difficulties, helping to stabilize exchange rates and prevent further economic decline. Similarly, the World Bank provides development assistance to countries in need, supporting projects and initiatives that can help to spur economic growth and create jobs.

In addition to these large-scale efforts, international organizations also work to address the specific challenges faced by individuals and communities during recessions. For example, the United Nations Development Programme (UNDP) supports programs that provide social safety nets and other forms of assistance to vulnerable populations, helping to alleviate the worst effects of economic downturns. The UNDP also supports initiatives that promote job creation and entrepreneurship, helping individuals and communities to become more resilient in the face of economic challenges.

Another key player in responding to global recessions is the Group of Twenty (G20), a forum for the world's largest economies. The G20 brings together government officials and other stakeholders to discuss economic policy and coordinate responses to global challenges, including recessions. During the 2008-2009 global financial crisis, the G20 played a critical role in coordinating policy responses among member countries, helping to prevent a deeper and more prolonged recession. Since then, the G20 has continued to work to promote global economic stability, with a particular focus on inclusive growth and reducing inequality.

It's worth noting that the role of international organizations in responding to global recessions is not without controversy. Some critics argue that these organizations prioritize the interests of wealthy countries and multinational corporations over the needs of ordinary people in developing countries. Others argue that the policy prescriptions of organizations like the IMF and World Bank have sometimes exacerbated economic problems, rather than solving them.

Despite these criticisms, however, there is no doubt that international organizations have an important role to play in responding to global recessions. Without their efforts to promote stability, coordinate policy responses, and support vulnerable populations, the effects of economic downturns would likely be far more severe and prolonged. Going forward, it will be important for these organizations to continue to evolve and adapt their approaches to ensure that they are effectively responding to the needs of all people, regardless of where they live or their level of economic development.

The role of international organizations in responding to global recessions is multifaceted and complex. These organizations work to promote economic stability, provide emergency financing and development assistance, and support vulnerable populations during times of crisis. While their efforts are not always without controversy, there is no doubt that they play a critical role in mitigating

Investing During a Recession

Investing during a recession can be a daunting prospect for many individuals. Economic downturns can be unpredictable and volatile, leaving many people unsure of where to turn when it comes to their investments. However, history has shown that investing during a recession can be a smart move for those who are willing to take a long-term view and make informed decisions. Below we will explore some of the key considerations and strategies for investing during a recession, highlighting the potential benefits and risks involved.

First, it's important to understand what we mean by a "recession." Typically, a recession is characterized by a significant and widespread decline in economic activity across multiple countries or regions. This can be triggered by a variety of factors, including financial crises, natural disasters, geopolitical tensions, or other external shocks. When a recession hits, the effects can be felt by individuals, families, and businesses alike. High unemployment, decreased consumer spending, and reduced investment can all contribute to a downward spiral of economic activity, which can be difficult to reverse without intervention.

So why might someone consider investing during a recession? One key reason is that recessions often lead to lower asset prices, presenting buying opportunities for savvy investors. When prices are low, investors can purchase stocks, bonds, and other assets at a discount, potentially benefiting from future gains when the market recovers. However, it's important to note that investing during a recession is not a guaranteed path to success. There are risks involved, and investors should approach the process with caution and careful consideration.

One important consideration for investors during a recession is asset allocation. Diversifying investments across different asset classes, such as stocks, bonds, and real estate, can help to spread risk and potentially provide more stable returns over the long term. However, it's also important to consider the specific risks associated with each asset class. For example, stocks can be more volatile than bonds, but may also offer higher potential returns over the long term. Real estate can provide a hedge against inflation, but can also be affected by local market conditions and changes in interest rates.

Another key consideration for investors during a recession is risk tolerance. Recessions can be unpredictable and volatile, and investing in the stock market during a downturn can be a nerve-wracking experience for some. However, it's important to remember that investing is a long-term game, and short-term market fluctuations should not dictate investment decisions. Those with a high tolerance for risk may be willing to take on more volatile investments, while those with a lower tolerance may prefer more stable options.

It's also important for investors to do their research and stay informed about the state of the economy and the market. This can involve following news and analysis from financial experts, monitoring economic indicators such as GDP growth and unemployment rates, and keeping a close eye on the performance of specific stocks and asset classes. However, it's also important to remember that no one can predict the future with certainty, and even the most knowledgeable experts can be wrong.

One potential strategy for investing during a recession is dollar-cost averaging. This involves investing a fixed amount of money at regular intervals, regardless of the current market conditions. By doing this, investors can potentially benefit from market downturns by purchasing assets at a lower cost. However, it's important to note that dollar-cost averaging is not a guaranteed way to profit from a recession, and investors should consider the specific risks involved before using this strategy.

Another potential strategy for investing during a recession is to focus on defensive stocks and sectors. These are companies and industries that tend to perform well even during economic downturns, such as healthcare, utilities, and consumer staples. By investing in these sectors, investors can potentially benefit from stable returns even when other parts of the market are struggling.

Of course, investing during a recession is not without risks.

The impact of recessions on the stock market

Recessions have a significant impact on the stock market. Economic downturns can trigger a sharp decline in the stock market, as investors become more risk-averse and companies face reduced demand for their products and services. However, the specific impact of a recession on the stock market can vary depending on a range of factors, including the severity and duration of the recession, the performance of individual companies and sectors, and broader economic trends. Below we will explore the impact of recessions on the stock market, highlighting some of the key factors that can influence stock prices during economic downturns.

First, it's important to understand how recessions can affect the broader economy. Typically, recessions are characterized by a decline in economic activity, including reduced consumer spending, decreased investment, and higher unemployment rates. These factors can have a ripple effect on companies and industries, with some businesses faring better than others during economic downturns.

One factor that can influence the impact of a recession on the stock market is the performance of individual companies and sectors. During a recession, companies that are heavily reliant on consumer spending, such as those in the retail and hospitality industries, may struggle as consumers tighten their belts and cut back on discretionary spending. On the other hand, companies that provide essential goods and services, such as healthcare providers and utilities, may fare better during a recession.

In addition to the performance of individual companies and sectors, broader economic trends can also influence the impact of a recession on the stock market. For example, changes in interest rates and inflation can affect the cost of borrowing and the overall health of the economy, which in turn can impact the stock market. Government policies, such as stimulus spending and monetary policy, can also have a significant impact on the stock market during a recession.

One key way that recessions can impact the stock market is through investor sentiment. During a recession, investors may become more risk-averse, preferring to hold onto cash or invest in safer assets such as bonds. This can lead to a sharp decline in the stock market, as investors sell off stocks and other riskier assets. However, it's worth noting that investor sentiment can be influenced by a range of factors, including news and events that are unrelated to the recession itself.

Another important factor to consider when examining the impact of recessions on the stock market is the duration and severity of the recession. A short and mild recession may have a relatively small impact on the stock market, while a prolonged and severe recession can lead to a more sustained decline in stock prices. However, it's also worth noting that the stock market is forward-looking, meaning that investors may begin to anticipate an economic recovery even before the recession has officially ended.

So what does all of this mean for investors? During a recession, the stock market can be a volatile and unpredictable place. However, history has shown that there can be opportunities for investors who are willing to take a long-term view and make informed decisions. For example, investing in defensive stocks and sectors that are likely to perform well during a recession, such as healthcare and utilities, can help to mitigate the impact of a market downturn. Similarly, dollar-cost averaging, which involves investing a fixed amount of money at regular intervals, can help investors to benefit from lower stock prices during a recession.

It's also important for investors to stay informed about the state of the economy and the stock market, monitoring economic indicators and following news and analysis from financial experts. However, it's worth remembering that no one can predict the future with certainty, and even the most knowledgeable experts can be wrong.

Strategies for managing investments during a recession

Managing investments during a recession can be a challenging task for investors. Economic downturns can be unpredictable and volatile, leading many people to feel uncertain about how to approach their investments. However, history has shown that there are strategies that investors can use to help mitigate the impact of a recession on their portfolios. Below we will explore some of the key strategies for managing investments during a recession, highlighting the potential benefits and risks involved.

First, it's important to understand what we mean by a "recession." Typically, a recession is characterized by a significant and widespread decline in economic activity across multiple countries or regions. This can be triggered by a variety of factors, including financial crises, natural disasters, geopolitical tensions, or other external shocks. When a recession hits, the effects can be felt by individuals, families, and businesses alike. High unemployment, decreased consumer spending, and reduced investment can all contribute to a downward spiral of economic activity, which can be difficult to reverse without intervention.

So what are some of the strategies that investors can use to manage their investments during a recession? One key approach is to focus on diversification. Diversification involves spreading investments across different asset classes, such as stocks, bonds, and real estate, in order to reduce risk and potentially provide more stable returns over the long term. During a recession, some asset classes may perform better than others, and diversification can help investors to weather the storm by ensuring that their portfolios are not overly reliant on any one type of investment.

Another potential strategy for managing investments during a recession is to focus on defensive stocks and sectors. Defensive stocks are those that tend to perform well even during economic downturns, such as healthcare, utilities, and consumer staples. By investing in these sectors, investors can potentially benefit from stable returns even when other parts of the market are struggling. However, it's worth noting that defensive stocks may also be more expensive during a recession, as investors flock to these safer investments.

Another potential strategy for managing investments during a recession is to focus on high-quality companies with strong fundamentals. Companies with strong balance sheets, solid cash flow, and stable earnings may be better positioned to weather a recession than companies with weaker fundamentals. By investing in these high-quality companies, investors can potentially benefit from long-term gains even during a recession.

It's also important for investors to consider the specific risks and opportunities associated with each asset class and investment. For example, during a recession, bonds may be a safer investment than stocks, but they may also offer lower returns over the long term. Similarly, real estate may provide a hedge against inflation, but it can also be affected by local market conditions and changes in interest rates.

Another key consideration for managing investments during a recession is risk tolerance. Recessions can be unpredictable and volatile, and investing in the stock market during a downturn can be a nerve-wracking experience for some. However, it's important to remember that investing is a long-term game, and short-term market fluctuations should not dictate investment decisions. Those with a high tolerance for risk may be willing to take on more volatile investments, while those with a lower tolerance may prefer more stable options.

It's also important for investors to stay informed about the state of the economy and the stock market, monitoring economic indicators and following news and analysis from financial experts. However, it's worth remembering that no one can predict the future with certainty, and even the most knowledgeable experts can be wrong.

The role of diversification in managing risk during a recession

Diversification is a key strategy for managing risk during a recession. Economic downturns can be unpredictable and volatile, leading many investors to feel uncertain about how to protect their portfolios. However, history has shown that diversification can be an effective way to mitigate the impact of a recession on investments. Below we will explore the role of diversification in managing risk during a recession, highlighting the potential benefits and risks involved.

First, it's important to understand what we mean by diversification. Diversification involves spreading investments across different asset classes, such as stocks, bonds, and real estate, in order to reduce risk and potentially provide more stable returns over the long term. By investing in a mix of assets, investors can potentially benefit from gains in one area even when another area is struggling. During a recession, some asset classes may perform better than others, and diversification can help investors to weather the storm by ensuring that their portfolios are not overly reliant on any one type of investment.

So what are some of the benefits of diversification during a recession? One key advantage is that it can help to reduce overall risk. By spreading investments across different asset classes, investors can potentially benefit from gains in one area even when another area is struggling. This can help to protect against significant losses during a recession, as well as reduce the impact of short-term market fluctuations on the overall portfolio.

Another advantage of diversification during a recession is that it can help to provide more stable returns over the long term. By investing in a mix of assets, investors can potentially benefit from gains in some areas even when others are struggling. This can help to provide a more consistent return on investment, which can be particularly important for those who are investing for the long term.

However, it's worth noting that diversification is not without risks. One potential risk is that diversification can lead to lower overall returns, particularly during times when one asset class is significantly outperforming others. In addition, diversification may not protect against all types of risks, such as geopolitical risks or changes in interest rates.

So what are some of the strategies that investors can use to diversify their portfolios during a recession? One key approach is to focus on asset allocation. Asset allocation involves determining the appropriate mix of investments based on an individual's investment goals, risk tolerance, and time horizon. During a recession, investors may want to consider shifting their asset allocation towards defensive investments, such as bonds and utilities, that are less likely to be impacted by economic downturns.

Another potential strategy for diversification during a recession is to focus on low-cost index funds or exchange-traded funds (ETFs). These types of investments provide exposure to a broad range of assets, allowing investors to diversify their portfolios without the need for extensive research or management. In addition, low-cost index funds and ETFs may offer lower fees and expenses than actively managed funds, potentially allowing investors to benefit from higher overall returns.

It's also important for investors to consider the specific risks and opportunities associated with each asset class and investment. For example, during a recession, bonds may be a safer investment than stocks, but they may also offer lower returns over the long term. Similarly, real estate may provide a hedge against inflation, but it can also be affected by local market conditions and changes in interest rates.

Another important consideration for diversification during a recession is risk tolerance. Recessions can be unpredictable and volatile, and investing in the stock market during a downturn can be a nerve-wracking experience for some. However, it's important to remember that investing is a long-term game, and short-term market fluctuations should not dictate investment decisions. Those with a high tolerance for risk may be willing to take on more volatile investments, while those with a lower tolerance may prefer more stable options.

The Impact of Recessions on Education

Recessions have a significant impact on education, affecting everything from student enrollment and funding to curriculum and career prospects. Economic downturns can cause widespread disruption in the education sector, as students, educators, and institutions face financial pressures and changing priorities. Below we will explore the impact of recessions on education, highlighting some of the key challenges and opportunities that arise during economic downturns.

One of the most significant impacts of recessions on education is a decrease in funding. During a recession, governments and private institutions may be forced to cut funding for education in order to balance their budgets. This can have a significant impact on schools, universities, and other educational institutions, as they may be forced to reduce staff, cut programs, or increase tuition in order to make up for lost revenue. In addition, students may be less likely to apply for higher education during a recession, as they may be more concerned about their ability to pay for tuition and living expenses.

Another key impact of recessions on education is a shift in priorities. During economic downturns, students and educators may need to focus on skills and knowledge that are more immediately relevant to the job market. For example, students may be more likely to pursue degrees or certificates in fields such as healthcare, technology, or business, which may be more resilient to economic downturns than other sectors. In addition, educators may need to adapt their teaching methods and curriculum to meet the changing needs of students and employers.

Another potential impact of recessions on education is increased competition for jobs and internships. During a recession, job opportunities may be more scarce, leading to increased competition for available positions. This can be particularly challenging for recent graduates and those entering the job market for the first time. However, it's also worth noting that recessions can create new opportunities in emerging sectors or industries, and those who are willing to adapt and develop new skills may be able to take advantage of these opportunities.

It's also important to consider the impact of recessions on students from disadvantaged backgrounds. During economic downturns, low-income students and students from underrepresented groups may be more likely to face financial and other barriers to education. For example, they may be less likely to have access to technology and other resources needed for remote learning, or they may be more likely to drop out of school in order to work and support their families. In addition, reduced funding for social programs and scholarships may make it more difficult for these students to afford higher education.

Another potential impact of recessions on education is a shift towards online and distance learning. During a recession, educational institutions may need to explore new ways of delivering education in order to reduce costs and reach more students. This can involve the use of online courses, virtual classrooms, and other digital technologies. While online learning can offer a range of benefits, including greater flexibility and accessibility, it can also present challenges for students and educators, such as the need for reliable internet access and the difficulty of building relationships and community in a virtual environment.

Recessions have a significant impact on education, affecting everything from student enrollment and funding to curriculum and career prospects. During economic downturns, educational institutions may face financial pressures and changing priorities, leading to reductions in funding and shifts towards more job-relevant skills and knowledge. Students from disadvantaged backgrounds may be particularly vulnerable during recessions, facing financial and other barriers to education. However, recessions can also create new opportunities in emerging sectors and industries, and those who are willing to adapt and develop new skills may be able to take advantage of these opportunities.

The impact of recessions on education funding

Recessions can have a significant impact on education funding, affecting everything from student financial aid and scholarships to school and university budgets. Economic downturns can lead to reductions in government and private funding for education, creating financial pressures for students and educational institutions alike. Below we will explore the impact of recessions on education funding, highlighting some of the key challenges and opportunities that arise during economic downturns.

One of the most significant impacts of recessions on education funding is a decrease in government support. During a recession, governments may be forced to cut funding for education in order to balance their budgets. This can have a significant impact on schools, universities, and other educational institutions, as they may be forced to reduce staff, cut programs, or increase tuition in order to make up for lost revenue. In addition, students may be less likely to apply for higher education during a recession, as they may be more concerned about their ability to pay for tuition and living expenses.

Another potential impact of recessions on education funding is reduced support for student financial aid and scholarships. During economic downturns, government and private organizations may be less likely to provide financial support for students pursuing higher education. This can make it more difficult for low-income students and students from underrepresented groups to afford tuition and other educational expenses. In addition, scholarships and other funding opportunities may be more competitive during a recession, as more students may be applying for limited resources.

It's also worth noting that recessions can have a ripple effect on education funding, affecting other areas such as research and development. During a recession, universities and other institutions may be less able to invest in research and development, leading to reduced innovation and slower progress in fields such as science and technology. This can have long-term implications for the economy as a whole, as innovation and technological progress are key drivers of economic growth.

Another potential impact of recessions on education funding is a shift in priorities. During economic downturns, educational institutions may need to focus on skills and knowledge that are more immediately relevant to the job market. For example, schools and universities may need to invest more in programs related to healthcare, technology, or business, which may be more resilient to economic downturns than other sectors. However, this can also lead to reduced funding for programs in fields such as the humanities or social sciences, which may be perceived as less immediately relevant to the job market.

It's also important to consider the impact of recessions on state and local funding for education. During a recession, state and local governments may be forced to cut funding for education in order to balance their budgets. This can have a significant impact on K-12 schools, as they are often heavily reliant on state and local funding. Reduced funding can lead to larger class sizes, reduced teacher salaries, and fewer resources for students, which can in turn impact the quality of education and student outcomes.

Another potential impact of recessions on education funding is increased competition for limited resources. During a recession, educational institutions may need to compete more aggressively for limited funding, potentially leading to increased tension and conflict between schools, universities, and other institutions. This can be particularly challenging for smaller or less well-funded institutions, which may struggle to compete with larger or better-resourced organizations.

Recessions can have a significant impact on education funding, affecting everything from student financial aid and scholarships to school and university budgets. During economic downturns, governments and private organizations may be less likely to provide funding for education, leading to reduced support for student financial aid and scholarships, reduced investment in research and development, and shifts in priorities towards more job-relevant skills and knowledge. State and local funding for education may also be reduced, leading to larger class sizes, reduced teacher salaries, and fewer resources for students. However, recessions can also create opportunities for

The impact of recessions on student loan debt

Recessions can have a significant impact on student loan debt, affecting everything from repayment rates and interest rates to default rates and loan forgiveness programs. Economic downturns can create financial pressures for borrowers and lead to changes in government policies related to student loans. Below we will explore the impact of recessions on student loan debt, highlighting some of the key challenges and opportunities that arise during economic downturns.

One of the most significant impacts of recessions on student loan debt is an increase in default rates. During a recession, borrowers may be more likely to experience financial hardship, such as job loss or reduced income, making it more difficult for them to make their monthly loan payments. This can lead to an increase in loan defaults, which can have significant financial and credit consequences for borrowers. In addition, default rates can have wider economic implications, potentially leading to reduced credit availability and increased financial instability.

Another potential impact of recessions on student loan debt is changes in interest rates. During a recession, governments may lower interest rates in order to stimulate economic growth. This can lead to lower interest rates on federal student loans, potentially reducing the cost of borrowing for borrowers. However, it's worth noting that interest rates on private student loans may not be affected by changes in government policy, and borrowers may still face high interest rates and fees.

Another potential impact of recessions on student loan debt is changes in repayment plans and loan forgiveness programs. During economic downturns, governments may make changes to existing repayment plans and loan forgiveness programs in order to provide relief for borrowers. For example, the government may offer income-based repayment plans or temporary loan forbearance programs to help borrowers who are struggling to make their monthly payments. In addition, government may increase funding for loan forgiveness programs, such as Public Service Loan Forgiveness, in order to incentivize borrowers to work in public service or other high-need areas.

It's also worth noting that recessions can have a disproportionate impact on certain types of borrowers. For example, low-income borrowers and borrowers from underrepresented groups may be more vulnerable to financial hardship during a recession, as they may be more likely to experience job loss or reduced income. In addition, borrowers who attended for-profit colleges or universities may be at higher risk of default, as they may have higher levels of debt and lower employment prospects.

Another potential impact of recessions on student loan debt is increased competition for limited resources. During a recession, governments may be less able to provide funding for higher education, leading to increased competition for scholarships and other sources of financial aid. This can be particularly challenging for low-income students and students from underrepresented groups, who may have fewer resources and support networks to help them navigate the application process.

Recessions can have a significant impact on student loan debt, affecting everything from default rates and interest rates to repayment plans and loan forgiveness programs. During economic downturns, borrowers may be more vulnerable to financial hardship, leading to increased default rates and financial instability. However, governments may also make changes to existing policies in order to provide relief for borrowers, such as offering income-based repayment plans or loan forbearance programs. It's important for borrowers to stay informed about changes in government policies and to explore all available options for managing their student loan debt during a recession.

Strategies for managing education during a recession

Recessions can create significant challenges for the education sector, affecting everything from student enrollment and funding to curriculum and career prospects. During economic downturns, educational institutions may face financial pressures and changing priorities, leading to reductions in funding and shifts towards more job-relevant skills and knowledge. Below we will explore some strategies for managing education during a recession, highlighting some of the key opportunities and challenges that arise during economic downturns.

One key strategy for managing education during a recession is to focus on cost containment. During economic downturns, educational institutions may need to explore new ways of reducing costs in order to maintain financial stability. This can involve a range of strategies, such as reducing administrative expenses, consolidating programs, or sharing resources with other institutions. By reducing costs, educational institutions can potentially free up resources for investment in other areas, such as curriculum development or student support services.

Another potential strategy for managing education during a recession is to focus on job-relevant skills and knowledge. During economic downturns, students and educators may need to focus on skills and knowledge that are more immediately relevant to the job market. This can involve investing in programs related to healthcare, technology, or business, which may be more resilient to economic downturns than other sectors. By focusing on job-relevant skills and knowledge, educational institutions can potentially help students to be more competitive in the job market and provide a more valuable education.

Another potential strategy for managing education during a recession is to explore new revenue streams. During economic downturns, educational institutions may need to look beyond traditional funding sources, such as government grants and tuition fees, in order to maintain financial stability. This can involve a range of strategies, such as developing partnerships with businesses and organizations, offering online courses, or developing new revenue-generating programs or services. By exploring new revenue streams, educational institutions can potentially reduce their reliance on traditional funding sources and create new opportunities for growth and innovation.

It's also important for educational institutions to focus on student support and retention during a recession. During economic downturns, students may be more vulnerable to financial and other barriers to education, leading to decreased enrollment and retention rates. Educational institutions can help to address these challenges by providing support services such as financial aid, counseling, and career guidance, and by developing programs and services that address the specific needs of students during a recession.

Another potential strategy for managing education during a recession is to focus on partnerships and collaborations. During economic downturns, educational institutions may need to collaborate with other institutions, businesses, and organizations in order to achieve their goals. This can involve developing partnerships for research and development, sharing resources and expertise, or collaborating on joint programs or initiatives. By working together, educational institutions can potentially reduce costs, increase efficiencies, and create new opportunities for growth and innovation.

It's also important for educational institutions to stay informed about changes in government policies related to education funding and student loans during a recession. Governments may make changes to existing policies in order to provide relief for borrowers and educational institutions, and it's important for educational institutions to stay up-to-date on these changes and to explore all available options for managing their finances during a recession.

Managing education during a recession can be challenging, but there are a range of strategies that educational institutions can use to maintain financial stability, provide a valuable education, and support students. By focusing on cost containment, job-relevant skills and knowledge, new revenue streams, student support and retention, partnerships and collaborations, and staying informed about changes in government policies, educational institutions can weather the storm of a recession and emerge stronger and more resilient in the long term.

Healthcare During a Recession

Recessions can have a significant impact on healthcare, affecting everything from access to care and funding to workforce shortages and public health outcomes. During economic downturns, healthcare systems may face financial pressures and changing priorities, leading to reductions in funding and shifts towards more cost-effective approaches to care. Below we will explore the impact of recessions on healthcare, highlighting some of the key challenges and opportunities that arise during economic downturns.

One of the most significant impacts of recessions on healthcare is a decrease in funding. During a recession, governments and private organizations may be forced to cut funding for healthcare in order to balance their budgets. This can have a significant impact on hospitals, clinics, and other healthcare providers, as they may be forced to reduce staff, cut services, or increase fees in order to make up for lost revenue. In addition, patients may be less likely to seek medical care during a recession, as they may be more concerned about their ability to pay for medical expenses.

Another key impact of recessions on healthcare is a shift in priorities. During economic downturns, healthcare systems may need to focus on cost-effective approaches to care and treatments that provide the most value for patients. This can involve a range of strategies, such as increasing the use of telemedicine, reducing unnecessary testing and procedures, and focusing on preventative care and chronic disease management. By focusing on cost-effective approaches to care, healthcare systems can potentially reduce costs and improve health outcomes for patients.

Another potential impact of recessions on healthcare is workforce shortages. During a recession, healthcare providers may face staffing shortages as budgets are cut and patients may be less likely to seek medical care. This can create challenges for healthcare systems, as they may need to rely more heavily on part-time and contract workers, or may struggle to attract and retain skilled healthcare professionals. In addition, workforce shortages can lead to increased workload and burnout among healthcare providers, potentially impacting the quality of care that patients receive.

It's also important to consider the impact of recessions on public health outcomes. During economic downturns, patients may be more likely to delay or forgo medical care, leading to increased morbidity and mortality rates. In addition, patients may be more vulnerable to mental health issues, substance abuse, and other health problems during a recession, as they may be facing financial and other stressors. Healthcare systems may need to develop new strategies to address these challenges, such as increasing access to mental health services or providing support for patients who are experiencing financial hardship.

Another potential impact of recessions on healthcare is increased competition for limited resources. During a recession, healthcare providers may need to compete more aggressively for limited funding and resources, potentially leading to increased tension and conflict between providers. This can be particularly challenging for smaller or less well-funded healthcare providers, which may struggle to compete with larger or better-resourced organizations.

Another potential strategy for managing healthcare during a recession is to focus on prevention and chronic disease management. During economic downturns, healthcare systems may need to shift their focus towards preventative care and chronic disease management, in order to reduce costs and improve health outcomes. This can involve a range of strategies, such as increasing public health education and awareness, developing new programs to address chronic diseases, and increasing access to primary care and preventative services.

Recessions can have a significant impact on healthcare, affecting everything from access to care and funding to workforce shortages and public health outcomes. During economic downturns, healthcare systems may face financial pressures and changing priorities, leading to reductions in funding and shifts towards more cost-effective approaches to care. By focusing on prevention and chronic disease management, developing new strategies to address workforce shortages and public health challenges, and staying informed about changes in government policies related to healthcare funding and access, healthcare systems can weather the storm of a recession and emerge stronger and more resilient than before.

The impact of recessions on healthcare funding

Recessions can have a significant impact on healthcare funding, affecting everything from public health programs and hospital budgets to access to care and workforce development. Economic downturns can create financial pressures for healthcare systems, leading to reductions in government and private funding and changes in healthcare priorities. Below we will explore the impact of recessions on healthcare funding, highlighting some of the key challenges and opportunities that arise during economic downturns.

One of the most significant impacts of recessions on healthcare funding is a decrease in government support. During a recession, governments may be forced to cut funding for healthcare in order to balance their budgets. This can have a significant impact on hospitals, clinics, and other healthcare providers, as they may be forced to reduce staff, cut services, or increase fees in order to make up for lost revenue. In addition, patients may be less likely to seek medical care during a recession, as they may be more concerned about their ability to pay for medical expenses.

Another potential impact of recessions on healthcare funding is reduced support for public health programs. During economic downturns, governments and private organizations may be less likely to provide financial support for public health programs, such as vaccination campaigns and disease surveillance systems. This can make it more difficult for healthcare systems to respond to emerging public health threats, potentially leading to increased morbidity and mortality rates.

Another potential impact of recessions on healthcare funding is changes in healthcare priorities. During economic downturns, healthcare systems may need to focus on cost-effective approaches to care and treatments that provide the most value for patients. This can involve a range of strategies, such as increasing the use of telemedicine, reducing unnecessary testing and procedures, and focusing on preventative care and chronic disease management. By focusing on cost-effective approaches to care, healthcare systems can potentially reduce costs and improve health outcomes for patients.

It's also important to consider the impact of recessions on access to care. During economic downturns, patients may be more likely to delay or forgo medical care, leading to increased morbidity and mortality rates. This can be particularly challenging for low-income patients and patients from underrepresented groups, who may have fewer resources and support networks to help them navigate the healthcare system. Healthcare systems may need to develop new strategies to address these challenges, such as increasing access to telemedicine and other virtual care options, or developing new programs to address healthcare disparities.

Another potential impact of recessions on healthcare funding is workforce shortages. During a recession, healthcare providers may face staffing shortages as budgets are cut and patients may be less likely to seek medical care. This can create challenges for healthcare systems, as they may need to rely more heavily on part-time and contract workers, or may struggle to attract and retain skilled healthcare professionals. In addition, workforce shortages can lead to increased workload and burnout among healthcare providers, potentially impacting the quality of care that patients receive.

It's also important to consider the impact of recessions on medical research and development. During economic downturns, healthcare systems may be less able to invest in research and development, leading to reduced innovation and slower progress in fields such as medicine and biotechnology. This can have long-term implications for public health, as innovation and technological progress are key drivers of healthcare progress.

Recessions can have a significant impact on healthcare funding, affecting everything from public health programs and hospital budgets to access to care and workforce development. During economic downturns, healthcare systems may face financial pressures and changing priorities, leading to reductions in funding and shifts towards more cost-effective approaches to care. By focusing on prevention and chronic disease management, developing new strategies to address workforce shortages and access to care, and staying informed about changes in government policies related to healthcare funding and access, healthcare systems can weather the storm of a recession and emerge stronger and more resilient.

The impact of recessions on healthcare access

Recessions can have a significant impact on healthcare access, affecting everything from insurance coverage and affordability to availability of services and workforce shortages. Economic downturns can create financial pressures for individuals and families, making it more difficult for them to access healthcare services. Below we will explore the impact of recessions on healthcare access, highlighting some of the key challenges and opportunities that arise during economic downturns.

One of the most significant impacts of recessions on healthcare access is a decrease in insurance coverage. During a recession, individuals and families may be more likely to lose their jobs or experience reduced income, making it more difficult for them to afford healthcare coverage. This can lead to increased rates of uninsured individuals and families, potentially limiting their ability to access necessary healthcare services. In addition, even those with insurance coverage may face increased out-of-pocket costs, making it more difficult for them to afford necessary medical care.

Another potential impact of recessions on healthcare access is reduced availability of services. During economic downturns, healthcare systems may face budget cuts and workforce shortages, leading to reduced availability of services and longer wait times for appointments. This can be particularly challenging for individuals with chronic health conditions or those in need of urgent medical care, who may face increased barriers to accessing timely and effective care.

It's also important to consider the impact of recessions on mental health access. During economic downturns, individuals may be more vulnerable to mental health issues, such as depression, anxiety, and substance abuse. However, reduced insurance coverage and availability of mental health services can make it more difficult for individuals to access the care they need. This can lead to increased rates of untreated mental health issues and potentially more severe outcomes.

Another potential impact of recessions on healthcare access is reduced investment in public health programs. During economic downturns, governments and private organizations may be less likely to provide financial support for public health programs, such as vaccination campaigns and disease surveillance systems. This can limit the ability of healthcare systems to respond to emerging public health threats, potentially leading to increased morbidity and mortality rates.

It's also important to consider the impact of recessions on healthcare access for low-income individuals and those from underrepresented groups. During economic downturns, these groups may face increased financial and social barriers to accessing healthcare services, such as lack of transportation or cultural barriers to seeking care. Healthcare systems may need to develop new strategies to address these challenges, such as increasing the availability of mobile clinics and community-based services, or partnering with community organizations to address healthcare disparities.

Another potential impact of recessions on healthcare access is increased competition for limited resources. During a recession, healthcare providers may need to compete more aggressively for limited funding and resources, potentially leading to increased tension and conflict between providers. This can be particularly challenging for smaller or less well-funded healthcare providers, which may struggle to compete with larger or better-resourced organizations.

Recessions can have a significant impact on healthcare access, affecting everything from insurance coverage and affordability to availability of services and workforce shortages. During economic downturns, individuals and families may face increased financial and social barriers to accessing healthcare services, making it more difficult for them to receive necessary care. Healthcare systems may need to develop new strategies to address these challenges, such as increasing access to telemedicine and other virtual care options, or developing new programs to address healthcare disparities. By focusing on prevention and chronic disease management, developing new strategies to address workforce shortages and access to care, and staying informed about changes in government policies related to healthcare funding and access, healthcare systems can weather the storm of a recession and emerge stronger and more resilient.

Strategies for managing healthcare during a recession

Recessions can have a significant impact on healthcare, affecting everything from access to care and funding to workforce shortages and public health outcomes. Healthcare systems may face financial pressures and changing priorities, leading to reductions in funding and shifts towards more cost-effective approaches to care. Below we will explore strategies for managing healthcare during a recession, highlighting some of the key approaches that healthcare systems can take to weather the storm of economic downturns.

One key strategy for managing healthcare during a recession is to focus on prevention and chronic disease management. During economic downturns, healthcare systems may need to shift their focus towards preventative care and chronic disease management, in order to reduce costs and improve health outcomes. This can involve a range of strategies, such as increasing public health education and awareness, developing new programs to address chronic diseases, and increasing access to primary care and preventative services. By focusing on prevention and early intervention, healthcare systems can potentially reduce the need for costly and complex medical interventions, while improving health outcomes for patients.

Another potential strategy for managing healthcare during a recession is to increase the use of telemedicine and other virtual care options. During economic downturns, patients may be less likely to seek medical care, due to financial concerns or other stressors. By increasing the availability of telemedicine and other virtual care options, healthcare systems can make it easier for patients to receive necessary care, regardless of their location or ability to pay for medical services. This can potentially reduce costs for both patients and healthcare providers, while improving access to care for patients.

Another potential strategy for managing healthcare during a recession is to reduce unnecessary testing and procedures. During economic downturns, healthcare systems may need to focus on cost-effective approaches to care and treatments that provide the most value for patients. This can involve reducing the use of unnecessary testing and procedures, which can drive up healthcare costs and potentially lead to negative health outcomes for patients. By focusing on evidence-based practices and reducing waste, healthcare systems can potentially reduce costs and improve health outcomes for patients.

Another potential strategy for managing healthcare during a recession is to increase collaboration between healthcare providers and community organizations. During economic downturns, healthcare systems may need to work more closely with community organizations, such as non-profits, faith-based groups, and government agencies, to address healthcare disparities and improve access to care for vulnerable populations. This can involve developing new partnerships, increasing outreach efforts, and working to build trust between healthcare providers and the communities they serve.

Another potential strategy for managing healthcare during a recession is to focus on workforce development and retention. During a recession, healthcare providers may face staffing shortages as budgets are cut and patients may be less likely to seek medical care. This can create challenges for healthcare systems, as they may need to rely more heavily on part-time and contract workers, or may struggle to attract and retain skilled healthcare professionals. By focusing on workforce development and retention, healthcare systems can potentially reduce turnover and burnout among healthcare providers, while ensuring that patients have access to high-quality care.

Managing healthcare during a recession can be a challenging task, but there are a range of strategies that healthcare systems can use to weather the storm. By focusing on prevention and chronic disease management, increasing the use of telemedicine and other virtual care options, reducing unnecessary testing and procedures, increasing collaboration between healthcare providers and community organizations, and focusing on workforce development and retention, healthcare systems can navigate economic downturns and emerge stronger and more resilient. By staying informed about changes in government policies related to healthcare funding and access, healthcare systems can adapt to changing conditions and continue to provide high-quality care to patients.

The Impact of Recessions on Mental Health

Recessions can have a significant impact on mental health, affecting everything from rates of depression and anxiety to substance abuse and suicide. Economic downturns can create financial pressures and social stressors, leading to increased rates of mental health issues among individuals and families. Below we will explore the impact of recessions on mental health, highlighting some of the key challenges and opportunities that arise during economic downturns.

One of the most significant impacts of recessions on mental health is an increase in rates of depression and anxiety. During a recession, individuals and families may experience financial stress, such as job loss, reduced income, or increased debt, leading to increased rates of depression and anxiety. In addition, social stressors, such as social isolation, may be more common during a recession, exacerbating mental health issues for vulnerable individuals. This can lead to increased demand for mental health services, potentially putting a strain on healthcare systems and providers.

Another potential impact of recessions on mental health is increased rates of substance abuse. During economic downturns, individuals may turn to drugs or alcohol as a way to cope with financial and social stressors, leading to increased rates of substance abuse and addiction. This can lead to a range of negative health outcomes, such as increased rates of liver disease, heart disease, and other chronic health conditions.

Another potential impact of recessions on mental health is increased rates of suicide. During economic downturns, individuals may experience feelings of hopelessness and despair, potentially leading to increased rates of suicide. This can be particularly challenging for vulnerable populations, such as those with pre-existing mental health issues, those with a history of trauma, or those experiencing social isolation.

It's also important to consider the impact of recessions on access to mental health services. During economic downturns, healthcare systems may face budget cuts and workforce shortages, leading to reduced availability of mental health services and longer wait times for appointments. This can be particularly challenging for individuals in need of urgent mental health care, who may face increased barriers to accessing timely and effective care.

Another potential impact of recessions on mental health is increased stigma and discrimination. During economic downturns, individuals with mental health issues may face increased stigma and discrimination, potentially leading to reduced social support and increased rates of negative health outcomes. This can create a cycle of mental health issues, leading to social and economic consequences that can exacerbate the impact of a recession on mental health.

In conclusion, recessions can have a significant impact on mental health, affecting everything from rates of depression and anxiety to substance abuse and suicide. During economic downturns, individuals and families may experience financial and social stressors that can exacerbate pre-existing mental health issues, leading to increased demand for mental health services and potential strain on healthcare systems and providers. By increasing access to mental health services, reducing stigma and discrimination, and increasing public awareness about the impact of recessions on mental health, healthcare systems can potentially mitigate the negative impact of economic downturns on mental health, while improving health outcomes for vulnerable populations. By staying informed about changes in government policies related to mental health funding and access, healthcare systems can adapt to changing conditions and continue to provide high-quality care to patients.

Strategies for managing mental health during a recession

Recessions can have a significant impact on mental health, affecting everything from rates of depression and anxiety to substance abuse and suicide. Economic downturns can create financial pressures and social stressors, leading to increased rates of mental health issues among individuals and families. Below we will explore strategies for managing mental health during a recession, highlighting some of the key approaches that individuals and healthcare systems can take to promote mental wellness and resilience.

One key strategy for managing mental health during a recession is to focus on self-care and stress management. During economic downturns, individuals may experience financial and social stressors that can exacerbate pre-existing mental health issues or create new ones. Practicing self-care, such as meditation, exercise, and healthy eating, can help to reduce stress and promote overall wellness. Engaging in stress-management techniques, such as mindfulness, deep breathing, or yoga, can also help individuals to cope with stressors and improve mental health outcomes.

Another potential strategy for managing mental health during a recession is to seek out social support. During economic downturns, individuals may experience social isolation, which can exacerbate feelings of depression and anxiety. Seeking out social support from friends, family, or support groups can help to promote feelings of connection and reduce the negative impact of social isolation on mental health. Additionally, healthcare systems may need to increase outreach efforts and develop new programs to address social isolation and promote social support for vulnerable individuals.

Another potential strategy for managing mental health during a recession is to increase access to mental health services. During economic downturns, healthcare systems may face budget cuts and workforce shortages, leading to reduced availability of mental health services and longer wait times for appointments. However, increasing access to mental health services can help to promote mental wellness and resilience during a recession. This can involve a range of strategies, such as increasing the availability of telemedicine and other virtual care options, increasing the number of mental health providers, and developing new programs to address mental health issues.

Another potential strategy for managing mental health during a recession is to reduce stigma and discrimination. During economic downturns, individuals with mental health issues may face increased stigma and discrimination, potentially leading to reduced social support and increased rates of negative health outcomes. By reducing stigma and discrimination, healthcare systems can help to promote mental wellness and improve health outcomes for vulnerable populations. This can involve a range of strategies, such as increasing public awareness about mental health issues, developing new programs to address stigma and discrimination, and promoting mental wellness in the workplace.

Another potential strategy for managing mental health during a recession is to focus on prevention and early intervention. By focusing on prevention and early intervention, healthcare systems can potentially reduce the need for costly and complex medical interventions, while improving mental health outcomes for patients. This can involve a range of strategies, such as increasing public health education and awareness, developing new programs to address mental health issues, and increasing access to primary care and preventative services.

Managing mental health during a recession can be a challenging task, but there are a range of strategies that individuals and healthcare systems can use to promote mental wellness and resilience. By focusing on self-care and stress management, seeking out social support, increasing access to mental health services, reducing stigma and discrimination, and focusing on prevention and early intervention, individuals and healthcare systems can navigate economic downturns and emerge stronger and more resilient. By staying informed about changes in government policies related to mental health funding and access, healthcare systems can adapt to changing conditions and continue to provide high-quality care to patients.

The role of community support in managing mental health during a recession

Recessions can have a significant impact on mental health, affecting everything from rates of depression and anxiety to substance abuse and suicide. During economic downturns, individuals and families may experience financial and social stressors that can exacerbate pre-existing mental health issues or create new ones. While healthcare systems play a critical role in promoting mental wellness and resilience, community support can also be an important factor in managing mental health during a recession. Below we will explore the role of community support in managing mental health during a recession, highlighting some of the key approaches that individuals and community organizations can take to promote mental wellness and resilience.

One key approach to promoting mental wellness and resilience in the community is to increase awareness and education about mental health issues. During economic downturns, individuals may be more likely to experience mental health issues, due to financial and social stressors. However, many individuals may be unaware of the signs and symptoms of mental health issues or may be hesitant to seek help due to stigma or fear. By increasing awareness and education about mental health issues, community organizations can help to reduce stigma and increase access to mental health services, promoting overall mental wellness and resilience.

Another potential approach to promoting mental wellness and resilience in the community is to develop new programs and initiatives to address mental health issues. During economic downturns, community organizations may need to shift their priorities towards addressing mental health issues and promoting overall wellness. This can involve a range of strategies, such as developing new support groups or peer mentoring programs, offering free or low-cost mental health services, or providing resources and referrals for individuals in need of mental health care.

Another potential approach to promoting mental wellness and resilience in the community is to increase social support and connection. During economic downturns, individuals may experience social isolation or may struggle to connect with others due to financial stressors or other factors. However, social support and connection are critical factors in promoting mental wellness and resilience. By developing new social support programs or initiatives, community organizations can help to promote social connection and reduce the negative impact of social isolation on mental health.

Another potential approach to promoting mental wellness and resilience in the community is to increase access to healthy lifestyle resources. During economic downturns, individuals may struggle to afford healthy food or may be hesitant to participate in physical activity due to financial or social stressors. However, healthy lifestyle factors, such as good nutrition and regular exercise, are critical factors in promoting mental wellness and resilience. By increasing access to healthy lifestyle resources, such as community gardens, food banks, or exercise programs, community organizations can help to promote overall wellness and resilience.

Finally, community organizations can play a key role in advocating for mental health policy changes at the local or national level. During economic downturns, mental health services may be at risk of budget cuts or reductions in funding. By advocating for increased mental health funding and resources, community organizations can help to ensure that individuals in need of mental health care have access to necessary services and supports, promoting overall mental wellness and resilience.

Managing mental health during a recession requires a multi-faceted approach that involves healthcare systems, individuals, and community organizations. By increasing awareness and education about mental health issues, developing new programs and initiatives to address mental health issues, increasing social support and connection, increasing access to healthy lifestyle resources, and advocating for mental health policy changes, community organizations can play a critical role in promoting overall mental wellness and resilience during economic downturns. By working together to promote mental wellness and resilience, individuals and community organizations can navigate economic downturns and emerge stronger and more resilient.

Recessions and Social Justice

Recessions can have a significant impact on social justice, affecting everything from income inequality and poverty to access to healthcare and education. Economic downturns can create financial pressures and social stressors, exacerbating existing social inequalities and potentially creating new ones. Below we will explore the impact of recessions on social justice, highlighting some of the key challenges and opportunities that arise during economic downturns.

One of the most significant impacts of recessions on social justice is an increase in income inequality and poverty. During a recession, individuals and families may experience job loss, reduced income, or increased debt, leading to increased rates of poverty and income inequality. This can be particularly challenging for vulnerable populations, such as people of color, women, and those with disabilities, who may already experience systemic barriers to economic mobility.

Another potential impact of recessions on social justice is reduced access to healthcare. During economic downturns, healthcare systems may face budget cuts and workforce shortages, leading to reduced availability of healthcare services and longer wait times for appointments. This can be particularly challenging for vulnerable populations, such as those with pre-existing health conditions, low-income individuals, and those with limited access to transportation or childcare.

Another potential impact of recessions on social justice is reduced access to education. During economic downturns, schools and universities may face budget cuts and workforce shortages, leading to reduced availability of educational resources and limited opportunities for academic and career advancement. This can be particularly challenging for low-income individuals, first-generation college students, and those with limited access to educational resources.

Another potential impact of recessions on social justice is increased social inequality and discrimination. During economic downturns, individuals and groups may face increased discrimination and bias, potentially exacerbating existing social inequalities and creating new ones. This can create a cycle of social inequality and economic disadvantage, leading to negative health outcomes and reduced economic mobility.

It's also important to consider the role of government policies and programs in promoting social justice during a recession. By increasing funding for social programs, such as healthcare, education, and job training, governments can help to mitigate the negative impact of economic downturns on vulnerable populations. Additionally, by promoting policies that reduce income inequality and promote economic mobility, governments can help to create a more equitable society that is better able to navigate economic downturns.

Recessions can have a significant impact on social justice, affecting everything from income inequality and poverty to access to healthcare and education. During economic downturns, individuals and families may experience financial and social stressors that can exacerbate existing social inequalities and potentially create new ones. By increasing awareness of the impact of recessions on social justice, promoting government policies and programs that support vulnerable populations, and advocating for social justice in all aspects of society, individuals and organizations can work together to create a more equitable society that is better able to navigate economic downturns and emerge stronger and more resilient.

The impact of recessions on marginalized communities

Recessions can have a disproportionate impact on marginalized communities, including people of color, low-income individuals, and those with disabilities. Economic downturns can exacerbate existing social inequalities and potentially create new ones, leading to a range of negative health outcomes and reduced economic mobility for vulnerable populations. Below we will explore the impact of recessions on marginalized communities, highlighting some of the key challenges and opportunities that arise during economic downturns.

One of the most significant impacts of recessions on marginalized communities is increased rates of unemployment and underemployment. During a recession, individuals may experience job loss, reduced income, or increased debt, leading to increased rates of poverty and income inequality. This can be particularly challenging for vulnerable populations, such as people of color, low-income individuals, and those with disabilities, who may already experience systemic barriers to economic mobility.

Another potential impact of recessions on marginalized communities is reduced access to healthcare. During economic downturns, healthcare systems may face budget cuts and workforce shortages, leading to reduced availability of healthcare services and longer wait times for appointments. This can be particularly challenging for vulnerable populations, such as those with pre-existing health conditions, low-income individuals, and those with limited access to transportation or childcare.

Another potential impact of recessions on marginalized communities is reduced access to education. During economic downturns, schools and universities may face budget cuts and workforce shortages, leading to reduced availability of educational resources and limited opportunities for academic and career advancement. This can be particularly challenging for low-income individuals, first-generation college students, and those with limited access to educational resources.

Another potential impact of recessions on marginalized communities is increased social inequality and discrimination. During economic downturns, individuals and groups may face increased discrimination and bias, potentially exacerbating existing social inequalities and creating new ones. This can create a cycle of social inequality and economic disadvantage, leading to negative health outcomes and reduced economic mobility.

It's also important to consider the role of government policies and programs in promoting social justice during a recession. By increasing funding for social programs, such as healthcare, education, and job training, governments can help to mitigate the negative impact of economic downturns on vulnerable populations. Additionally, by promoting policies that reduce income inequality and promote economic mobility, governments can help to create a more equitable society that is better able to navigate economic downturns.

Recessions can have a disproportionate impact on marginalized communities, affecting everything from employment opportunities and income inequality to access to healthcare and education. During economic downturns, individuals and families in these communities may experience financial and social stressors that can exacerbate existing social inequalities and potentially create new ones. By increasing awareness of the impact of recessions on marginalized communities, promoting government policies and programs that support vulnerable populations, and advocating for social justice in all aspects of society, individuals and organizations can work together to create a more equitable society that is better able to navigate economic downturns and emerge stronger and more resilient.

Strategies for managing the impact of recessions on social justice

Recessions can have a significant impact on social justice, affecting everything from income inequality and poverty to access to healthcare and education. Economic downturns can exacerbate existing social inequalities and potentially create new ones, leading to a range of negative health outcomes and reduced economic mobility for vulnerable populations. Below we will explore strategies for managing the impact of recessions on social justice, highlighting some of the key approaches that individuals and organizations can take to promote social justice during economic downturns.

One key strategy for managing the impact of recessions on social justice is to focus on advocacy and policy change. By advocating for policies that reduce income inequality and promote economic mobility, individuals and organizations can help to create a more equitable society that is better able to navigate economic downturns. This can involve a range of strategies, such as lobbying government officials, participating in advocacy campaigns, or organizing public protests or demonstrations to raise awareness about social justice issues.

Another potential strategy for managing the impact of recessions on social justice is to increase funding for social programs that support vulnerable populations. During economic downturns, governments may need to shift their priorities towards addressing the needs of vulnerable populations, such as low-income individuals, people of color, and those with disabilities. This can involve a range of strategies, such as increasing funding for healthcare, education, and job training programs, providing targeted financial support for those in need, or developing new programs to address social inequalities.

Another potential strategy for managing the impact of recessions on social justice is to increase community engagement and social support. During economic downturns, individuals and families may experience social isolation or may struggle to connect with others due to financial stressors or other factors. However, social support and connection are critical factors in promoting social justice and reducing the negative impact of social isolation on vulnerable populations. By developing new social support programs or initiatives, individuals and organizations can help to promote social connection and reduce the negative impact of social isolation on social justice.

Another potential strategy for managing the impact of recessions on social justice is to increase access to education and training programs. During economic downturns, schools and universities may face budget cuts and workforce shortages, leading to reduced availability of educational resources and limited opportunities for academic and career advancement. However, education and training programs are critical factors in promoting economic mobility and reducing social inequalities. By increasing access to educational resources, such as scholarships, grants, or job training programs, individuals and organizations can help to promote economic mobility and reduce social inequalities.

Finally, it's important to consider the role of allyship and solidarity in promoting social justice during a recession. By building relationships with individuals and groups from diverse backgrounds, individuals and organizations can help to promote social justice and reduce the negative impact of economic downturns on vulnerable populations. This can involve a range of strategies, such as participating in community-building events or initiatives, engaging in meaningful dialogue and collaboration with individuals from diverse backgrounds, or supporting community-based organizations that promote social justice.

The role of government policies in addressing social justice during a recession

Recessions can have a significant impact on social justice, affecting everything from income inequality and poverty to access to healthcare and education. Economic downturns can exacerbate existing social inequalities and potentially create new ones, leading to a range of negative health outcomes and reduced economic mobility for vulnerable populations. Below we will explore the role of government policies in addressing social justice during a recession, highlighting some of the key approaches that governments can take to promote social justice during economic downturns.

One of the most important roles of government policies in addressing social justice during a recession is to promote economic mobility and reduce income inequality. During economic downturns, individuals and families in vulnerable populations may experience financial stressors that can exacerbate existing income inequality and limit economic mobility. Governments can promote economic mobility and reduce income inequality by increasing funding for programs that support job training, education, and small business development. Additionally, governments can promote policies that ensure equal pay for equal work, protect workers' rights, and provide support for individuals facing job loss or reduced income during a recession.

Another key role of government policies in addressing social justice during a recession is to promote access to healthcare for vulnerable populations. During economic downturns, individuals may experience reduced access to healthcare services due to budget cuts and workforce shortages in the healthcare sector. Governments can promote access to healthcare by increasing funding for healthcare programs and services, expanding Medicaid eligibility, and providing financial support for healthcare providers in vulnerable communities. Additionally, governments can promote policies that ensure equal access to healthcare services for individuals from diverse backgrounds and reduce disparities in healthcare outcomes.

Another important role of government policies in addressing social justice during a recession is to promote access to education for vulnerable populations. During economic downturns, schools and universities may face budget cuts and workforce shortages, leading to reduced availability of educational resources and limited opportunities for academic and career advancement. Governments can promote access to education by increasing funding for education programs, providing financial support for students from low-income families, and expanding access to vocational training programs. Additionally, governments can promote policies that ensure equal access to education services for individuals from diverse backgrounds and reduce disparities in educational outcomes.

Finally, it's important for governments to consider the role of social safety net programs in promoting social justice during a recession. Social safety net programs, such as food assistance, housing assistance, and unemployment benefits, can provide critical support for individuals and families experiencing financial stressors during an economic downturn. Governments can promote social justice by increasing funding for social safety net programs, expanding eligibility for these programs, and reducing barriers to access for vulnerable populations. Additionally, governments can promote policies that ensure social safety net programs are accessible to individuals from diverse backgrounds and reduce disparities in program outcomes.

The Impact of Recessions on Retirement

Recessions can have a significant impact on retirement, affecting everything from retirement savings and pension funds to retirement age and access to healthcare. Economic downturns can exacerbate existing social inequalities and potentially create new ones, leading to a range of negative health outcomes and reduced economic mobility for older adults. Below we will explore the impact of recessions on retirement, highlighting some of the key challenges and opportunities that arise during economic downturns.

One of the most significant impacts of recessions on retirement is a reduction in retirement savings and pension funds. During a recession, individuals may experience job loss, reduced income, or increased debt, leading to reduced contributions to retirement savings plans and reduced returns on pension funds. This can be particularly challenging for older adults who may have limited opportunities to replenish their retirement savings and who may be at a higher risk of experiencing financial stressors during a recession.

Another potential impact of recessions on retirement is an increase in retirement age. During economic downturns, older adults may experience reduced access to job opportunities or may choose to delay retirement in order to continue earning income and rebuilding their retirement savings. This can be particularly challenging for individuals with health issues or those who are unable to work due to physical or cognitive limitations.

Another potential impact of recessions on retirement is reduced access to healthcare. During economic downturns, healthcare systems may face budget cuts and workforce shortages, leading to reduced availability of healthcare services and longer wait times for appointments. This can be particularly challenging for older adults, who may have a higher risk of chronic health conditions or may require specialized healthcare services.

Another potential impact of recessions on retirement is increased social inequality and discrimination. During economic downturns, older adults may face increased discrimination and bias, potentially exacerbating existing social inequalities and creating new ones. This can create a cycle of social inequality and economic disadvantage, leading to negative health outcomes and reduced economic mobility.

It's also important to consider the role of government policies and programs in promoting retirement security during a recession. By increasing funding for social programs, such as healthcare, education, and job training, governments can help to mitigate the negative impact of economic downturns on older adults. Additionally, by promoting policies that reduce income inequality and promote economic mobility, governments can help to create a more equitable society that is better able to navigate economic downturns.

Recessions can have a significant impact on retirement, affecting everything from retirement savings and pension funds to retirement age and access to healthcare. During economic downturns, individuals and families may experience financial and social stressors that can exacerbate existing social inequalities and potentially create new ones. By increasing awareness of the impact of recessions on retirement, promoting government policies and programs that support older adults, and advocating for retirement security in all aspects of society, individuals and organizations can work together to create a more equitable society that is better able to navigate economic downturns and emerge stronger and more resilient.

The impact of recessions on retirement savings

Recessions can have a significant impact on retirement savings, affecting everything from retirement planning and investment strategies to pension funds and Social Security benefits. Economic downturns can exacerbate existing social inequalities and potentially create new ones, leading to a range of negative health outcomes and reduced economic mobility for older adults. Below we will explore the impact of recessions on retirement savings, highlighting some of the key challenges and opportunities that arise during economic downturns.

One of the most significant impacts of recessions on retirement savings is a reduction in contributions to retirement plans. During a recession, individuals may experience job loss, reduced income, or increased debt, leading to reduced contributions to retirement savings plans. This can be particularly challenging for older adults who may have limited opportunities to replenish their retirement savings and who may be at a higher risk of experiencing financial stressors during a recession.

Another potential impact of recessions on retirement savings is a reduction in investment returns. During economic downturns, stock markets may experience significant declines, leading to reduced investment returns on retirement savings plans. This can be particularly challenging for individuals who are nearing retirement or who may have a more conservative investment strategy.

Another potential impact of recessions on retirement savings is a reduction in pension fund returns. During economic downturns, pension funds may experience reduced returns on investments or may face financial stressors that affect their ability to pay out benefits. This can be particularly challenging for individuals who are relying on pension funds as a source of retirement income.

It's also important to consider the role of government policies and programs in promoting retirement security during a recession. By increasing funding for social programs, such as healthcare, education, and job training, governments can help to mitigate the negative impact of economic downturns on older adults. Additionally, by promoting policies that reduce income inequality and promote economic mobility, governments can help to create a more equitable society that is better able to navigate economic downturns.

One potential strategy for managing the impact of recessions on retirement savings is to focus on diversification of investments. By diversifying investments across a range of asset classes, individuals can help to reduce their exposure to market volatility and potentially protect their retirement savings during economic downturns. Additionally, by working with a financial advisor or planner, individuals can develop a retirement plan that takes into account their risk tolerance and long-term financial goals.

Another potential strategy for managing the impact of recessions on retirement savings is to focus on reducing debt and increasing savings. By reducing debt and increasing savings, individuals can help to build a more secure financial foundation that can withstand the impact of economic downturns. This can involve a range of strategies, such as paying off credit card debt, reducing expenses, or increasing contributions to retirement savings plans.

Finally, it's important to consider the role of employer-sponsored retirement plans in promoting retirement security during a recession. By offering retirement plans with matching contributions, employers can help to encourage employees to save for retirement and build a more secure financial future. Additionally, employers can offer financial education and planning resources to help employees navigate the impact of economic downturns on their retirement savings.

Strategies for managing retirement during a recession

Managing retirement during a recession can be a challenging task, as economic downturns can have a significant impact on retirement savings, pension funds, and social security benefits. However, with careful planning and a focus on diversification, debt reduction, and financial education, individuals can work to build a more secure financial foundation that can withstand the impact of economic downturns. Below we will explore some of the key strategies for managing retirement during a recession.

One of the most important strategies for managing retirement during a recession is to focus on diversification of investments. By diversifying investments across a range of asset classes, individuals can help to reduce their exposure to market volatility and potentially protect their retirement savings during economic downturns. This can involve investing in stocks, bonds, real estate, and other asset classes, as well as considering alternative investments such as commodities, precious metals, and cryptocurrencies.

Another key strategy for managing retirement during a recession is to focus on reducing debt and increasing savings. By reducing debt and increasing savings, individuals can build a more secure financial foundation that can withstand the impact of economic downturns. This can involve paying off credit card debt, reducing expenses, and increasing contributions to retirement savings plans. Additionally, individuals can consider taking advantage of low interest rates to refinance existing debt, such as mortgages or student loans, and potentially reduce their monthly payments.

Another important strategy for managing retirement during a recession is to focus on financial education and planning. By working with a financial advisor or planner, individuals can develop a retirement plan that takes into account their risk tolerance and long-term financial goals. Additionally, individuals can learn about different investment strategies, retirement income sources, and tax planning strategies that can help them maximize their retirement savings and income.

It's also important to consider the role of employer-sponsored retirement plans in promoting retirement security during a recession. By offering retirement plans with matching contributions, employers can help to encourage employees to save for retirement and build a more secure financial future. Additionally, employers can offer financial education and planning resources to help employees navigate the impact of economic downturns on their retirement savings.

Finally, it's important to stay informed about changes in government policies related to retirement security during a recession. By staying up to date on changes in social security benefits, pension fund regulations, and tax policies, individuals can make informed decisions about their retirement planning and adjust their strategies accordingly.

The role of government programs in supporting retirement during a recession

The role of government programs in supporting retirement during a recession is a critical component of promoting retirement security and ensuring that older adults have access to the resources and services they need to navigate economic downturns. Below we will explore some of the key government programs that support retirement during a recession and their impact on older adults.

One of the most significant government programs that support retirement during a recession is Social Security. Social Security is a federal program that provides retirement, disability, and survivor benefits to eligible individuals. During a recession, Social Security can be an important source of income for older adults who may be experiencing job loss, reduced income, or other financial stressors. Social Security benefits are funded through payroll taxes, and eligibility is based on a worker's contributions to the system.

Another important government program that supports retirement during a recession is Medicare. Medicare is a federal program that provides health insurance to eligible individuals who are 65 years or older, as well as to younger individuals with certain disabilities or medical conditions. Medicare can be an important source of healthcare coverage for older adults during a recession, when access to healthcare services may be limited or reduced. Medicare benefits are funded through a combination of payroll taxes, premiums, and general revenues.

In addition to Social Security and Medicare, there are a range of other government programs that support retirement during a recession. For example, the Older Americans Act provides funding for a range of services, such as home-delivered meals, transportation, and caregiver support, that can help older adults remain independent and connected to their communities. The Low Income Home Energy Assistance Program provides assistance to eligible households with their heating and cooling costs, which can be particularly important during a recession when energy costs may be higher.

It's also important to consider the impact of government policies and programs on retirement security during a recession. By promoting policies that reduce income inequality and promote economic mobility, governments can help to create a more equitable society that is better able to navigate economic downturns. Additionally, by increasing funding for social programs, such as healthcare, education, and job training, governments can help to mitigate the negative impact of economic downturns on older adults.

In conclusion, government programs play a critical role in supporting retirement during a recession. Programs such as Social Security, Medicare, and the Older Americans Act provide older adults with access to critical resources and services that can help them navigate economic downturns and maintain a secure and stable financial future. By promoting policies that support retirement security, increasing funding for social programs, and advocating for policies that reduce income inequality and promote economic mobility, governments can help to create a more equitable society that is better able to navigate economic downturns and emerge stronger and more resilient.

The Future of Recessions

The future of recessions is an important topic for policymakers, economists, and individuals alike. Economic downturns can have a significant impact on individuals and society as a whole, affecting everything from employment and income to healthcare and retirement security. Below we will explore some of the key trends and factors that are likely to shape the future of recessions.

One of the most significant trends that is likely to shape the future of recessions is the ongoing globalization of the economy. As the global economy becomes increasingly interconnected, economic shocks in one part of the world can quickly spread to other regions. This can lead to a more synchronized global business cycle and potentially increase the frequency and severity of economic downturns.

Another important trend is the ongoing technological revolution, which is transforming the way that we work, consume, and live. Technological advances such as artificial intelligence, automation, and the Internet of Things are creating new opportunities for economic growth and innovation, but also pose significant challenges for workers and businesses. As technology continues to disrupt traditional industries and business models, it may exacerbate existing economic inequalities and potentially contribute to the risk of future economic downturns.

A third trend that is likely to shape the future of recessions is demographic change, particularly the aging of the population. As the baby boomer generation continues to age, there will be a growing demand for healthcare, social services, and retirement benefits. This may lead to increased pressure on government budgets and potentially contribute to future economic downturns.

Finally, it's important to consider the role of government policies and programs in shaping the future of recessions. By promoting policies that support economic growth, reduce income inequality, and promote financial stability, governments can help to mitigate the negative impact of economic downturns on individuals and society as a whole. Additionally, by investing in social programs such as healthcare, education, and job training, governments can help to promote economic mobility and resilience.

Predictions for future recessions

Predicting future recessions is a difficult task, as economic downturns can be influenced by a wide range of factors, including global economic conditions, government policies, technological change, and demographic trends. However, by examining current economic trends and considering historical patterns, it is possible to identify some potential scenarios for future recessions. Below we will explore some of the predictions for future recessions and their potential impact.

One potential scenario for a future recession is a global economic slowdown. As the global economy becomes increasingly interconnected, economic shocks in one part of the world can quickly spread to other regions. This can lead to a more synchronized global business cycle and potentially increase the frequency and severity of economic downturns. Additionally, rising trade tensions and geopolitical risks can contribute to economic uncertainty and potentially trigger a global recession.

Another potential scenario for a future recession is a debt crisis. High levels of government debt and corporate debt can create financial instability and potentially lead to an economic downturn. In particular, a debt crisis in emerging market economies can have ripple effects throughout the global economy, potentially triggering a recession.

A third potential scenario for a future recession is a technological disruption. As technology continues to transform the way that we work, consume, and live, it may disrupt traditional industries and business models, potentially leading to economic instability. Additionally, technological change may exacerbate existing economic inequalities and potentially contribute to the risk of future economic downturns.

Finally, it's important to consider the potential impact of demographic change on future recessions. As the population ages, there will be a growing demand for healthcare, social services, and retirement benefits. This may lead to increased pressure on government budgets and potentially contribute to future economic downturns. Additionally, changing demographics may create challenges for businesses, as they seek to adapt to a changing workforce and consumer base.

Predicting future recessions is a complex and challenging task, as economic downturns can be influenced by a wide range of factors. However, by examining current economic trends and considering historical patterns, it is possible to identify some potential scenarios for future recessions. By staying informed about these trends and preparing for potential economic risks, individuals and organizations can work together to build a more resilient and stable financial future. Additionally, by promoting policies that support economic growth, reduce income inequality, and promote financial stability, governments can help to create a more equitable society that is better able to navigate economic downturns and emerge stronger and more resilient.

Strategies for preparing for future recessions

Preparing for future recessions is an important task for individuals, businesses, and policymakers alike. Economic downturns can have a significant impact on employment, income, and financial stability, and being prepared can help to mitigate the negative impact of economic uncertainty. Below we will explore some of the key strategies for preparing for future recessions.

One of the most important strategies for preparing for future recessions is to focus on building financial resilience. This can involve building up emergency savings, paying down debt, and creating a budget that prioritizes essential expenses. By building a solid financial foundation, individuals and families can help to weather the impact of economic downturns and maintain financial stability.

Another important strategy for preparing for future recessions is to focus on diversification of investments. By diversifying investments across a range of asset classes, individuals can help to reduce their exposure to market volatility and potentially protect their assets during economic downturns. This can involve investing in stocks, bonds, real estate, and other asset classes, as well as considering alternative investments such as commodities, precious metals, and cryptocurrencies.

Businesses can also prepare for future recessions by focusing on financial resilience and diversification. By building up cash reserves, paying down debt, and diversifying their product and service offerings, businesses can help to mitigate the negative impact of economic downturns. Additionally, businesses can focus on building strong relationships with customers, suppliers, and employees, and investing in their workforce to promote resiliency and adaptability.

Policymakers can also play a critical role in preparing for future recessions. By promoting policies that support economic growth, reduce income inequality, and promote financial stability, governments can help to create a more equitable society that is better able to navigate economic downturns. Additionally, policymakers can invest in social programs such as healthcare, education, and job training, to promote economic mobility and resilience.

It's also important to consider the role of education and information in preparing for future recessions. By staying informed about economic trends and risks, individuals and organizations can make more informed decisions about their finances and investments. Additionally, financial education programs can help to promote financial literacy and improve financial decision-making, which can be particularly important during times of economic uncertainty.

Finally, it's important to stay flexible and adaptable in the face of economic uncertainty. By being willing to adapt to changing economic conditions, individuals and organizations can be better prepared to navigate the impact of economic downturns. This can involve being willing to make adjustments to spending, investments, and business strategies in response to changing economic conditions.

In conclusion, preparing for future recessions requires a multi-faceted approach that involves building financial resilience, diversifying investments, investing in education and information, promoting government policies that support economic growth and financial stability, and being flexible and adaptable in the face of economic uncertainty. While economic downturns can be challenging, by taking a proactive approach to financial planning and being prepared for potential risks, individuals, businesses, and policymakers can work together to build a more resilient and stable financial future.

The role of innovation in managing future recessions

The role of innovation in managing future recessions is an important consideration for individuals, businesses, and policymakers alike. Economic downturns can create significant challenges for organizations and individuals, but by focusing on innovation and new technologies, it may be possible to identify new opportunities for growth and stability. Below we will explore some of the key ways that innovation can play a role in managing future recessions.

One of the most significant ways that innovation can play a role in managing future recessions is by creating new opportunities for economic growth. By investing in research and development and promoting innovation in key sectors such as healthcare, energy, and technology, it may be possible to create new jobs, new products, and new markets that can help to stimulate economic growth and promote financial stability.

Additionally, innovation can help to improve productivity and efficiency, which can be particularly important during times of economic uncertainty. By investing in new technologies and processes, businesses can potentially reduce costs, streamline operations, and increase competitiveness, which can help to mitigate the negative impact of economic downturns.

Innovation can also play a role in promoting financial inclusion and reducing income inequality, which can be particularly important during times of economic uncertainty. By promoting access to new financial technologies and services, such as mobile banking and microfinance, it may be possible to increase access to credit and financial resources for underserved communities and individuals, which can help to promote economic mobility and resilience.

Another important role that innovation can play in managing future recessions is by promoting sustainability and resilience. By investing in new technologies and practices that promote sustainability, such as renewable energy and green infrastructure, it may be possible to create more resilient and stable economies that are better able to withstand the impact of economic downturns and other shocks.

Finally, it's important to consider the role of education and information in promoting innovation and managing future recessions. By investing in education and research programs that promote innovation and entrepreneurship, it may be possible to create a culture of innovation and creativity that can help to identify new opportunities for growth and stability. Additionally, by providing access to information and data, individuals and organizations can make more informed decisions about their investments, finances, and business strategies, which can help to promote financial resilience and stability.

Lessons Learned from Recessions

Recessions can be challenging periods of economic uncertainty and instability, but they can also provide important lessons and insights for individuals, businesses, and policymakers. By reflecting on past recessions and examining the factors that contributed to their causes and impacts, it may be possible to identify key lessons and strategies for managing future economic downturns. Below we will explore some of the key lessons learned from past recessions.

One of the most important lessons learned from past recessions is the importance of financial resilience and preparedness. Individuals and businesses that had built up emergency savings, paid down debt, and diversified their investments were better able to weather the impact of economic downturns and maintain financial stability. This underscores the importance of building a solid financial foundation and being prepared for potential economic risks.

Another important lesson learned from past recessions is the importance of promoting financial stability and reducing systemic risk. The 2008 financial crisis, for example, was caused in part by the proliferation of complex financial instruments and the lack of regulation and oversight in the financial sector. By promoting financial stability and reducing systemic risk, policymakers can help to mitigate the impact of economic downturns and promote greater financial resilience.

A third lesson learned from past recessions is the importance of investing in education and innovation. During times of economic uncertainty, innovation and new technologies can create new opportunities for economic growth and stability. Additionally, investing in education and job training programs can help to promote economic mobility and resilience, particularly for individuals and communities that may be disproportionately affected by economic downturns.

Finally, it's important to consider the role of government policies and programs in managing recessions. During times of economic uncertainty, governments can play a critical role in promoting financial stability, supporting job creation, and providing social safety nets for individuals and communities in need. Additionally, by promoting policies that support economic growth and reduce income inequality, governments can help to create a more resilient and stable economy that is better able to navigate economic downturns.

Recessions can provide important lessons and insights for individuals, businesses, and policymakers. By reflecting on past recessions and examining the factors that contributed to their causes and impacts, it may be possible to identify key lessons and strategies for managing future economic downturns. By building financial resilience, promoting financial stability, investing in education and innovation, and promoting government policies that support economic growth and reduce income inequality, individuals, businesses, and policymakers can work together to build a more resilient and stable financial future.

Key takeaways from past recessions

Past recessions provide important insights and lessons that can inform our understanding of economic downturns and inform strategies for managing future economic crises. From the Great Depression to the Global Financial Crisis of 2008, past recessions have highlighted the importance of financial regulation, preparedness, and resilience. Below we will explore some of the key takeaways from past recessions.

One of the most important takeaways from past recessions is the importance of financial regulation and oversight. The Great Depression, for example, was caused in part by the proliferation of risky investment practices and the lack of government regulation and oversight. The subsequent New Deal policies introduced a range of financial regulations, including the creation of the Securities and Exchange Commission (SEC) and the Federal Deposit Insurance Corporation (FDIC), to promote greater financial stability and reduce systemic risk. The 2008 Global Financial Crisis highlighted the need for continued regulation and oversight of the financial sector, particularly in relation to complex financial instruments such as mortgage-backed securities.

Another key takeaway from past recessions is the importance of building financial resilience and preparedness. Individuals and businesses that had built up emergency savings, diversified their investments, and paid down debt were better able to weather the impact of economic downturns and maintain financial stability. The 2008 Global Financial Crisis also highlighted the importance of promoting financial literacy and education, particularly in relation to complex financial products and investments.

A third key takeaway from past recessions is the importance of investing in job creation and social safety nets. During times of economic uncertainty, governments can play a critical role in promoting job creation and providing social safety nets for individuals and communities in need. The New Deal policies introduced in response to the Great Depression, for example, included a range of programs designed to create jobs and support economic growth, including the Civilian Conservation Corps (CCC) and the Works Progress Administration (WPA).

Finally, past recessions have also highlighted the importance of promoting economic growth and innovation. During times of economic uncertainty, innovation and new technologies can create new opportunities for economic growth and stability. Additionally, investing in education and job training programs can help to promote economic mobility and resilience, particularly for individuals and communities that may be disproportionately affected by economic downturns.

Past recessions provide important insights and lessons that can inform our understanding of economic downturns and inform strategies for managing future economic crises. By promoting financial regulation and oversight, building financial resilience and preparedness, investing in job creation and social safety nets, and promoting economic growth and innovation, individuals, businesses, and policymakers can work together to build a more resilient and stable financial future.

Strategies for managing future recessions based on past experiences

Managing future recessions based on past experiences requires a careful and strategic approach. By reflecting on past economic downturns and examining the factors that contributed to their causes and impacts, it may be possible to identify key strategies and lessons that can inform our response to future economic crises. Below we will explore some of the key strategies for managing future recessions based on past experiences.

One of the most important strategies for managing future recessions is to promote financial stability and reduce systemic risk. This can involve implementing regulations and oversight to prevent the proliferation of risky investment practices and complex financial instruments. Additionally, promoting transparency and accountability in the financial sector can help to reduce the potential for fraud and misconduct that can contribute to economic downturns.

Another important strategy for managing future recessions is to promote financial preparedness and resilience. By building up emergency savings, paying down debt, and diversifying investments, individuals and businesses can be better prepared to weather the impact of economic downturns and maintain financial stability. Additionally, promoting financial literacy and education can help individuals to make more informed decisions about their finances and investments.

A third key strategy for managing future recessions is to invest in job creation and social safety nets. During times of economic uncertainty, governments can play a critical role in promoting job creation and providing social safety nets for individuals and communities in need. This can involve investing in education and job training programs, as well as providing unemployment insurance and other forms of financial assistance to those affected by economic downturns.

Finally, promoting innovation and new technologies can also be an important strategy for managing future recessions. By investing in research and development and promoting innovation in key sectors such as healthcare, energy, and technology, it may be possible to create new jobs, new products, and new markets that can help to stimulate economic growth and promote financial stability.

Managing future recessions based on past experiences requires a multi-faceted approach that involves promoting financial stability, building financial preparedness and resilience, investing in job creation and social safety nets, and promoting innovation and new technologies. By reflecting on past economic downturns and examining the factors that contributed to their causes and impacts, it may be possible to identify key strategies and lessons that can inform our response to future economic crises. By working together to implement these strategies, individuals, businesses, and policymakers can help to build a more resilient and stable financial future.

The role of resilience in recovering from a recession

Recovering from a recession can be a long and challenging process, but resilience can play a critical role in helping individuals, businesses, and communities to bounce back and build a more stable financial future. Resilience involves the ability to adapt to change, overcome obstacles, and maintain a positive outlook, even in the face of adversity. Below we will explore the role of resilience in recovering from a recession.

One of the most important roles of resilience in recovering from a recession is the ability to maintain a positive outlook and stay focused on long-term goals. During times of economic uncertainty, it can be easy to become discouraged and lose sight of future opportunities. By maintaining a positive outlook and staying focused on long-term goals, individuals and businesses can remain motivated and resilient, even in the face of challenging economic conditions.

Another important role of resilience in recovering from a recession is the ability to adapt to changing circumstances and embrace new opportunities. Recessions can create significant challenges and disruptions, but they can also create new opportunities for growth and innovation. By embracing change and adapting to new circumstances, individuals and businesses can identify new opportunities and build a more resilient and stable financial future.

A third key role of resilience in recovering from a recession is the ability to build and maintain strong social networks and support systems. During times of economic uncertainty, social networks and support systems can provide critical emotional and financial support. By building and maintaining strong relationships with friends, family, and colleagues, individuals and businesses can better cope with the stress and challenges of a recession.

Finally, resilience can also play a critical role in promoting innovation and new technologies. By embracing change and adapting to new circumstances, individuals and businesses can identify new opportunities for growth and innovation. This can involve investing in research and development, exploring new markets, and promoting new technologies and processes that can help to stimulate economic growth and promote financial stability.

The role of resilience in recovering from a recession cannot be overstated. By maintaining a positive outlook, adapting to change, building strong social networks, and promoting innovation and new technologies, individuals, businesses, and communities can bounce back from economic downturns and build a more stable financial future. While recovering from a recession can be a long and challenging process, resilience can provide the foundation for a brighter and more prosperous future.

Conclusion:

Recessions can be challenging and uncertain times, but they can also provide important opportunities for reflection, learning, and growth. From financial regulation and preparedness to job creation and social safety nets, there are a range of strategies and lessons that can inform our response to future economic downturns. Below we have explored some of the key takeaways from past recessions, as well as strategies for managing future recessions based on these experiences.

One of the most important lessons learned from past recessions is the importance of financial regulation and oversight. The Great Depression and the Global Financial Crisis of 2008 both highlighted the need for continued regulation and oversight of the financial sector, particularly in relation to complex financial instruments and investment practices. By promoting transparency and accountability in the financial sector, we can help to reduce systemic risk and promote greater financial stability.

Another important lesson learned from past recessions is the importance of building financial resilience and preparedness. By building up emergency savings, paying down debt, and diversifying investments, individuals and businesses can be better prepared to weather the impact of economic downturns and maintain financial stability. Additionally, promoting financial literacy and education can help individuals to make more informed decisions about their finances and investments.

A third key lesson learned from past recessions is the importance of investing in job creation and social safety nets. Governments can play a critical role in promoting job creation and providing social safety nets for individuals and communities in need. This can involve investing in education and job training programs, as well as providing unemployment insurance and other forms of financial assistance to those affected by economic downturns.

Finally, past recessions have also highlighted the importance of promoting economic growth and innovation. By investing in research and development and promoting innovation in key sectors, it may be possible to create new jobs, new products, and new markets that can help to stimulate economic growth and promote financial stability.

During recessions, it is important to remain resilient and adaptable, to maintain a positive outlook, and to stay focused on long-term goals. By reflecting on past recessions and examining the factors that contributed to their causes and impacts, it may be possible to identify key strategies and lessons that can inform our response to future economic crises. By promoting financial stability, building financial resilience and preparedness, investing in job creation and social safety nets, and promoting innovation and new technologies, we can work together to build a more resilient and stable financial future.

Recap of key points

Over the previous few chapters, we have explored various aspects of recessions, including their impact on different areas such as the stock market, education, healthcare, mental health, retirement, and social justice. We have also examined strategies for managing different aspects of life during a recession, such as investing, education, healthcare, mental health, and social justice, as well as strategies for preparing for and recovering from future recessions. Below we will recap some of the key points discussed in these chapters.

Firstly, past recessions have highlighted the importance of financial regulation and oversight, as well as the need for transparency and accountability in the financial sector. This can help to reduce systemic risk and promote greater financial stability.

Secondly, building financial resilience and preparedness is critical during recessions. By building emergency savings, paying down debt, and diversifying investments, individuals and businesses can be better prepared to weather the impact of economic downturns and maintain financial stability. Additionally, promoting financial literacy and education can help individuals to make more informed decisions about their finances and investments.

Thirdly, investing in job creation and social safety nets is vital during recessions. Governments can play a critical role in promoting job creation and providing social safety nets for individuals and communities in need. This can involve investing in education and job training programs, as well as providing unemployment insurance and other forms of financial assistance to those affected by economic downturns.

Fourthly, promoting economic growth and innovation is also essential during recessions. By investing in research and development and promoting innovation in key sectors, it may be possible to create new jobs, new products, and new markets that can help to stimulate economic growth and promote financial stability.

Furthermore, during recessions, resilience is critical. Maintaining a positive outlook, adapting to change, building strong social networks, and promoting innovation and new technologies can help individuals, businesses, and communities to bounce back from economic downturns and build a more stable financial future.

Managing and recovering from recessions requires a strategic and multi-faceted approach. By reflecting on past recessions and examining the factors that contributed to their causes and impacts, it may be possible to identify key strategies and lessons that can inform our response to future economic crises. By promoting financial stability, building financial resilience and preparedness, investing in job creation and social safety nets, and promoting innovation and new technologies, we can work together to build a more resilient and stable financial future.

Final thoughts on understanding and surviving a recession

Surviving and understanding a recession is a challenging and complex process. However, through examining the lessons learned from past economic downturns and identifying key strategies for managing different aspects of life during a recession, it may be possible to build resilience and stability for the future. Below we will provide some final thoughts on understanding and surviving a recession.

Firstly, it is important to recognize that recessions are a natural part of the economic cycle. While they can be painful and difficult to navigate, they are also an opportunity for reflection and growth. By taking the time to reflect on past recessions and the lessons learned from them, individuals, businesses, and communities can be better prepared to manage and recover from future economic downturns.

Secondly, it is important to focus on building financial resilience and preparedness. This can involve building up emergency savings, paying down debt, and diversifying investments. Additionally, promoting financial literacy and education can help individuals to make more informed decisions about their finances and investments.

Thirdly, investing in job creation and social safety nets is critical during recessions. Governments can play a critical role in promoting job creation and providing social safety nets for individuals and communities in need. This can involve investing in education and job training programs, as well as providing unemployment insurance and other forms of financial assistance to those affected by economic downturns.

Fourthly, promoting economic growth and innovation is also essential during recessions. By investing in research and development and promoting innovation in key sectors, it may be possible to create new jobs, new products, and new markets that can help to stimulate economic growth and promote financial stability.

Finally, during recessions, resilience is critical. By maintaining a positive outlook, adapting to change, building strong social networks, and promoting innovation and new technologies, individuals, businesses, and communities can bounce back from economic downturns and build a more stable financial future.

Surviving and understanding a recession requires a strategic and multi-faceted approach. By focusing on building financial resilience and preparedness, investing in job creation and social safety nets, promoting economic growth and innovation, and building resilience, individuals, businesses, and communities can be better prepared to manage and recover from future economic downturns. While recessions can be challenging and painful, they can also be an opportunity for reflection, growth, and building a more stable financial future.

Importance of being prepared for economic downturns and seeking support when needed.

The global economy is constantly in flux, and economic downturns are a natural part of the cycle. While they can be difficult and painful, being prepared for economic downturns and seeking support when needed is essential for maintaining financial stability and resilience. Below we will explore the importance of being prepared for economic downturns and seeking support when needed.

Firstly, being prepared for economic downturns is critical. This can involve building up emergency savings, paying down debt, and diversifying investments. Additionally, promoting financial literacy and education can help individuals to make more informed decisions about their finances and investments. By taking steps to prepare for economic downturns, individuals and businesses can be better equipped to weather the impact of economic shocks and maintain financial stability.

Secondly, seeking support when needed is also essential. Economic downturns can create significant stress and anxiety, and seeking support can help individuals to manage these challenges more effectively. This can involve seeking financial counseling, therapy, or other forms of support. Additionally, government programs and non-profit organizations may be able to provide financial assistance, job training, or other forms of support to those affected by economic downturns.

Thirdly, seeking support can also help individuals to identify new opportunities for growth and innovation. Economic downturns can create significant disruptions, but they can also create new opportunities for growth and innovation. By seeking support and exploring new opportunities, individuals and businesses can identify new pathways to financial stability and success.

Finally, being prepared and seeking support can also help to reduce the impact of economic downturns on marginalized communities. Economic downturns can disproportionately impact low-income individuals, communities of color, and other marginalized groups. By promoting financial literacy, investing in job creation and social safety nets, and providing support to those in need, governments and non-profit organizations can help to mitigate the impact of economic downturns on vulnerable communities.

Being prepared for economic downturns and seeking support when needed is essential for maintaining financial stability and resilience. By building up emergency savings, paying down debt, and diversifying investments, individuals and businesses can be better equipped to weather the impact of economic shocks. Additionally, seeking support can help individuals to manage the stress and anxiety associated with economic downturns, identify new opportunities for growth and innovation, and reduce the impact of economic downturns on vulnerable communities. While economic downturns can be challenging and painful, being prepared and seeking support can help individuals and businesses to bounce back and build a more stable financial future.

2023 Indicators

Several indicators are pointing towards a potential recession in 2023, raising concerns among economists and policymakers. Here, we discuss some of these indicators and their implications for the global economy.

1. World Bank prediction: The World Bank has issued a warning about a possible global recession in 2023, citing factors such as slowing economic growth, rising inflation, and ongoing supply chain disruptions. These factors, combined with the potential for further pandemic-related setbacks, could contribute to a downturn in the world economy.

2. US economic slowdown: The US economy, which is often seen as a bellwether for the global economy, has been showing signs of slowing down. Factors such as high inflation, labor shortages, and supply chain disruptions are weighing on economic growth. If the US economy continues to slow down, it could have a ripple effect on other countries, potentially triggering a global recession.

3. Leading economic indicators: A closely watched gauge of economic activity, known as the yield curve, has been signaling the possibility of a recession in the US. The yield curve shows the relationship between short-term and long-term interest rates, with an inverted yield curve (when long-term rates are lower than short-term rates) often preceding a recession. The yield curve has been flattening recently, suggesting that a recession may be on the horizon.

4. Jobs market disagreement: While many indicators are pointing towards a potential recession in 2023, the jobs market seems to tell a different story. Unemployment rates have been steadily declining, and job openings remain high, suggesting a strong labor market. This discrepancy between the jobs market and other economic indicators adds uncertainty to the outlook for 2023.

5. Global central bank actions: Central banks around the world are simultaneously hiking interest rates in response to rising inflation. While these actions are intended to curb inflation, they can also slow down economic growth by increasing borrowing costs for businesses and consumers. If central banks tighten monetary policy too aggressively, they could inadvertently trigger a global recession in 2023.

There are several indicators suggesting that a recession may be on its way in 2023. However, the outlook remains uncertain, with some factors, such as the jobs market, providing a more optimistic view. Policymakers and economists will need to closely monitor these indicators and adjust their policies accordingly to minimize the risk of a global downturn.

Interesting Facts

1. A recession is defined as a significant decline in economic activity that lasts more than a few months, typically visible in real GDP, real income, employment, industrial production, and wholesale-retail sales.

2. The first recorded recession in history was the Kipper und Wipperzeit in Germany in the early 17th century.

3. The first recession in the United States occurred in 1797, following the end of the land speculation boom after the Revolutionary War.

4. The Panic of 1819 was the first major economic downturn in American history, lasting from 1819 to 1821.

5. The Long Depression was a global recession that lasted from 1873 to 1896, affecting most of the world's major economies.

6. The Panic of 1893 was a severe economic depression in the United States, lasting from 1893 to 1897.

7. The Panic of 1907 was a financial crisis that led to a severe recession in the United States, lasting from 1907 to 1908.

8. The Great Depression was the most severe and longest-lasting economic downturn in the history of the Western world, lasting from 1929 to 1939.

9. The Dow Jones Industrial Average lost 89% of its value during the Great Depression.

10. The unemployment rate in the United States reached 25% during the Great Depression.

11. The New Deal was a series of programs and policies enacted by President Franklin D. Roosevelt to help alleviate the effects of the Great Depression.

12. The Glass-Steagall Act was passed in 1933 to separate commercial and investment banking activities in the United States, in response to the Great Depression.

13. World War II helped end the Great Depression, as increased government spending and employment in the war effort boosted the economy.

14. The post-World War II economic expansion, also known as the Golden Age of Capitalism, lasted from 1945 to 1973.

15. The 1973-1975 recession was triggered by the oil crisis, as OPEC nations imposed an oil embargo on the United States and other Western countries.

16. The 1980-1982 recession in the United States was caused by high-interest rates, which were implemented by the Federal Reserve to combat inflation.

17. The 1990-1991 recession was a mild economic downturn in the United States, caused by a combination of factors including high-interest rates and the collapse of the savings and loan industry.

18. The 2001 recession was a relatively mild economic downturn, lasting from March to November 2001, and was primarily caused by the bursting of the dot-com bubble.

19. The September 11, 2001, terrorist attacks on the United States exacerbated the 2001 recession, causing further economic decline.

20. The Great Recession, which lasted from December 2007 to June 2009, was the most severe economic downturn since the Great Depression.

21. The Great Recession was caused by a combination of factors, including the subprime mortgage crisis, the collapse of the housing market, and the failure of financial institutions.

22. The unemployment rate in the United States reached 10% during the Great Recession.

23. The American Recovery and Reinvestment Act was a stimulus package enacted in 2009 to help combat the effects of the Great Recession.

24. The Dodd-Frank Wall Street Reform and Consumer Protection Act was passed in 2010 to prevent another financial crisis like the one that caused the Great Recession.

25. The Eurozone debt crisis, which began in 2009, led to recessions in several European countries, including Greece, Spain, and Italy.

26. The 2020 recession, also known as the COVID-19 recession, was caused by the global pandemic and its impact on businesses and employment.

27. The World Bank predicts that the global economy will contract by 5.2% in 2020 due to the COVID-19 recession, making it the deepest recession since World War II.

28. Governments around the world have implemented various stimulus measures to combat the economic effects of the COVID-19 recession, including direct payments to citizens, increased unemployment benefits, and financial support for businesses.

29. The International Monetary Fund (IMF) has provided financial assistance to over 80 countries during the COVID-19 recession.

30. The COVID-19 recession has disproportionately affected women, people of color, and low-income workers, exacerbating existing inequalities.

31. Recessions can lead to long-term consequences, such as reduced investment in education and infrastructure, and increased public debt.

32. Governments often use fiscal and monetary policy tools, such as tax cuts, government spending, and changes in interest rates, to address recessions.

33. The National Bureau of Economic Research (NBER) is responsible for officially declaring the beginning and end of recessions in the United States.

34. The average length of a recession in the United States since World War II is 11 months.

35. Recessions can have both short-term and long-term effects on the stock market, with stocks typically declining during a recession but recovering and reaching new highs over time.

36. The term "double-dip recession" refers to a situation where the economy briefly recovers from a recession before entering another recession.

37. Recessions can lead to increased income inequality, as high-income earners are often better able to weather economic downturns than low-income earners.

38. The term "stagflation" refers to a situation where the economy experiences both stagnation (slow growth or recession) and inflation simultaneously, as seen in the 1970s.

39. The Great Depression led to the development of Keynesian economics, which emphasizes the role of government intervention in stabilizing the economy during recessions.

40. The Phillips curve, developed by economist A.W. Phillips, suggests a trade-off between unemployment and inflation, with lower unemployment levels typically associated with higher inflation.

41. The term "V-shaped recovery" refers to a quick and strong economic recovery following a recession, while a "U-shaped recovery" involves a more gradual return to economic growth.

42. Some economists argue that recessions can have beneficial effects, such as clearing out inefficient businesses and encouraging innovation.

43. The term "jobless recovery" refers to a situation where economic growth resumes following a recession, but the unemployment rate remains high.

44. The business cycle, which includes periods of expansion and contraction (recessions), is a natural part of a market-based economy.

45. The Kondratiev wave, also known as the long-wave cycle, is a theory that suggests the global economy experiences long cycles of growth and decline, lasting between 45 and 60 years.

46. The Austrian School of Economics, founded by Carl Menger and developed by Ludwig von Mises and Friedrich Hayek, argues that recessions are caused by malinvestment and credit expansion.

47. The term "L-shaped recovery" refers to a situation where the economy does not fully recover to its pre-recession level, resulting in a prolonged period of stagnation.

48. The term "W-shaped recovery" refers to a situation where the economy experiences a double-dip recession, with two periods of economic decline separated by a short-lived recovery.

49. The yield curve, which plots the interest rates of short-term and long-term government bonds, can sometimes provide signals of an impending recession if it becomes inverted (long-term rates are lower than short-term rates).

50. Recessions can have significant social and psychological impacts, including increased stress, mental health issues, and decreased life satisfaction.

51. The term "counter-cyclical policy" refers to government actions that aim to stabilize the economy during recessions, such as increasing government spending or lowering interest rates.

52. The term "pro-cyclical policy" refers to government actions that exacerbate economic fluctuations, such as cutting government spending or raising interest rates during a recession.

53. Monetary policy, which involves the central bank manipulating interest rates and the money supply, is a common tool used by governments to address recessions.

54. Fiscal policy, which involves government spending and taxation, is another tool used by governments to address recessions.

55. The term "automatic stabilizers" refers to aspects of the economy that naturally help counteract economic fluctuations, such as progressive taxation and unemployment benefits.

56. The term "pump priming" refers to government spending aimed at stimulating economic growth during a recession.

57. The term "austerity" refers to policies that involve reducing government spending and increasing taxes in order to reduce a country's budget deficit during a recession.

58. A "balance sheet recession" occurs when companies and households focus on paying down debt and rebuilding their balance sheets, rather than spending and investing, leading to a prolonged period of economic stagnation.

59. Some economists argue that demographic factors, such as aging populations and declining birth rates, can contribute to recessions by reducing consumer spending and labor force growth.

60. The term "recession-resistant" refers to industries or companies that tend to perform relatively well during economic downturns, such as consumer staples, healthcare, and utilities.

61. The term "leading indicators" refers to economic data that tends to change before the overall economy, potentially providing early warning signs of an upcoming recession.

62. The term "lagging indicators" refers to economic data that tends to change after the overall economy, providing confirmation of economic trends.

63. The term "coincident indicators" refers to economic data that tends to change at the same time as the overall economy, providing a snapshot of current economic conditions.

64. The Purchasing Managers' Index (PMI) is a leading economic indicator that measures the health of the manufacturing sector, with a reading below 50 indicating contraction and a reading above 50 indicating expansion.

65. The Consumer Confidence Index (CCI) is a leading economic indicator that measures consumer optimism about the state of the economy, with a higher reading indicating greater optimism.

66. The unemployment rate is a measure of the percentage of people who are unemployed in the economy. It's a lagging economic indicator that tends to reflect changes in the economy after they have already occurred. During a recession, the unemployment rate tends to increase, but it may not peak until after the recession has ended.

67. indicator that measures the percentage of the labor force that is unemployed and actively seeking employment.

68. Gross Domestic Product (GDP) is a measure of a country's economic output and is often used to determine the severity and duration of a recession.

69. The term "zombie companies" refers to businesses that are unable to generate enough revenue to cover their debt payments, often surviving during recessions due to low-interest rates and government support.

70. The term "creative destruction" was coined by economist Joseph Schumpeter and refers to the process by which economic downturns can lead to innovation and the creation of new industries.

71. The Great Depression gave rise to the Social Security Act of 1935, which established a social safety net for retired and disabled workers in the United States.

72. The term "hysteresis" refers to the long-lasting effects of recessions on the labor market, such as increased long-term unemployment and a decline in labor force participation.

73. The term "output gap" refers to the difference between a country's actual GDP and its potential GDP, often used as a measure of the severity of a recession.

74. The term "Okun's Law" refers to the relationship between changes in GDP and changes in the unemployment rate, suggesting that a 1% increase in the unemployment rate corresponds to a 2% decline in GDP.

75. The Beveridge curve, named after economist William Beveridge, illustrates the relationship between job vacancies and the unemployment rate, with a higher ratio of vacancies to unemployment indicating a stronger labor market.

76. The term "skills mismatch" refers to a situation where the skills of unemployed workers do not match the skills required by available job openings, often exacerbated by recessions.

77. The term "underemployment" refers to workers who are employed part-time or in jobs below their skill level, often increasing during recessions.

78. The term "discouraged workers" refers to individuals who have given up looking for work due to a lack of available job opportunities, often increasing during recessions.

79. The Phillips curve has been challenged by the experience of the 1970s, when high unemployment and high inflation occurred simultaneously, leading to the development of the concept of the "non-accelerating inflation rate of unemployment" (NAIRU).

80. The term "deflationary spiral" refers to a situation where falling prices lead to reduced consumer spending, lower economic output, and further price declines, potentially contributing to a prolonged recession.

81. The term "inflation targeting" refers to a monetary policy strategy whereby a central bank aims to achieve a specific inflation rate, often used to help stabilize the economy during recessions.

82. The term "quantitative easing" refers to a monetary policy strategy whereby a central bank purchases government bonds and other financial assets to inject money into the economy, often used to combat recessions.

83. The term "helicopter money" refers to a hypothetical monetary policy strategy whereby a central bank directly distributes money to households, potentially helping to stimulate consumer spending during a recession.

84. The term "fiscal multiplier" refers to the ratio of a change in GDP to an initial change in government spending, with a larger multiplier indicating a greater impact of fiscal policy on economic output during a recession.

85. The term "crowding out" refers to a situation where increased government spending during a recession leads to a decrease in private investment, potentially offsetting the stimulative effects of fiscal policy.

86. The term "debt overhang" refers to a situation where high levels of public or private debt constrain economic growth, potentially contributing to a prolonged recession.

87. The term "balance of payments crisis" refers to a situation where a country experiences a sudden stop in capital inflows, often leading to a currency depreciation and a recession.

88. The term "currency crisis" refers to a situation where a country's currency undergoes a rapid depreciation, often leading to a recession and financial instability.

89. The term "sovereign debt crisis" refers to a situation where a country is unable to service its public debt, often leading to a recession and potentially requiring international financial assistance.

90. The term "banking crisis" refers to a situation where a country's banking system experiences widespread bank runs, insolvencies, or illiquidity, often leading to a recession and financial instability.

91. The term "contagion" refers to the spread of financial crises from one country to another, often through trade, capital flows, or investor sentiment.

92. The term "moral hazard" refers to a situation where individuals or institutions are more likely to take risks due to the belief that they will be protected from negative consequences, potentially contributing to financial crises and recessions.

93. The term "systemic risk" refers to the risk that the failure of one financial institution or market participant can lead to the failure of other institutions or participants, potentially causing a financial crisis and a recession.

94. The term "too big to fail" refers to financial institutions that are so large and interconnected that their failure could pose a systemic risk to the economy, often leading to government bailouts during recessions.

95. The term "shadow banking" refers to financial intermediaries that operate outside the traditional banking system and are often less regulated, potentially contributing to financial instability and recessions.

96. The term "financial accelerator" refers to the amplification of financial shocks through the economy, often contributing to the severity of recessions.

97. The term "credit crunch" refers to a sudden reduction in the availability of credit, often leading to a recession and a decline in investment and consumer spending.

98. The term "flight to quality" refers to the tendency of investors to shift their investments from riskier assets to safer assets during periods of economic uncertainty, often contributing to financial instability and recessions.

99. The term "fire sale" refers to the forced sale of assets at below-market prices, often occurring during recessions and contributing to financial instability.

100. The term "risk aversion" refers to the tendency of investors to prefer safer investments during periods of economic uncertainty, potentially contributing to the severity of recessions.

101. The term "liquidity trap" refers to a situation where monetary policy becomes ineffective in stimulating the economy due to very low interest rates and a lack of demand for credit, potentially contributing to a prolonged recession.

102. The term "fiscal cliff" refers to a sudden and large reduction in government spending and/or increase in taxes, potentially leading to a recession.

103. The term "deleveraging" refers to the process of reducing debt levels, often occurring during recessions as households and businesses attempt to rebuild their balance sheets.

104. The term "capital buffer" refers to the additional capital that banks are required to hold during periods of economic growth to help absorb losses during recessions.

105. The term "macroprudential policy" refers to regulatory measures aimed at reducing systemic risk and promoting financial stability, often used in conjunction with monetary and fiscal policy to address recessions.

106. The term "stress test" refers to an assessment of a financial institution's ability to withstand economic shocks, often used by regulators to identify potential vulnerabilities during recessions.

107. The term "forward guidance" refers to a central bank's communication about its future policy actions, often used to influence market expectations and promote economic stability during recessions.

108. The term "asset price bubble" refers to a situation where the price of an asset rises rapidly and significantly above its fundamental value, potentially contributing to recessions when the bubble bursts.

109. The term "commodity price shock" refers to a sudden and large change in the price of a commodity, often leading to a recession if the shock is negative and affects a country's terms of trade.

110. The term "terms of trade" refers to the ratio of a country's export prices to its import prices, with a decline in the terms of trade potentially leading to a recession if it reduces national income and purchasing power.

111. The term "global imbalances" refers to persistent differences in current account balances between countries, often contributing to financial instability and recessions.

112. The term "current account" refers to a country's balance of trade in goods and services, net income from abroad, and net current transfers, with a deficit potentially indicating a reliance on foreign borrowing and vulnerability to recessions.

113. The term "capital account" refers to a country's balance of financial flows, including foreign direct investment, portfolio investment, and other investments, with a surplus potentially indicating a reliance on domestic borrowing and vulnerability to recessions.

114. The term "twin deficits" refers to a situation where a country has both a budget deficit and a current account deficit, potentially contributing to financial instability and recessions.

115. The term "external debt" refers to the total amount of debt owed by a country to foreign creditors, with high levels of external debt potentially increasing a country's vulnerability to financial crises and recessions.

116. The term "debt sustainability" refers to a country's ability to service its debt without incurring further debt, with unsustainable debt levels potentially leading to a debt crisis and a recession.

117. The term "fiscal space" refers to the difference between a country's current level of public debt and its debt limit, with limited fiscal space potentially constraining a country's ability to implement counter-cyclical policies during a recession.

118. The term "structural reforms" refers to changes in a country's economic institutions and policies aimed at promoting long-term growth and stability, often implemented in response to recessions.

119. The term "labor market flexibility" refers to the ease with which workers can move between jobs and industries, with greater flexibility potentially reducing the severity of recessions by facilitating the reallocation of labor.

120. The term "product market flexibility" refers to the ease with which firms can adjust their production and prices in response to changes in demand, with greater flexibility potentially reducing the severity of recessions by facilitating the reallocation of resources.

121. The term "financialization" refers to the increasing role of financial markets and institutions in the economy since the 1980s. It has both positive and negative effects, such as increased access to credit and income inequality. Some criticize it for leading to speculation and erosion of social safety nets, while others see it as necessary for economic growth and innovation.

122. market flexibility" refers to the ease with which financial institutions can adjust their lending and borrowing activities in response to changes in economic conditions, with greater flexibility potentially reducing the severity of recessions by facilitating the flow of credit.

123. The term "labor market policies" refers to government interventions aimed at improving the functioning of the labor market, such as unemployment benefits, job training programs, and minimum wage laws, which can help mitigate the effects of recessions.

124. The term "automatic stabilizers" refers to government programs and policies, such as unemployment benefits and progressive taxation, that automatically increase government spending or reduce taxes during a recession, helping to stabilize the economy.

125. The term "aggregate demand" refers to the total demand for goods and services in an economy, with a decline in aggregate demand often contributing to the onset of a recession.

126. The term "aggregate supply" refers to the total supply of goods and services in an economy, with a decline in aggregate supply potentially leading to a recession if it is not matched by a corresponding decline in aggregate demand.

127. The term "supply-side economics" refers to a school of thought that emphasizes the role of policies aimed at increasing aggregate supply, such as tax cuts and deregulation, in promoting economic growth and combating recessions.

128. The term "demand-side economics" refers to a school of thought that emphasizes the role of policies aimed at increasing aggregate demand, such as government spending and monetary policy, in promoting economic growth and combating recessions.

129. The term "monetarism" refers to a school of thought that emphasizes the role of the money supply in determining economic growth and inflation, with monetarists often advocating for tight control of the money supply to combat recessions.

130. The term "neoliberalism" refers to a set of economic policies and ideas that emphasize free markets, deregulation, and limited government intervention, often associated with a focus on supply-side economics and a reluctance to use fiscal policy during recessions.

131. The term "endogenous growth theory" refers to a set of economic models that incorporate the effects of technological progress, human capital, and innovation on economic growth, suggesting that appropriate policies can help promote long-term growth and reduce the likelihood of recessions.

132. The term "trade-off" refers to the idea that there are often costs associated with pursuing one policy objective, such as reducing inflation, which may conflict with other objectives, such as maintaining low unemployment during a recession.

133. The term "policy mix" refers to the combination of monetary policy, fiscal policy, and structural policies used by a government to address economic challenges, such as recessions.

134. The term "policy coordination" refers to the process by which governments and central banks work together to achieve common policy objectives, potentially helping to reduce the severity of recessions.

135. The term "globalization" refers to the increasing integration of national economies through trade, investment, and the exchange of ideas, potentially contributing to the spread of financial crises and recessions across countries.

136. The term "financial integration" refers to the growing interconnectedness of financial markets and institutions across countries, potentially increasing the risk of contagion during recessions.

137. The term "regional economic integration" refers to the process by which countries within a geographic region cooperate to promote trade, investment, and economic growth, potentially helping to reduce the severity of recessions within the region.

138. The term "currency union" refers to a group of countries that share a common currency, such as the euro in the Eurozone, potentially increasing the risk of contagion during recessions but also promoting trade and investment among member countries.

139. The term "economic governance" refers to the institutions and processes that guide economic policymaking and implementation, with effective governance potentially helping to reduce the likelihood and severity of recessions.

140. The term "economic resilience" refers to the ability of an economy to withstand shocks and recover quickly from recessions, with factors such as diversification, flexibility, and strong institutions potentially contributing to resilience.

141. The term "economic diversification" refers to the process by which an economy becomes less dependent on a single industry or sector, potentially reducing the impact of sector-specific shocks and recessions.

142. The term "export-led growth" refers to a development strategy that focuses on promoting exports as a source of economic growth, potentially increasing a country's vulnerability to external shocks and recessions.

143. The term "import substitution" refers to a development strategy that focuses on promoting domestic industries to replace imported goods, potentially reducing a country's vulnerability to external shocks and recessions.

144. The term "structural adjustment" refers to a set of economic policies, often implemented as a condition of international financial assistance, aimed at promoting economic growth and reducing fiscal imbalances, potentially contributing to short-term recessions but promoting long-term stability.

145. The term "poverty trap" refers to a situation where poor economic conditions, such as low income, limited access to education, and poor health, perpetuate poverty and reduce the ability of individuals and countries to recover from recessions.

146. The term "inclusive growth" refers to the idea that economic growth should be broad-based, benefiting all segments of society, potentially helping to reduce the severity of recessions and promote long-term development.

147. The term "sustainable development" refers to the idea that economic growth should be balanced with social and environmental concerns, potentially helping to reduce the likelihood of resource depletion and environmental crises that can contribute to recessions.

148. The term "human development" refers to the process of improving the well-being and capabilities of individuals, with investments in areas such as education, health, and social protection potentially helping to reduce the severity of recessions and promote long-term growth.

149. The term "development aid" refers to financial and technical assistance provided by developed countries to support economic development in low- and middle-income countries, potentially helping to reduce the impact of recessions and promote long-term growth.

150. The term "global economic governance" refers to the institutions and processes that guide international economic policymaking, with effective governance potentially helping to reduce the likelihood and severity of global recessions and financial crises.

Asset Bubbles

Tulip Mania (1634-1637): The first recorded speculative bubble, this occurred in the Dutch Republic when the prices of tulip bulbs soared to unsustainable levels and then dramatically collapsed.

The South Sea Bubble (1719-1720): A British stock market bubble, driven by speculation in the shares of the South Sea Company, which collapsed and caused widespread financial ruin.

Mississippi Company Bubble (1719-1720): A French financial bubble driven by speculation in the shares of the Mississippi Company, leading to an economic collapse and the introduction of paper money.

The British Railway Mania (1840s): A speculative bubble in the UK's railway industry, with overinvestment in railway companies, followed by a financial collapse.

The 1860s Gold Bubble (Australia): A speculative bubble in gold mining shares in the Australian colonies during the 1860s gold rush, leading to a financial panic and market collapse.

The Brazilian Coffee Boom (1880s-1920s): A period of excessive production and investment in the Brazilian coffee industry, followed by a market collapse and an economic crisis.

The Roaring Twenties (1920-1929): A period of economic prosperity and excessive speculation in the U.S., leading up to the 1929 stock market crash and the Great Depression.

The Florida Land Boom (1920s): A real estate bubble in Florida during the 1920s, driven by speculative investment and overdevelopment, leading to a collapse in land prices and a subsequent recession.

The Great Depression Stock Market Crash (1929): The U.S. stock market crash in October 1929, which marked the beginning of the Great Depression and a prolonged economic downturn.

The Nifty Fifty Bubble (1970s): A period of excessive valuation of 50 popular large-cap U.S. stocks, followed by a significant market correction in the mid-1970s.

The Poseidon Nickel Bubble (1969-1970): A mining bubble in Australia driven by the discovery of nickel deposits, leading to a rapid rise and subsequent fall in mining company share prices.

The Silver Thursday Crash (1980): The Hunt brothers' attempt to corner the silver market led to a rapid increase in silver prices, followed by a sharp decline and financial ruin for the brothers.

Nordic Banking Crisis (1980s-1990s): A period of deregulation in the Nordic banking sector, followed by a collapse in property prices and widespread bank failures.

The 1980s Savings and Loan Crisis (U.S.): A financial crisis in the U.S. savings and loan industry, driven by deregulation and risky investments, leading to numerous bank failures and a government bailout.

Japanese Asset Price Bubble (1986-1991): A period of excessive valuation of real estate and stocks in Japan, followed by a prolonged economic stagnation known as the "Lost Decade."

The 1990s Biotech Bubble: A period of excessive valuation of biotechnology stocks, driven by optimism around new technologies and potential medical breakthroughs, followed by a market correction.

The Asian Financial Crisis (1997-1998): A financial crisis that began in Thailand and spread throughout East Asia, resulting in currency devaluations, stock market crashes, and economic contractions.

The Beanie Baby Bubble (1995-1999): A speculative bubble in the market for collectible Beanie Babies plush toys, resulting in inflated prices and a subsequent crash when the craze faded.

The Dot-com Bubble (1995-2000): A stock market bubble driven by excessive speculation in internet-based companies, which burst in 2000 and led to a sharp decline in technology stocks.

Irish Property Bubble (1995-2007): A significant rise in Irish property prices, followed by a severe crash, contributing to Ireland's banking crisis and a prolonged recession.

The U.S. Housing Bubble (2002-2007): A period of excessive valuation of real estate in the United States, fueled by easy credit and subprime mortgages, leading to the 2008 financial crisis.

The Chinese Stock Market Bubble (2007): A sharp increase in stock prices on the Shanghai and Shenzhen stock exchanges, followed by a rapid decline, leading to tightened regulations on margin trading.

Spanish Property Bubble (1997-2008): A sharp increase in Spanish real estate prices, followed by a collapse that contributed to the European sovereign debt crisis.

Bitcoin and Cryptocurrency Bubble (2017): A rapid increase in the value of various cryptocurrencies, including Bitcoin, followed by a sharp decline in 2018, raising concerns about the stability and viability of these digital assets.

Australian Property Bubble (1990s-2018): A prolonged period of escalating real estate prices in Australia, raising concerns about housing affordability and potential economic consequences if the bubble bursts.

Frequently Asked Questions.

What happens in a recession?

When the economy weakens and fewer goods and services are bought and sold, this is called a recession. The decrease in spending can lead to lost jobs and income as well as less money for investments, which can further hurt the economy. In a recession, businesses may produce less, hire fewer workers, or even close down entirely. People who have lost their jobs may struggle to find new ones. The decrease in spending can also lead to less money for investments, which can further hurt the economy. A recession can last for a few months or even a few years. During this time, people may cut back on their spending even further, which can make it difficult for the economy to recover. Recessions can be difficult times for everyone, but there are things that can be done to help. Governments may provide support to businesses and individuals through stimulus packages. This can help to encourage spending and prevent further job losses. It is important to remember that economies always go through ups and downs. While a recession can be a difficult time, it is not the end of the world. With the right support, the economy can recover and people can start to improve their lives once again.

What would a recession mean?

A recession is defined as two consecutive quarters of negative economic growth.While it is technically possible for the US to experience a recession, it is unlikely in the near future. However, if a recession were to happen, what would it mean? A recession would have a number of consequences. First and foremost, it would mean a decrease in economic activity. This would lead to a decrease in production and a decrease in jobs. As businesses saw their profits decline, they would be forced to cut costs, and that would mean layoffs. Unemployment would begin to rise, and with it, poverty. A recession would also have an impact on the stock market. Stocks would fall as businesses lost value, and people would lose money. This would lead to a decrease in consumer confidence, and a decrease in spending. The housing market would also be affected, as people would be less likely to buy homes or take out mortgages. A recession would have a ripple effect on the economy, and it would be felt by everyone. Businesses would suffer, consumers would suffer, and the government would suffer. The effects of a recession would be far-reaching and long-lasting.

What is a recession vs depression?

A recession is typically defined as two consecutive quarters of negative economic growth, as measured by a country's gross domestic product (GDP). A depression, on the other hand, is a more severe economic downturn that can last for several years and be characterized by widespread unemployment and financial instability. While a recession is typically seen as a normal part of the business cycle, a depression is a more severe event that can have far-reaching effects on an economy. recessions can be caused by a variety of factors, including tight monetary policies, oil price shocks, and financial crises. A depression, on the other hand, is often the result of a more severe shock to the economy, such as a major financial crisis or a prolonged period of high unemployment. While a recession typically lasts for a few months or a couple of years, a depression can last for several years. The most recent depression, the Great Depression of the 1930s, lasted for more than a decade. While recessions are generally seen as normal, albeit unpleasant, part of the business cycle, depressions are more severe and can have far-reaching effects on an economy.

How long do recessions last?

A recession is typically defined as two consecutive quarters of negative economic growth, as measured by a country's gross domestic product (GDP). However, the effects of a recession can be felt long after the GDP has begun to rebound. Unemployment, for example, often takes much longer to recover. So how long do recessions typically last? The short answer is that it varies. Some recessions are over in a matter of months, while others can drag on for years. The average length of a recession in the United States since World War II has been just under 10 months. However, there have been some very lengthy recessions, such as the early 1980s recession, which lasted more than two years. There are a number of factors that can influence the length of a recession. One is the severity of the economic downturn. A recession that is triggered by a financial crisis, for example, tend to be deeper and longer-lasting than those that are sparked by a less severe event. Another factor is the response of policy makers. If they act quickly and decisively, they can help to limit the duration and severity of a recession. So while there is no definitive answer to the question, the length of a recession can vary depending on the underlying causes and the response of policymakers.

What is a recession

A recession is a period of economic decline, typically lasting for around six months, when GDP falls and unemployment rises. It is generally considered to be caused by a combination of factors, such as a decrease in consumer spending, an increase in taxes or interest rates, or a decrease in exports. During a recession, businesses often cut back on their investment and hiring, which can lead to even further economic decline and higher unemployment. However, there are also some positive aspects to recessions, such as a decrease in inflation and an increase in savings. There are a number of different ways to measure a recession, but one of the most common is by looking at GDP growth. If GDP growth is negative for two consecutive quarters, then this is generally considered to be a recession. Recessions can have a major impact on people's lives, both in the short and long term. In the short term, people may lose their jobs or see their hours reduced, which can lead to financial difficulties. In the long term, people may find it harder to get a job, or may experience lower wages even if they are in work. Recessions can also have a knock-on effect on other areas of life, such as mental health, crime rates and divorce rates. It is important to remember that recessions are a natural part of the economic cycle, and will eventually come to an end. However, this doesn't mean that they don't have serious consequences for those affected by them.

What should you not do in a recession?

A recession is when the economy shrinks for two consecutive quarters. This means that there is less money being made and fewer jobs available. When this happens, people start to worry about their financial future and how they will make ends meet. There are a lot of things that people should not do during a recession, but here are five of the most important things to avoid: 1. Don't quit your job: Even if you hate your job, it's important to hang onto it during a recession. This is because jobs are hard to come by and you don't want to put yourself in a position where you're competing with hundreds of other people for the same role. If you do lose your job, make sure you take the time to look for another one before quitting. 2. Don't overspend: It's easy to get caught up in a spending spree when times are good, but during a recession it's important to reign in your spending and focus on saving money. This means cutting back on unnecessary expenses like nights out, new clothes, and vacations. 3. Don't take on too much debt: One of the worst things you can do during a recession is to take on more debt than you can handle. This can be in the form of credit card debt, loans, or even a mortgage. Not only will this put a strain on your finances, but it could also ruin your credit score. 4. Don't invest in risky ventures: Many people think that they can make a quick buck by investing in something risky during a recession, but this is rarely the case. In fact, it's often a good idea to steer clear of any investments that you don't understand or that seem too good to be true. 5. Don't panic: It's normal to feel a little anxious during a recession, but it's important not to panic. This is because making rash decisions can often lead to financial problems down the road. Instead, take a deep breath and assess your situation before making any decisions.

Who suffers the most during a recession?

When the economy dips and we slip into a recession, a lot of people feel the pinch. But some groups suffer more than others. For example, young people just starting out in their careers can find it hard to get their foot on the ladder during a recession. With fewer job opportunities available, they may have to take unpaid internships or low-paid jobs that don't give them the chance to progress. Recessions can also hit certain sectors of the workforce harder than others. People working in manufacturing or construction, for example, may lose their jobs as businesses cut back on investment. Women are also often disproportionately affected by recessions. They are more likely to work in sectors like healthcare and education, which are often hit by public spending cuts. And they are more likely to work part-time or in temporary jobs, which are often the first to go when businesses start to make redundancies. Those on low incomes are also particularly vulnerable during a recession. With less money to go around, they may have to cut back on essentials like food and heating. And they may be pushed into debt or homelessness as a result. Of course, recessions also have a knock-on effect on families and communities. When people lose their jobs, it can put a strain on relationships. And as businesses close and unemployment rises, whole communities can be left feeling despondent and without hope. So, while we all feel the effect of a recession, some of us feel it more than others. And it's often the most vulnerable members of society who suffer the most.

The recession has been hard on everyone, but there are some things that you can do to help ease the pain. First, try to save as much money as you can. This will help you in the long run if you lose your job or have to take a pay cut. Second, try to stay positive and think of the recession as a challenge that you can overcome. Lastly, be sure to help out others who are struggling during this difficult time. By working together, we can get through the recession and come out stronger on the other side.

Who benefits in a recession?

In a recession, there are a few different types of people who can benefit. The first type is people who are able to hoard their money. These are the people who have a lot of savings and are able to put away even more during a recession. They benefit because they can use their money to buy things when prices are low and then sell them later when prices have recovered. Another type of person who benefits from a recession is someone who has a lot of debt. This might seem counterintuitive, but during a recession, people with debt can actually benefit. This is because interest rates tend to go down during a recession, meaning that people with debt can save money on their payments. Finally, there are people who benefit from a recession because they are able to find a job. Although it might be harder to find a job during a recession, there are still some companies that are hiring. And, because there are fewer people looking for jobs, those who are looking have a better chance of getting hired. So, who benefits from a recession? People who have a lot of money, people with a lot of debt, and people who are looking for a job.

Does recession mean crash?

A recession is defined as two consecutive quarters of negative economic growth, as measured by a country's Gross Domestic Product (GDP). In other words, it's when the economy shrinks for six months or more. A recession is not the same thing as a crash, although a recession can lead to a crash. A crash is a sudden, sharp decline in asset prices, usually in the stock market. A recession is a sustained period of economic decline. The cause of a recession is not always clear, but it is usually the result of a combination of factors. A slowdown in consumer spending is often a major factor, as is a decrease in business investment. Other factors can include a decrease in exports, an increase in imports, and a rise in interest rates. A recession can have a number of negative effects on an economy. One is that it can lead to a rise in unemployment, as businesses lay off workers in an effort to cut costs. This can in turn lead to a further decrease in consumer spending, as people have less money to spend. A recession can also lead to an increase in government debt, as the government is often called upon to provide financial assistance to those suffering from the effects of the recession. A recession is often followed by a period of economic growth, as businesses and consumers alike adjust to the new economic reality. However, it is possible for a recession to turn into a depression, which is a much longer and more severe period of economic decline.

Are we headed for a depression in 2023?

The U.S. National Bureau of Economic Research defines a recession as "a significant decline in economic activity spread across the economy, lasting more than a few months, normally visible in real GDP, real income, employment, industrial production, and wholesale-retail sales." There is no set definition of what constitutes a depression, but it is generally considered to be a more severe and prolonged recession. The National Bureau of Economic Research has only declared three depressions in U.S. history: the Great Depression of 1929-1933, the depression of 1873-1879, and the depression of 1883-1885. Some economists are warning that the U.S. could be headed for another depression in 2023. They point to a number of factors, including: -The increasing level of debt held by the U.S. government, businesses, and households. -The aging of the Baby Boomer generation and the resulting decline in consumer spending. -The rising costs of health care and education. -The globalization of the economy and the increasing competition from low-wage countries. -The increasing inequality of income and wealth. -The declining role of manufacturing in the economy. -The slow growth of the U.S. economy in recent years. These factors have led some economists to warn that the U.S. could be headed for another depression in 2023. While there is no guarantee that this will happen, it is certainly a possibility that should be taken seriously.

How do you survive a recession?

A recession can be a difficult time for everyone, but there are ways to survive it. Here are some tips: -Cut back on unnecessary spending: This is the time to be more mindful about your spending and to cut back on any unnecessary expenses. -Create a budget: Now is the time to be extra diligent about tracking your income and expenses and creating a budget. This will help you to stay on top of your finances and make informed decisions about your spending. -Save money: Try to put away as much money as you can each month into savings. This will help you to have a buffer in case of tough times. -Look for ways to make extra money: If you have some extra time, look for ways to make extra money. This could include picking up a part-time job or taking on freelance work. -Be mindful of your debt: Be careful about taking on new debt during a recession. If possible, try to pay off any existing debt. -Make a plan: Having a plan can help to ease anxiety during a recession. Try to plan your finances and spending so that you know what to expect. This can help you to stay on track and make informed decisions.

How do you prepare for a recession?

When it comes to preparing for a recession, there are a few key things you can do to ensure you weather the storm. Firstly, it's important to have an emergency fund in place. This will give you a cushion to fall back on if you lose your job or experience a drop in income. Secondly, it's wise to make sure you have a good handle on your finances and are living within your means. This will make it easier to cut back on spending if necessary. Finally, it's a good idea to diversify your income sources. This way, if one stream of income dries up, you'll still have others to fall back on. While there's no way to completely avoid the fallout from a recession, following these steps can help you weather the storm and come out the other side in better shape.

What jobs will be affected by a recession?

In any recession, there are certain sectors of the job market which are always hit the hardest. These are the jobs which are deemed to be 'non-essential', and are usually the first to go when companies start making cuts. The following jobs are typically most affected by a recession: - Retail and customer service positions are often amongst the first to go during a recession. This is because spending slows down significantly during economic downturns, meaning that many stores and businesses struggle to keep up with profits. As a result, they start making cuts to their workforce in order to stay afloat.

- Hospitality and tourism jobs are also typically affected by a recession. This is because people are less likely to want to travel and take holidays when money is tight. As a result, businesses in these sectors start to make cuts to their staff. - Manufacturing jobs can also be hit hard during a recession. This is because businesses start to look for ways to cut costs, and one way to do this is by outsourcing manufacturing to cheaper countries. This can lead to job losses in the manufacturing sector. - Administrative and support jobs can also be affected by a recession. This is because businesses start to streamline their operations and reduce their overhead costs. This can lead to job losses in the administrative and support sectors. A recession can have a major impact on the job market, with many people losing their jobs as businesses start to make cuts. The sectors which are most affected are typically those which are considered to be 'non-essential'. Retail, customer service, hospitality, tourism, manufacturing and administrative jobs are all at risk during a recession.

How long did 2008 recession last?

The 2008 recession was a global economic crisis that affected many countries around the world. The United States, in particular, was hit hard by the recession, with many people losing their jobs and homes. The recession lasted for several years, finally coming to an end in 2010. The cause of the 2008 recession was largely due to the housing market crash. In the years leading up to the recession, home prices had been steadily increasing. This led to more and more people taking out loans to buy homes, with the hope that they would be able to sell the home for a profit down the road. However, when the housing market crashed, home prices plummeted and many people were left with mortgages that were worth more than their homes. This caused a ripple effect throughout the economy, as people lost their jobs and businesses struggled. The recession had a major impact on the United States economy. GDP growth slowed, unemployment rose, and home prices fell. The stock market also took a hit, with the Dow Jones Industrial Average losing nearly 50% of its value. The recession was a difficult time for many people, but the United States has since made a recovery. GDP growth has returned to pre-recession levels and unemployment has fallen. The stock market has also rebounded, though not to its pre-recession highs. Despite the challenges of the recession, the United States economy is now in a much better place than it was a decade ago.

The current recession has been tough on everyone, but there are things that can be done to help ease the financial burden. things like cutting back on spending, finding ways to make extra money, and living within your means. It's important to remember that we're all in this together and that things will eventually get better.

Should you sell before a recession?

A recession is defined as a significant decline in economic activity lasting more than a few months. It is typically accompanied by a rise in unemployment. A recession can occur when there is a widespread drop in spending (demand), often triggered by a financial shock. Statistically, recessions tend to be fairly rare events. The U.S. has experienced just nine recessions since 1945. Given their rarity, it can be difficult to know how to best prepare for a recession. One common question is whether it makes sense to sell investments before a recession hits. Selling investments before a recession may help to avoid losses in the value of those investments. However, it is important to remember that a recession is not necessarily synonymous with a stock market crash. The stock market may continue to rise during a recession, as it did during the 2001 and 2008 recessions. Additionally, selling investments before a recession may mean missing out on opportunities for gains when the economy eventually recovers. It can be difficult to predict when a recession will end, so selling investments too early may mean missing out on potential gains. Of course, there is no one-size-fits-all answer to the question of whether to sell before a recession. The best decision will depend on each individual investor's unique circumstances. However, selling investments before a recession is not generally recommended as a long-term strategy.

What will happen if the world goes into recession?

The economists define a recession as "a significant decline in economic activity spread across the economy, lasting more than a few months, normally visible in real gross domestic product (GDP), real personal income, employment (non-farm payrolls), industrial production, and wholesale-retail sales". In layman's terms, this simply means that there is less money and economic activity circulating around. There are many factors that contribute to a recession. The most common reason is an over-extension of credit. This can lead to a build-up of debt, which in turn can lead to defaults and foreclosures. When this happens, it reduces the amount of available credit, which then leads to a decrease in spending and investment. This decrease in spending can lead to a decrease in production, which then leads to a decrease in wages and incomes. All of this can then lead to a negative feedback loop, where the decrease in spending leads to a further decrease in production, and so on. A recession can also be caused by a sharp decrease in demand, either due to a change in consumer preferences or a sudden decrease in disposable incomes. This can lead to a decrease in production and a decrease in jobs, which can then lead to a decrease in spending and a further decrease in production. This can also create a negative feedback loop.

Interestingly, a recession can also be caused by an increase in supply. This might happen if there is a technological breakthrough that leads to a sudden increase in production. This increase in production can lead to a decrease in prices, which can lead to a decrease in demand and a decrease in jobs. Again, this can create a negative feedback loop. So what will happen if the world goes into recession? In the short-term, we can expect to see a decrease in economic activity and a decrease in jobs. This will lead to a decrease in spending, and a further decrease in economic activity. This will create a negative feedback loop, which will magnify the effects of the recession. In the long-term, we can expect to see a recovery, but the magnitude and timing of the recovery will depend on the underlying causes of the recession.

Will the world go into recession 2023?

The current state of the world economy is tumultuous, to say the least. Political factors such as Brexit, the trade war between the United States and China, and the overall instability of many countries' governments are just some of the issues that are causing concern for economists. One of the big questions on everyone's mind is whether or not the world will go into recession in 2023. There are a number of factors that will play into this decision. One is the strength of the US dollar. If the dollar weakens, it could lead to inflation, which would in turn hurt the US economy and potentially trigger a recession. Another factor is the increasing debt levels in both the US and Chinese governments. As debt levels increase, it becomes more difficult for countries to repay their debts, which could lead to default and a recession. There are also a number of positive factors that could prevent a recession. One is the recent tax cuts in the US, which are expected to increase consumer spending and boost the economy. Another is the increasing price of oil, which is helping to improve the finances of many oil-producing countries. So, what will the world economy look like in 2023? Nobody can say for sure. However, there are a number of factors that will play a role in whether or not a recession occurs. Whether or not the world goes into recession in 2023 will depend on a number of factors, including the strength of the US dollar, the increasing debt levels in the US and China, and the recent tax cuts in the US.

How long will the 2023 recession last?

In 2023, the US economy will hit a recession. It is difficult to say how long this recession will last, as it will largely depend on the policies that are put in place in response to the recession. If the government implements policies that help to stimulate the economy, then the recession may not last very long. However, if the government does not take action to improve the economy, then the recession could last for several years.

What to buy in recession?

When it comes to recession, there are a lot of different opinions on what to do. Some people think that you should spend less money, while others believe that you should continue to spend money but be more mindful of where it goes. Ultimately, the decision of what to buy during a recession comes down to each individual and their own personal circumstances. For those who are looking to save money during a recession, there are a few things that can be done. One option is to buy generic brands instead of name brands. This can be done for items such as food, cleaning supplies, and personal care products. Another option is to purchase items that are on sale. This could mean waiting for a holiday sale or looking for clearance items. Additionally, people can save money by buying used items instead of new. This could include shopping at thrift stores, garage sales, or online marketplaces. For those who are looking to continue spending money during a recession, it is important to be mindful of where the money is going. One way to do this is to create a budget and stick to it. This budget should include all necessary expenses, such as housing, food, transportation, and utilities. Once all of the necessary expenses are accounted for, any additional money can be spent on discretionary items. When it comes to discretionary spending, it is important to choose wisely. Perhaps instead of buying a new piece of clothing, the money could be spent on a concert ticket or going out to eat. The goal is to still enjoy life during a recession, but to be mindful of where the money is being spent. In the end, what to buy during a recession is a personal decision. Some people may choose to save money while others may choose to continue spending. The most important thing is to be aware of your own financial situation and make the best decision for you.

Is my money safe during a recession?

Is my money safe during a recession? This is a question on many people's minds as we enter another recession. The last recession was harsh on many people, causing them to lose their jobs, homes, and savings. So, is your money safe during a recession? The answer is, it depends. If you keep your money in a savings account or cash, then it is safe from inflation. However, the interest rates on these accounts are very low, so your money may not grow as much as you would like. Investing your money is a riskier proposition during a recession, but it can also lead to higher rewards. Many people lost money in the stock market during the last recession, but those who held on to their investments or even bought more during the downturn ultimately made a lot of money when the market recovered. So, what is the best way to protect your money during a recession? The best strategy is to diversify your investments and to have a mix of cash, stocks, and other assets. This way, if one area of the market takes a hit, you will still have other investments to cushion the blow. No investment is 100% safe, but by diversifying your portfolio, you can minimize your risks and maximize your chances of weathering a recession.

What is best to hold in a recession?

A recession is a general slowdown in economic activity. When economic activity slows, businesses may start to lay off workers or cut back on hours. Consumers may start to spend less money. All of this can lead to even slower economic activity and higher unemployment. There are a lot of different opinions on what is best to hold in a recession. Some people believe that cash is king and that you should hold onto as much cash as possible. Others believe that you should invest in assets that will hold their value or even increase in value during a recession. The truth is that there is no one-size-fits-all answer to this question. It depends on your individual circumstances and what your goals are. If you are retired or close to retirement, you may want to hold more cash so that you don't have to sell investments during a time when they may be worth less. On the other hand, if you are young and have a long time to invest, you may be more comfortable with taking on some risk in hopes of making money during a recession. No matter what your situation is, it's important to remember that recessions are a normal part of the business cycle. They don't last forever and eventually the economy will start to recover. So, don't make any rash decisions out of fear. Instead, work with a financial advisor to come up with a plan that makes sense for you and your family.

The article concludes that the recession was caused by a number of factors, including the housing market crash, subprime mortgage crisis, and high oil prices. The recession has had a devastating effect on the economy, with millions of Americans losing their jobs and homes. The article urges readers to learn from the mistakes of the past and to be prepared for the next economic downturn.

Who will be hit hardest by recession?

The recession will have a big impact on different groups of people in different ways. Some will be hit much harder than others. Generally, those who are on lower incomes will suffer most during a recession. This is because they are more likely to lose their jobs or have their hours cut. This can lead to debt and financial problems, as well as anxiety and mental health issues. Young people are also likely to be affected badly by a recession. They are more likely to be in low-paid, insecure work, and so are more likely to lose their jobs. They may also find it harder to get a job after the recession. Householders will also be affected, as the value of their homes may fall and they may find it harder to get a mortgage. This could lead to negative equity, where people owe more to the bank than their home is worth. The recession will also have an impact on businesses. Small businesses are particularly vulnerable, as they may not have the resources to weather a downturn. This can lead to businesses going bust, and people losing their jobs. The knock-on effect of all this is that the economy as a whole will suffer. GDP will fall, and unemployment will rise. This will have a negative impact on everyone, even those who have not been directly affected by the recession.

Who gets laid off in a recession?

In a recession, employers across the board tend to lay off workers. But there are certain groups of workers who are more likely to be laid off than others. For example, workers in industries that are particularly sensitive to economic downturns, such as construction and manufacturing, are more likely to be laid off than workers in other industries. Also, workers who are employed in temporary or contract positions are more likely to be laid off than those with permanent jobs. And finally, workers who are already employed in precarious or low-wage jobs are more likely to be laid off than those who are employed in better-paying jobs.

What is the biggest problem in a recession?

A recession can be defined as a period of negative economic growth, when trade and businesses contract and unemployment rises. The biggest problem in a recession is that it can act as a self-fulfilling prophecy. As people lose their jobs or become worried about losing their jobs, they spend less. This reduced demand can lead to businesses making less profit, and so they invest less and may lay off staff. The knock-on effect of this is that even more people lose their jobs, and the economy goes into further decline. Recessions can also have a long-lasting effect on people's lives. For example, people who lose their jobs during a recession may find it difficult to get another job that pays as well, or they may be forced to take lower-paid jobs. This can lead to a spiral of decline, as people on lower incomes are less likely to have the disposable income to spend on goods and services. This can further damage the economy, as businesses see a drop in demand for their products. Governments can try to mitigate the effects of a recession by implementing economic policies such as stimulus packages. This involves pumping money into the economy in the hope that this will encourage people to spend, and so help to boost demand and kick-start the economy. However, there is no guarantee that these measures will be successful, and often they can take a long time to have an effect. In the meantime, people are still suffering the consequences of job losses, pay cuts and the like. This can lead to social problems such as crime and homelessness, as well as mental health problems such as anxiety and depression. In conclusion, the biggest problem in a recession is that it can have a devastating and long-lasting impact on people's lives.

Do people lose money during a recession?

A recession is typically defined as two consecutive quarters of negative economic growth, as measured by a country's gross domestic product (GDP). A recession can also be triggered by a stock market crash, a natural disaster, or a major political event. During a recession, people may lose their jobs, have their hours reduced, or see their wages cut. This can lead to a decrease in spending power and an increase in debt. The decrease in spending can lead to businesses closing their doors and, in turn, further job losses. Recessions can be difficult times for people, but there are ways to weather the storm. One of the best things you can do is to save money. Having a cushion of savings can help you make it through a period of unemployment or underemployment. Another key is to try to reduce your expenses. This can be difficult if your income has been cut, but it's important to remember that every little bit helps. It's also important to keep perspective during a recession. A recession is not the end of the world, and it is certainly not the end of your financial life. With careful planning and a little bit of luck, you can make it through a recession without too much damage.

Do I lose money in a recession?

It is a common misconception that one automatically lose money during a recession. While it is true that recessions can cause a decrease in the value of stocks and other investments, there are many ways to protect oneself from such losses. For example, one can diversify their portfolio by investing in different types of assets, including bonds and cash. Additionally, one can increase their savings during a recessionary period in order to have a cushion in case their income decreases. There are a number of different ways to measure a recession. The most common method is to look at the gross domestic product (GDP), which is the total value of all goods and services produced in a country. When the GDP decreases for two consecutive quarters, it is typically considered to be in a recession. Another method is to look at the unemployment rate, which tend to increase during a recession as businesses lay off workers. A recession can have a variety of different causes, but it is typically brought about by a combination of factors. For example, a decrease in consumer spending can lead to a decrease in production, which in turn can lead to layoffs and an increase in unemployment. Additionally, a decrease in business investment can lead to a decrease in demand for goods and services, which can further contribute to a decrease in production. Recessions can have a number of different effects on people's lives. For example, they can lead to a decrease in the value of investments, such as stocks and real estate. Additionally, they can lead to an increase in unemployment, as businesses lay off workers in order to cut costs. Finally, recessions can also lead to a decrease in wages as businesses strive to remain profitable. Despite the negative effects of a recession, there are a number of ways to protect oneself from economic decline. For example, one can diversify their portfolio by investing in different types of assets, including bonds and cash. Additionally, one can increase their savings during a recessionary period in order to have a cushion in case their income decreases. By taking these measures, one can weather the storm of a recession and come out ahead financially.

What are the signs of a recession coming?

There are a few key signs that can indicate that a recession may be on the horizon. One such sign is an increase in unemployment. When people start losing their jobs, they have less money to spend, which can lead to a decrease in consumer spending and a decrease in economic activity. Another sign of a recession is a decrease in housing prices. This can be caused by a decrease in demand for housing, which can lead to a decrease in construction and a decrease in home values. Finally, another sign of a recession is an increase in interest rates. This can lead to a decrease in investment and a decrease in economic activity.

How long will 2023 recession last?

The 2023 recession is projected to last for two full years. This is based on current projections of the economy's growth. However, there are a number of variables that could affect the length of the recession. The first variable is the depth of the recession. A deeper recession will last longer because it takes longer to recover from a larger drop in economic activity. The second variable is the response of policymakers. If they respond quickly and effectively, the recession will likely be shorter. The third variable is the strength of the global economy. A stronger global economy can help the US economy recover more quickly. The 2023 recession is projected to be milder than the Great Recession of 2008-2009. However, it will still be a significant downturn. It is important to remember that projections are never exact, and the actual length of the recession could be different than what is currently projected.

What happens if we go into recession?

If the economy weakens and economic activity slows, this is called a recession. A recession is typically defined as two consecutive quarters of negative economic growth, as measured by a country's gross domestic product (GDP). During a recession, businesses may cut back on production and investment, which can lead to layoffs and higher unemployment. Consumer spending usually declines as well, as people tighten their belts and prioritize spending on essential items. While a recession can be painful in the short-term, there are some silver linings. For example, a recession can lead to lower interest rates and inflation, as well as create opportunities to buy assets at a discount. In the long-run, recoveries from recessions are typically strong. After peaking, the economy usually bounces back quickly and growth resumes. However, there is no guarantee that this will happen, and some countries take longer to recover than others. A recession can also have a ripple effect on the rest of the world. For example, if a country's exports decline, this can hurt other countries that depend on those exports. Recessions are often caused by a variety of factors, including financial bubbles, tighter monetary policy, and shocks to the system (such as a natural disaster or terrorist attack). They can also be caused by a slowdown in productivity growth or a decrease in consumer confidence. While there is no surefire way to avoid a recession, there are things that can be done to lessen the impact. For example, countries can implement policies that encourage investment and consumer spending. In the end, a recession is a natural part of the business cycle and is something that all countries will experience at some point. While they can be painful, they also present opportunities for growth and renewal.

What does a recession do to the average person?

In the United States, a recession is defined as a significant decline in economic activity lasting more than a few months.1 It is characterized by a fall in gross domestic product (GDP), higher unemployment, and lower consumer spending and Applies to countries across the globe.2 A recession has different effects on different people, but there are some generalities that can be made. A recession hits the average person in a number of ways. First, there is the obvious decrease in income. This can come about in a variety of ways. People can lose their jobs, have their hours reduced, or see their investments lose value. All of these lead to less money coming in, which can make it difficult to make ends meet. Another way that a recession affects people is through inflation. Inflation is when prices for goods and services rise, but wages do not. This leaves people with less purchasing power, as their money does not go as far. This can be a particular problem for people on fixed incomes, such as pensioners. A recession can also lead to an increase in crime. This is often due to the fact that people are desperate and will do whatever it takes tosurvive. This can include things like theft, violence, and prostitution. A recession can have a number of other effects on people as well. It can lead to mental health problems, as people struggle to cope with the financial stress. It can also put a strain on relationships, as people argue about money. A recession is a difficult time for everyone, but it is especially difficult for the average person. They must contend with a decrease in income, inflation, and an increased crime rate. It is important to be aware of these effects and do what you can to protect yourself.

Who benefits from a recession?

A recession occurs when there is a decrease in economic activity for a sustained period of time. This can be caused by a number of factors, including a decrease in consumer spending, an increase in taxes, or a decrease in exports. A recession can have both positive and negative effects on different groups of people. For example, a recession may cause a decline in the stock market, which can lead to a loss of retirement savings for some people. On the other hand, a recession may also cause an increase in the unemployment rate, which can lead to financial hardship for families. In general, there are a few groups of people who tend to benefit from a recession. Firstly, people who have cash savings tend to benefit from a recession, as the value of their savings increases when the economy slows down. Secondly, people who own assets such as property or stocks may also see the value of their assets increase during a recession. Finally, people who have low levels of debt tend to benefit from a recession, as the interest rates on their debt decrease. However, it is important to remember that a recession can have negative effects on even the groups of people who typically benefit from them. For example, a decrease in the stock market can lead to a loss of retirement savings, and an increase in the unemployment rate can lead to financial hardship. Therefore, it is important to be aware of the potential benefits and drawbacks of a recession before making any decisions.

Who suffers most in a recession?

A recession is an economic downturn that usually lasts for a few months. It is marked by a decrease in the gross domestic product (GDP), an increase in unemployment, and a decline in the stock market. The most recent recession in the United States began in December 2007 and lasted until June 2009. During a recession, consumers spending decreases, which leads to a decrease in production and jobs. The decrease in spending is usually caused by a combination of factors, such as an increase in taxes, a decrease in wages, and an increase in the cost of living. As a result of the decrease in production, businesses suffer and may go bankrupt. This can lead to an increase in unemployment. Recessions can be difficult for everyone, but they often hit the most vulnerable members of society the hardest. The poor and the unemployed are often the first to feel the effects of a recession. As businesses close and jobs are lost, they find it increasingly difficult to make ends meet. In a recession, the rich may also suffer, but they are usually better equipped to weather the storm. They often have investments that can be liquidated to provide them with extra cash, and they may have multiple sources of income. The poor, on the other hand, often have only one source of income, and are less likely to have savings or other assets to fall back on. While recessions can be difficult for everyone, they often have the most severe consequences for the most vulnerable members of society. The poor and the unemployed are often the first to lose their jobs and homes, and they often find it the most difficult to recover from the economic downturn.

How long do recessions usually last?

A recession is typically defined as two consecutive quarters of negative economic growth, as measured by a country's gross domestic product (GDP). However, the length of a recession can vary significantly. The longest recession on record lasted for more than a decade, from 1973 to 1985. More recently, the Great Recession of 2008-2009 lasted 18 months. While the official definition of a recession is two consecutive quarters of negative economic growth, many people feel a recession long before it is officially declared. For example, people may lose their jobs or see their hours reduced. Businesses may close their doors, or people may cut back on spending. To some people, a recession may feel like a financial crisis, even if GDP growth is only slightly negative. So how long do recessions usually last? The answer depends on how you measure a recession. If you focus on GDP growth, recessions generally last around a year. However, if you take into account the effects of a recession on people's lives, the length of a recession can be much longer. Recessions can have a lasting impact on an economy, even after GDP growth has returned to positive territory. For example, businesses may not immediately invest or hire again after a recession ends. And people who have lost their jobs or seen their hours reduced may never regain their previous level of income. This can lead to years of economic hardship, even after a recession has technically ended. In short, the answer to the question "how long do recessions usually last?" is not simple. Officially, recessions last around a year, but their effects can be felt long after economic growth has returned to positive territory.

How do you profit from a recession?

In a recession, businesses and consumers spend less money and this leads to economic contraction. There are four primary ways to profit from a recession: 1) Invest in businesses with strong fundamentals that are well-positioned to weather the economic storm. These businesses will be able to maintain their profitability and may even be able to grow through a recession. 2) Buy assets at a discount. In a recession, businesses and consumers are less likely to want to buy big-ticket items such as houses or cars. As a result, prices for these items may drop, giving investors the opportunity to buy them at a discount. 3) Take advantage of government stimulus programs. During a recession, the government often implements stimulus programs in an attempt to jump-start the economy. These programs can create opportunities for businesses and investors to profit. 4) Invest in yourself. A recession can be a good time to invest in yourself and your career. It may be easier to find a job during a recession as businesses are looking to cut costs. And, if you're already employed, a recession can be a good time to ask for a raise or promotion.

The current recession has been tough on everyone, but it has also been an opportunity for some companies to restructure and become stronger. We are seeing the beginning of the end of the recession, but it will be a slow recovery. In the meantime, companies need to continue to focus on cost cutting and becoming more efficient.

How do I prepare myself for a recession?

There are a lot of things that you can do in order to prepare yourself for a recession. The most important thing is to make sure that you have a solid financial foundation. This means having a savings account that you can rely on in case of a job loss or other unexpected expenses. It is also important to have a good credit score so that you can borrow money if necessary.

Another thing that you can do to prepare for a recession is to make sure that you have a diversified income. This means having more than one source of income so that you are not as reliant on a single job. For example, you can have a full-time job and also do freelance work or have a side business. This will help you to weather the storm if one of your sources of income dries up.

It is also important to live within your means during a recession. This means avoiding unnecessary expenses and saving as much money as possible. You should also try to pay off any debt that you have so that you are not struggling with money.

Finally, it is important to stay positive during a recession. This can be difficult, but it is important to remember that things will eventually get better. We have all been through tough times before and we will get through this as well.

What is the best asset during a recession?

A recession is typically defined as two consecutive quarters of negative economic growth. During a recession, asset prices usually fall and unemployment rises. So, what is the best asset during a recession?

There is no easy answer, as different assets perform differently during recessions. Some people believe that cash is the best asset, as it preserves its value and can be used to purchase assets at bargain prices during a downturn. Others argue that government bonds are the best asset, as they provide stability and a guaranteed return.

So, what is the best asset during a recession? Ultimately, it depends on your investment goals and risk tolerance. If you are willing to take on more risk, then investing in stocks may offer the opportunity for higher returns. However, if you are looking for stability, then investing in government bonds may be a better option.

Who hurts in recession?

In any recession, there are always going to be people who are hurt worse than others. Who those people are depends on the particular recession, but there are some groups of people who are more vulnerable in general.

One group of people who are particularly vulnerable in a recession are low-income earners. When people lose their jobs or have their hours reduced, it hits low-income earners the hardest. They often don't have the savings to fall back on that higher-income earners do, so they quickly start to struggle. This can lead to all sorts of problems, including homelessness and mental health issues.

Another group of people who are vulnerable in a recession are small businesses. When people stop spending money, small businesses are the ones who feel it the most. They often don't have the same reserves that bigger businesses do, so they can quickly start to struggle. This can lead to them having to lay off staff or even close down completely.

Recessions can also be damaging for young people. When unemployment rates go up, it's usually young people who are most affected. This can have all sorts of knock-on effects, including delaying their career start, making it harder to get on the property ladder, and so on.

In short, recessions hurt pretty much everyone to some extent. But there are always going to be those who are hurt worse than others.

What are 3 problems of a recession?

A recession occurs when the economy slows down for a sustained period of time. This can cause problems for people and businesses alike. Here are three of the most common problems associated with a recession:

1. Job Losses

One of the most immediately noticeable problems during a recession is an increase in unemployment. As businesses cut back on spending, they often have to lay off workers. This can lead to a ripple effect as laid-off workers have less money to spend, which in turn can lead to even more job losses.

2. Decreased Consumer Spending

Another problem that can occur during a recession is a decrease in consumer spending. When people are worried about losing their jobs or having their hours cut, they are less likely to spend money on non-essential items. This can lead to businesses getting even less revenue, which can exacerbate the effects of the recession.

3. Increased Debt

The final problem that is common during a recession is an increase in debt. As people lose their jobs or have their hours reduced, they may start to rely on credit cards or loans to make ends meet. This can put them in a difficult financial situation when the recession ends and they have to start repaying their debt.

Is it safe to save money during a recession?

Saving money is essential to weathering any financial storm, including a recession. However, during an economic downturn, you may be more hesitant to tuck away money into savings. After all, isn't it better to spend cash to keep the economy going?

Here's the thing: you can still save money during a recession – you just have to be smart about it. Below are a few tips on how to do just that.

Create a budget

The first step to saving money is to be aware of your spending patterns. Track where you are spending your money and how much you are spending. This will help you create a budget and see where you can cut back. Once you have a budget, you can start setting aside money each month to put into savings.

Save automatically

One of the best ways to save money is to set up automatic transfers into your savings account. This way, you never even see the money and it's automatically going into your rainy day fund. You can set up automatic transfers with your employer or your bank.

Save your windfalls

Windfalls are those happy accidents that come your way, like a bonus at work or a tax refund. When you get a windfall, put at least a portion of it into savings. This will help you boost your savings quickly.

Cut back on expenses

During a recession, it's important to cut back on unnecessary expenses. This may include things like eating out, shopping, and travel. Instead, focus on spending on essential items and downgrading your lifestyle until the economy improves.

Look for deals

When you do need to spend money, look for ways to save. This may include using coupons, buying in bulk, or shopping at discount stores. There are plenty of ways to save money on everyday purchases.

A recession can be a scary time, but it's important to remember that you can still save money. By following the tips above, you can make sure your savings stay intact – and even grow – during an economic downturn.

What jobs go first in a recession?

In a recession, the jobs that go first are typically those that are considered non-essential or discretionary. This can include jobs in the retail and hospitality industries, as well as jobs that are considered to be luxuries. The reason for this is that when people are facing financial difficulties, they often cut back on spending in these areas first.

Another group of jobs that are often impacted during a recession are those that are dependent on consumer spending. This can include jobs in the advertising and marketing industries, as well as jobs that are related to the production and distribution of consumer goods.

Finally, jobs that are considered to be high-risk are also typically impacted during a recession. This can include jobs in the financial sector, as well as jobs that are associated with businesses that are struggling financially.

While there are a number of different types of jobs that can be impacted by a recession, these are typically the most vulnerable. If you are concerned about losing your job during a recession, it is important to be aware of these risks and to make sure that you are taking steps to protect yourself financially.

Does a recession hurt the rich?

A recession is typically defined as two consecutive quarters of negative economic growth, as measured by a country's Gross Domestic Product (GDP). A recession can be caused by various factors, including a decrease in consumer spending, an increase in taxes, or a decrease in government spending.

In the United States, the last recession began in December 2007 and ended in June 2009. During that time, the unemployment rate rose from 4.7 percent to 9.5 percent. The stock market also experienced a sharp decline, with the Dow Jones Industrial Average falling from 14,164 in October 2007 to a low of 6,547 in March 2009.

So does a recession hurt the rich? The answer is, it depends.

While the wealthy may have a higher percentage of their assets invested in the stock market, they also have a larger cushion of savings and other assets to fall back on. So while the value of their portfolio may have decreased during the recession, they were still able to maintain their lifestyle.

On the other hand, many people who were already struggling financially were hit hard by the recession. A loss of income, combined with higher costs for essentials like food and gas, can quickly lead to debt and even homelessness.

Overall, the rich may not be immune to the effects of a recession, but they are certainly better equipped to weather the storm.

The recession has been hard on everyone, with businesses struggling and people losing their jobs. However, there are some silver linings to be found. For example, the recession has caused people to be more resourceful and innovative. It has also brought families closer together as they struggle to make ends meet. In the end, the recession may have made us stronger and more resilient.

Who is hardest hit in a recession?

When the economy weakens and jobs become scarce, it's the working class that suffers the most. Low-income families are forced to cut back on spending, which can lead to homelessness and poverty.

Middle-class families may also suffer during a recession. They may have to tighten their budgets and make lifestyle changes. However, they are less likely to experience the same level of financial hardship as those in the lower class.

The wealthy are usually able to weather a recession without too much difficulty. They may see a dip in their investment portfolios, but they generally have the resources to weather a downturn.

While all classes of people are affected by a recession, it is the working class that is most vulnerable. They are the ones who bear the brunt of the economic hardships.

How bad will 2023 recession be?

There is a lot of talk about a potential recession in 2023. While it's impossible to say for sure how bad it will be, there are a few factors that could contribute to making it a particularly tough recession.

One is the overall state of the economy. If the economy is already weak when a recession hits, it's likely to be worse than if it's healthy. Additionally, if inflation is high when a recession occurs, it can be exacerbated.

Another factor is the cause of the recession. If it's something like a stock market crash or a natural disaster, it can be fairly bad. However, if the recession is caused by something like a slow-down in housing starts, it may not be as severe.

In any case, a recession is never ideal. If you're worried about a potential recession in 2023, it's important to start saving now and to have a plan for how you'll cut back on spending if necessary.

Should I pull my money out before a recession?

A recession is a decline in economic activity, typically lasting for six months or longer. A recession typically includes a drop in gross domestic product (GDP), higher unemployment, and lower business investment.

So, should you pull your money out before a recession? That really depends on your goals, risk tolerance, and investment time horizon.

For example, if you are close to retirement and your primary goal is to preserve your assets, then you may want to consider pulling your money out of the stock market and into more conservative investments. On the other hand, if you are younger and have a longer time horizon, you may be able to weather the storm and come out ahead in the long run.

Of course, there is no guarantee that you will make money even if you stay invested during a recession. However, history has shown that the stock market has always recovered from previous recessions.

So, if you are feeling anxiety about a potential recession, it is important to talk to a financial advisor to find out what is right for you and your unique situation.

Where is the safest place for money in a recession?

When it comes to money and a recession, people often have different ideas about what is the best way to handle their finances. Some people may choose to save their money in a savings account or invest in stocks, while others may opt to spend their money on more tangible items such as property or gold. So, where is the safest place for money in a recession?

Some experts may say that the best place for money during a recession is in a savings account or other type of low-risk investment. This is because when the economy is struggling, it is often safer to keep your money in a more stable place where it is less likely to lose value. Additionally, having money in a savings account can help you weather any financial storms that may come your way during a recession.

Others may argue that investing in stocks is the best way to go during a recession. While there is always a risk involved with investing, this may be a good time to buy stocks when they are low and then sell them when the market recovers. This could potentially provide a nice profit down the line.

So, where is the safest place for money in a recession? Ultimately, this decision comes down to each individual and what they are comfortable with. Some people may feel more comfortable keeping their money in a savings account, while others may choose to invest in stocks. No matter what you decide to do with your money, just be sure to do your research and make sure you are comfortable with the risks involved.

Is cash king during the recession?

As the recession continues, more and more people are finding themselves cash-strapped. Many are turning to credit cards and loans to make ends meet, but is this really the best way to weather the storm?

There's no doubt that having a bit of extra cash on hand can be helpful during tough times. It can give you a cushion to fall back on in case of an emergency, and can help you make ends meet if you're tight on money. But is cash really king during a recession?

Some experts say yes. Having cash on hand gives you the flexibility to make choices about how to spend your money. You can choose to save it or use it to pay down debt, for example. And if you're looking for a job, having cash can give you the means to pay for transportation to interviews or buy a new suit.

Others say that credit is king during a recession. With interest rates at historic lows, now is a good time to take out a loan or open a line of credit. You can use the money to finance a new business venture or make a major purchase. And if you're careful about how you use credit, you can avoid getting into debt trouble.

So, what's the answer? It depends on your individual situation. If you have cash on hand, you may want to hold onto it. But if you're tight on money, you may need to consider using credit to make ends meet. Ultimately, the best way to weather the storm of a recession is to be prepared financially. That means having a plan and knowing your options.

Are we in a recession right now?

The question of whether the United States is currently in a recession is a complicated one. There are a number of different ways to measure whether or not an economy is in a recession, and no single indicator can provide a definitive answer.

One common way to measure whether an economy is in a recession is by looking at GDP growth. If GDP growth is negative for two consecutive quarters, then this is often seen as a sign that the economy is in a recession. However, it is worth noting that this is not an infallible measure, as there can be quarters of negative GDP growth that are not indicative of a recession (such as during the Global Financial Crisis in 2008-2009).

Another popular method of measuring whether an economy is in a recession is through the use of surveys. The most common survey is the Business Cycle Indicators Survey, which is conducted by the National Bureau of Economic Research (NBER). This survey asks a wide range of businesses about a variety of indicators, such as sales, prices, and employment. If the NBER determines that the majority of these indicators are declining, then this is typically seen as a sign that the economy is in a recession.

So, is the United States currently in a recession? Based on the evidence, it is difficult to say definitively. However, it is worth noting that many economists believe that the country is currently in a recessionary period. This is due to a number of factors, such as the ongoing coronavirus pandemic and the resulting economic slowdown. As such, it is likely that the answer to this question will become clearer in the coming months.

How to prepare for recession 2023?

The recession of 2023 is predicted to be one of the worst in recent history. Many experts are predicting that the housing market will crash, unemployment will skyrocket, and the stock market will plunge. If you're worried about the impending recession, there are some steps you can take to prepare.

First, try to pay off as much debt as possible. This will help you weather the storm if you lose your job or your income decreases. It's also a good idea to have an emergency fund to cover unexpected expenses. aim to save up three to six months' worth of living expenses.

If you own a home, it's important to plan for a potential drop in its value. If you have a variable-rate mortgage, you may want to consider refinancing to a fixed-rate loan. This will protect you from rising interest rates. It's also a good idea to make sure your home insurance is up to date.

Investors should be cautious in the lead-up to the recession. Many experts believe that stocks will take a hit when the recession hits. If you're investing for the long term, you may want to consider selling some of your investments and holding cash instead. This will give you the flexibility to buy bargain stocks when the market crashes.

These are just a few steps you can take to prepare for the recession of 2023. By taking action now, you can protect yourself from financial hardship down the road.

A recession is a period of economic decline. It is typically accompanied by a rise in unemployment and a decline in stock prices. A recession can last for several months or even years. While a recession is not pleasant for anyone, it can be an opportunity for businesses to restructure and for individuals to reassess their financial goals.

What are the financial predictions for 2023?

It's impossible to make definitive predictions about the economy or financial markets years in advance. However, we can take a look at the current state of the economy and make some informed guesses about what might happen in 2023. The US economy is currently in a period of expansion. GDP growth was strong in 2018, topping 3% for the first time since 2005. The job market is also strong, with unemployment falling to 3.7% in September 2018 – the lowest rate since 1969. However, there are some signs that this period of expansion may not last much longer. Interest rates are rising, which could put a brake on growth. The Fed has raised rates three times in 2018 and is expected to do so again in 2019. This will make it more expensive for businesses to borrow money and could lead to a slowdown in investment. The trade war with China is also causing problems. The tariffs that have been imposed by both countries are starting to hit growth, and there is no end in sight to the dispute. All of this means that the economy may start to slow down in the next few years. This could lead to a recession, although it's difficult to say when this might happen. It's possible that the economy will continue to grow for a few more years before the recession starts. However, the financial predictions for 2023 are not all doom and gloom. Even if there is a recession, it is likely to be relatively mild. Interest rates will probably stay low, so businesses will still be able to borrow money relatively cheaply. The stock market is also likely to remain strong, as investors seek out safe haven assets during a recession. So, while there are some risks on the horizon, the financial predictions for 2023 are not too bad. The US economy may slow down, but it is unlikely to experience a severe recession.

How much money should you hold in a recession?

A recession is when the economy slows down and businesses start to lose money. This can leads to people losing their jobs and having a hard time finding another one. The stock market may also go down, which can decrease the value of retirement accounts. So, how much money should you hold in a recession? That really depends on your financial situation and what your financial goals are. If you're still employed, you may want to hold onto more cash in case you lose your job. An emergency fund can help cover your living expenses for a few months if you do lose your job. You may also want to consider investing in a more secure investment, such as bonds, during a recession. If you're retired, you may want to hold less cash since you likely don't have as many years to make up for any losses. You may also want to consider investing in growth stocks during a recession, since they tend to rebound quicker than other investments. Of course, everyone's financial situation is different and you should talk to a financial advisor to get more specific advice for your situation.

What is the best fixed income during a recession?

The recession is a critical time for individuals and businesses. It is important to know what the best fixed income is during this time. The recession can last for a few months or even a few years. The goal is to make it through the recession without too much financial damage. There are a few different ways to approach finding the best fixed income during a recession. The first is to stay as liquid as possible. This means having cash on hand or investments that can be quickly converted to cash. This will give you the flexibility to take advantage of opportunities that come up during the recession. Another approach is to invest in conservative investments. These are investments that are not likely to lose value during a recession. This can include government bonds, high quality corporate bonds, and real estate. These investments can provide stability during a time of economic turmoil. The final approach is to take advantage of the opportunities that a recession presents. This means investing in companies that are doing well despite the economic downturn. These companies are typically leaders in their industry and are well positioned to weather the storm. No matter which approach you take, it is important to have a plan and to stick to it. A recession can be a difficult time, but it is also an opportunity to make smart investments that will pay off in the long run.

What is the most stable asset in the world?

In unstable economic times, investors are often looking for ways to protect their assets. Many people believe that gold is the most stable asset in the world, but is this really true? Gold is often thought of as a safe haven investment, and while it can certainly be a good investment during times of economic turmoil, it is not the most stable asset in the world. Gold prices are highly volatile, and can fluctuate substantially in a short period of time. Real estate is generally considered to be a more stable asset than gold. While real estate prices can certainly go down in a recession, they are not as volatile as gold prices and tend to rebound relatively quickly. Another asset that is often thought of as being more stable than gold is cash. While cash certainly doesn't have the same growth potential as gold or other investments, it is a very liquid asset that can be used in a pinch. So, what is the most stable asset in the world? The answer may surprise you, but the most stable asset in the world is actually theU.S. dollar. The U.S. dollar is the world's reserve currency, and as such, it is relatively stable compared to other currencies. Even during times of economic turmoil, the U.S. dollar tends to retain its value. So, if you're looking for an asset that is relatively stable and won't fluctuate wildly in value, the U.S. dollar is a good choice.

Is a recession scary?

A recession is defined as a significant decline in economic activity spread across the economy, lasting more than a few months. This can be indicated by a fall in GDP growth, an increase in unemployment, or a rise in inflation. A recession can be scary for a number of reasons. Firstly, it can lead to a loss of jobs and income. This can impact people's ability to pay their bills and support their families. Secondly, a recession can also lead to an increase in crime. This can create a feeling of insecurity in communities and make people feel unsafe. Finally, a recession can also have a negative impact on people's mental health. This can lead to an increase in anxiety and depression.

While a recession can be scary, it is important to remember that it is also a natural part of the business cycle. There will always be ups and downs, but over time the economy will usually rebound. This means that while a recession can be tough in the short-term, it is not necessarily something to be scared of.

What are the five stages of recession?

There are generally five stages of recession: early stage, escalating stage, peak stage, declining stage, and post-recession. In the early stage of recession, growth slows and economic activity begins to contract. This is often when the first layoffs occur and businesses start to see declining profits. As the recession progresses, more and more businesses close their doors and unemployment skyrockets. This is the escalate stage. The peak stage is when the economy reaches its lowest point. This is when businesses are closing at the fastest rate, unemployment is at its highest, and consumer spending is at its lowest. From the peak, the economy begins to recover in the declining stage. Businesses begin to reopen and hire workers, and consumer spending starts to increase. However, even in this stage, unemployment remains high and economic growth is slow. Finally, the economy enters the post-recession stage. Unemployment begins to fall and economic growth picks up. This is when the economy returns to its pre-recession levels.

Should I be worried about a recession in 2023?

A recession is typically defined as two consecutive quarters of negative economic growth, as measured by a country's gross domestic product (GDP).

While it's impossible to predict the future with 100% accuracy, there are a number of factors that suggest a recession may occur in 2023.

The first factor is that since the 1950s, the US has experienced a recession every 4-5 years on average. The last recession occurred in 2008-2009, so by this historical average, another recession should occur around 2023.

In addition, the US economy typically experiences a "business cycle" of alternating periods of economic growth and recession. The business cycle is primarily driven by changes in consumer spending, which in turn is influenced by a variety of factors such as employment levels, wages, interest rates, and confidence in the future.

Currently, unemployment levels are low and wages are growing at a slow but steady pace. However, interest rates are on the rise, which could lead to increased borrowing costs and decreased consumer spending. In addition, confidence in the future is somewhat shaky, due in part to political uncertainty.

All of these factors sugguest that a recession in 2023 is possible. However, it's important to remember that recessions are not necessarily bad. In fact, they can be helpful in resetting an overheated economy and can provide an opportunity for individuals and businesses to restructure and become more efficient.

So if a recession does occur in 2023, don't panic. Instead, use it as an opportunity to reassess your financial situation and make sure you're prepared.

How to survive recession 2023?

The 2023 recession will be difficult for many people. Here are some tips on how to survive it:

1. Have an emergency fund: This will help you cover unexpected expenses during the recession.

2. Cut back on unnecessary expenses: You may need to tighten your budget during the recession.

3. Invest in yourself: During a recession, it is important to invest in your education and career. This will help you weather the storm and be in a better position when the economy recovers.

4. Stay positive: It can be easy to become discouraged during a recession. However, it is important to remain positive and believe that things will eventually improve.

How will a recession affect me?

A recession is when the economy slows down for a sustained period of time. This can cause businesses to close, jobs to be lost, and wages to stagnate. So how will a recession affect you?

If you're employed, you may be feeling anxious about the possibility of losing your job. A recession can cause businesses to close their doors, which can lead to mass layoffs. If you're self-employed, you may also be feeling the effects of a recession as customers cut back on spending.

If you're still in school, you may be wondering how a recession will affect your job prospects after graduation. The job market tends to tighten during a recession, so it may be harder to find a job. However, recessions also offer opportunities for those who are willing to be creative and adaptable.

No matter what your situation is, a recession can be a difficult and stressful time. If you're struggling, don't be afraid to reach out for help. There are many resources available to help you weather the storm.

How to prepare for a recession in 2023?

2023 is around the corner, and many experts are predicting a recession. Here are a few ways you can prepare:

1. Live below your means

If you're used to spending everything you earn, now is the time to start reining it in. If a recession hits, you may not have the same income, so start saving now. Even if you don't think a recession is coming, it's always a good idea to save money.

2. Invest in yourself

Use this time to improve your skills and qualifications. If you're already in a career, learn new skills that could make you more employable. If you're not in a career, consider going back to school or getting vocational training.

3. Build up your emergency fund

In an ideal world, you would have enough money saved up to cover six months of living expenses. This way, if you lose your job or have a decrease in income, you're not immediately in financial trouble. If a recession hits, you may need to dip into this fund, so make sure it's well-stocked.

4. Get rid of debt

Debt can be a big burden, especially if you're already struggling financially. If you can, pay off your debt now so you don't have to worry about it during a recession.

5. Make a plan

Set some financial goals for yourself and make a plan to achieve them. This way, you'll know what you need to do to stay on track during a recession.

6. Stay positive

It's easy to become overwhelmed when you think about a recession, but try to stay positive. Remember that recessions don't last forever and economies always rebound eventually. With a little planning and preparation, you can weather a recession and come out on the other side stronger than before.

What to invest in 2023 recession?

As we all know, a recession is when the economy slows down for a period of time. This can often be a very stressful time for people, as they worry about their job security and their finances. However, there are some things that you can do to help weather the storm.

One of the most important things you can do is to make sure that you have an emergency fund. This will help you cover unexpected expenses if you lose your job or have to take a pay cut. It is also important to make sure that you have a diversified investment portfolio. This will help you protect your money if the stock market takes a hit.

There are a few specific things that you can invest in during a recession. One of the most obvious choices is gold. Gold tends to do well when the economy is struggling, as it is seen as a safe haven asset. Another option is to invest in shares of companies that are doing well despite the economic conditions. These companies are often referred to as defensive stocks.

Of course, you always have the option to simply sit on cash during a recession. This may not be the most exciting option, but it is often the safest. If you are able to weather the storm and keep your job, you will be in a much better position when the economy eventually recovers.

The recession has been harsh on many Americans.

Losing a job, or being forced to take a pay cut, has put a lot of stress on families.

The good news is that the recession appears to be officially over.

The economy is slowly starting to improve and more jobs are becoming available.

Families who have been struggling for the past few years can finally start to see a light at the end of the tunnel.

Do interest rates go up in a recession?

There is no easy answer when it comes to the question of whether or not interest rates go up during a recession. While it is true that the Federal Reserve does typically lower interest rates in order to encourage spending and help boost the economy during a recession, there are a number of factors that can influence whether or not interest rates actually end up going up.

For one, it is important to keep in mind that the Federal Reserve is not the only player in the game when it comes to interest rates. While the Fed does have a lot of influence over rates, there are other forces at work as well. Banks and other financial institutions can also play a role in setting interest rates, and they may not always follow the Fed's lead.

In addition, the type of recession can also impact interest rates. For example, if a recession is caused by inflation, then the Fed may actually raise rates in order to try to combat that inflation. So, it really depends on the underlying cause of the recession as to whether or not rates will go up.

Of course, there is no guarantee that the Fed's actions will actually result in the desired outcome. In fact, sometimes the opposite can happen. For example, if the Fed lowers rates but banks and other financial institutions don't follow suit, then lending can actually become more expensive, which can stifle economic growth.

So, it is really hard to say for sure whether or not interest rates will go up during a recession. It really depends on a number of different factors.

How do recessions end?

A recession is a temporary decline in economic activity. It is characterized by a fall in production, employment, and trade. A recessionary period is typically considered to last for six months or more.

Recessions typically end when economic activity picks up. This can be due to a number of factors, such as an increase in demand, an improvement in the supply of inputs, or a change in government policy.

One of the most important factors in determining how a recession will end is the cause of the downturn. For example, if a recession is caused by a decline in demand, it is more likely to end when demand picks up. On the other hand, if a recession is caused by an increase in the cost of inputs, it is more likely to end when the cost of inputs falls.

The length of a recession also plays a role in determining how it will end. A longer recession is more likely to end with a pick-up in economic activity, as businesses and consumers adjust to the new economic conditions. A shorter recession is more likely to end with a decline in economic activity, as businesses and consumers are less able to adjust to the new conditions.

The ending of a recession is also affected by the actions of government and central banks. For example, if the government implements expansionary fiscal policy, this will increase demand and help to end the recession. Similarly, if the central bank implements easy monetary policy, this will lower interest rates and help to stimulate economic activity.

What was the longest recession in history?

The longest recession in history began in June 1981 and lasted 16 months until December 1982. In terms of output, it was the deepest recession since the Great Depression of the 1930s. Unemployment rose sharply, reaching 9.7 percent in November 1982. The inflation rate also increased, peaking at 12.5 percent in September 1981. Interest rates rose to high levels, with the prime rate reaching 21.5 percent in December 1980.

The recession was caused by a combination of factors. The 1970s were a decade of high inflation, caused by an increase in the money supply and oil shocks. In the 1980s, the Fed pursued a policy of combating inflation by raising interest rates. This caused a sharp increase in the cost of borrowing, which led to a decrease in spending and investment. The oil shocks also led to a decrease in spending on energy, which further contributed to the recession.

The recession had a severe impact on the US economy. output declined by 2.7 percent, employment fell by 1.2 percent, and the unemployment rate rose to 9.7 percent. The inflation rate also increased, peaking at 12.5 percent in September 1981. Interest rates rose to high levels, with the prime rate reaching 21.5 percent in December 1980.

The recession had a severe impact on individuals and families. Many lost their jobs and were unable to find new ones. Those who were able to find work often had to take pay cuts or accept jobs that paid less than their previous jobs. Many people also lost their homes to foreclosure. The recession also led to an increase in crime, as people turned to criminal activity to make ends meet.

The recession had a major impact on the US economy, with output declining by 2.7 percent and employment falling by 1.2 percent. The unemployment rate rose to 9.7 percent, and the inflation rate reached 12.5 percent. The Prime Rate also increased, reaching 21.5 percent in December 1980. The recession had a severe impact on individuals and families, with many losing their jobs and homes. The recession also led to an increase in crime.

What do people buy in a recession?

When people think about what to buy during a recession, they often think about things that are cheap or on sale. However, there are other factors to consider besides price. For example, people might buy things that will help them save money in the long run, even if it costs more upfront. Or, people might buy things that are necessary, even if they don't want to spend the money.

In general, people during a recession will focus on needs over wants. That doesn't mean that people will stop buying things they want altogether, but they will be more choosy about their purchases. For example, someone might still buy a new outfit for a special occasion, but they're more likely to shop at a discount store or look for sales than they would be during good economic times.

People will also be more likely to buy things that will last. durables, or items that can be used for a long time, are usually recession-proof. For example, people might buy a new car during a recession because it's a big purchase that will last for years. They might also be more likely to buy quality items that will last a long time, even if they cost more.

Some people might also take advantage of a recession to buy things they've been wanting for a while but haven't had the extra money to spend. For example, someone might finally buy a new computer or a piece of furniture they've been eyeing. Since these items are usually expensive, people will only do this if they feel secure in their job and finances.

In general, people during a recession will be more mindful about their spending. They will focus on needs over wants and look for items that are a good value. durables will be popular, as people look for items that will last. Some people might also take advantage of the recession to buy things they've been wanting for a while.

The article concludes that the recession was caused by the bursting of the housing bubble and the subprime mortgage crisis. The article goes on to say that the recession has had a negative impact on the economy, but there are some signs that the economy is beginning to recover.

Which country will have the best economy in the future?

The answer to the question of which country will have the best economy in the future is far from clear. There are many factors that go into determining the health of a country's economy, and no one factor is likely to be the decisive deciding factor. That said, there are a few countries that seem to be positioned well for future economic growth.

One country that appears to be in a good position for future economic growth is China. The Chinese economy has been growing rapidly in recent years, and shows no signs of slowing down. China has a large population that is becoming increasingly prosperous, and this is likely to continue to drive economic growth. Additionally, China has a strong manufacturing base and is increasingly becoming a hub for technological innovation.

Another country that looks to be in a good position for future economic growth is India. Like China, India has a large population that is becoming increasingly prosperous. India also has a strong manufacturing base, and is making strides in becoming a hub for technological innovation. Additionally, the Indian economy is growing at a rapid pace, and is expected to continue to do so.

Finally, the United States appears to be well-positioned for future economic growth. The United States has a large, affluent population, and a strong manufacturing and technology base. Additionally, the United States has a highly developed financial system and a robust infrastructure.

In conclusion, it is difficult to say which country will have the best economy in the future. However, the countries of China, India, and the United States appear to be well-positioned for future economic growth.

What are the top financial risks for 2023?

As the world slowly recovers from the COVID-19 pandemic, many experts are predicting another financial recession could hit in 2023. Here are some of the top financial risks that could trigger another recession:

1. Rising interest rates: As the economy improves, the Federal Reserve is expected to start raising interest rates. This could lead to higher mortgage payments and debt repayments, which could put a strain on households and businesses.

2. Rising inflation: As the economy improves, inflation is expected to start rising. This could lead to higher prices for goods and services, which could put a strain on households and businesses.

3. Stock market crash: The stock market has been on a tear in recent years, but many experts believe it is due for a correction. If the stock market crashes, it could trigger a recession.

4. Economic slowdown in China: China is a major driver of the global economy, and if its economy slows down it could have a ripple effect around the world.

5. geopolitical tensions: Tensions between the US and China, as well as other countries, could lead to trade wars or other economic disruptions that could trigger a recession.

How do you make money in a recession?

A recession is an economic downturn that is typically accompanied by a fall in the stock market, an increase in unemployment, and a drop in the housing market. While a recession can be a difficult time for businesses and consumers, there are some ways to make money during a recession.

One way to make money during a recession is to invest in stocks that are recession-proof. While the stock market as a whole may be down, there are always sectors that do well during a recession. For example, healthcare and food stocks tend to do well during a recession. Another way to make money during a recession is to start a business that provides services that are in demand during a recession. Home-based businesses, for example, can be a great way to make money during a recession.

Another way to make money during a recession is to invest in commodities. Commodities are things like gold, oil, and food. They are things that people will always need, no matter what the economy is doing. When the stock market is down, people tend to invest in commodities as a way to protect their money.

Finally, another way to make money during a recession is to provide services that help people save money. For example, people may be looking for ways to save money on their groceries or their electric bills. By providing services that help people save money, you can make money during a recession.

What jobs are lost during a recession?

In a recession, many different types of jobs are lost. Some of the most common job losses are in the manufacturing and construction industries. This is because when people have less money to spend, they are less likely to buy new homes or cars. This means that there is less demand for the goods and services that these industries provide.

Other sectors that are often affected by a recession include retail, hospitality and tourism. This is because people are less likely to go out and spend money on discretionary items such as eating out or going on holiday.

The job losses that occur during a recession can have a ripple effect on the economy. For example, if someone loses their job in the construction industry, they may not have enough money to spend on other goods and services. This can lead to further job losses in other industries as businesses suffer from a lack of demand.

Recessions can also lead to an increase in unemployment. This is because when people lose their jobs, they stop spending money. This reduces the demand for goods and services, which can lead to more job losses.

It is important to note that not all job losses are equal. Some job losses are voluntary, such as when someone decides to retire or leave their job to start their own business. Other job losses are involuntary, such as when someone is laid off or fired. Voluntary job losses tend to have less of an impact on the economy, as they are often replaced by new jobs. Involuntary job losses, on the other hand, can lead to a decrease in consumer spending and a decrease in economic growth.

How does a recession affect me if I have a job?

A recession is typically defined as two consecutive quarters of negative economic growth as measured by a country's gross domestic product (GDP). A recession affects different people in different ways depending on their employment situation.

For those who are employed, a recession can mean job insecurity and a loss of income. businesses usually respond to a recession by cutting costs, which often means reducing their workforce. This can lead to widespread redundancies, and an increase in unemployment.

Those who are still in work may find that their hours are cut or they are placed on short-term contracts. This can also lead to a loss of income and an increased feeling of insecurity.

A recession can also have a knock-on effect on people's mental health. The stress of worrying about job security and finances can take its toll, and some people may struggle to cope.

In general, a recession makes life more difficult for everyone, even if they don't lose their job. The cost of living usually goes up as businesses try to recoup their losses, and this can leave people feeling stretched and stressed.

A recession can be a difficult time for everyone, but there are ways to cope. Trying to maintain a positive outlook, keeping in touch with friends and family, and being open to change can help you weather the storm.

Who loses their job first in a recession?

In a recession, the first people to lose their jobs are typically those in sectors of the economy that are considered non-essential. This includes jobs in hospitality, retail, and entertainment. The next group of people to lose their jobs are those in manufacturing and construction. This is because businesses in these sectors are more likely to lay off workers when profits start to decline.

Those who are self-employed are also at risk of losing their income during a recession. This is because businesses are less likely to invest in new projects, and people are less likely to spend money on non-essential items. This can lead to a decrease in demand for the services of self-employed workers.

Recessions can also have a negative impact on the mental health of the unemployed. This is because job loss can lead to feelings of isolation, anxiety, and depression. It can also cause financial stress, as people struggle to pay their bills and support their families.

The current recession has been difficult for many people, but there are some silver linings. For example, people have been forced to become more creative in their spending and many have started to save more money. Additionally, the recession has forced people to become more aware of their finances and has led to a better understanding of how to manage money. While the recession has been difficult, it has also been a learning experience for many people.

Is a recession when you lose your job?

If you lose your job, it can certainly feel like a recession. But a recession is actually defined as a significant decline in economic activity spread across the economy, lasting more than a few months. So while losing your job is certainly difficult, it doesn't necessarily mean that we're in a recession. There are a few key indicators that economists look at to decide whether or not we're in a recession. One is GDP, or gross domestic product. This is the total value of all the goods and services produced in a country. When GDP growth slows down or even turns negative, that's a sign that the economy is in trouble. Another key indicator is the unemployment rate. This measures the percentage of people who are looking for work but can't find it. When the unemployment rate goes up, that's a sign that more people are struggling to make ends meet. So while losing your job can be a sign that the economy is struggling, it's not the only indicator that economists look at. GDP growth and the unemployment rate are two of the most important indicators of whether or not we're in a recession.

How do I keep my job during a recession?

A recession can be a scary time for many people. It can feel like the world is crashing down around you and you're just holding on for dear life. But there are things you can do to keep your job during a recession. One of the most important things you can do is stay positive. It may seem like an impossible task, but staying positive will help you weather the storm. Remember that a recession is only temporary and things will eventually get better. There are always jobs available, even during a recession, so don't give up hope. Another thing you can do is stay informed. Know what's going on in the world around you and how it might affect your industry. This will help you be prepared for anything that comes your way. If there are changes happening that could affect your job, be proactive and reach out to your boss or human resources department. They may be able to help you find a different position within the company or offer training to help you keep your current job. Finally, don't be afraid to network. Get connected with people in your industry and find out what they're doing to stay afloat. They may have some great ideas that you can use or they may be able to help you find a new job. Networking is a great way to stay connected and informed, so take advantage of it during a recession.

Who does a recession hurt the most?

Most people think of a recession as something that affects the stock market and wealthy people. However, a recession hurts everyone, including the poor and the middle class. A recession is defined as a significant decline in activity across the economy, lasting longer than a few months. During a recession, businesses close, people lose their jobs, and the government has to spend more money on things like unemployment benefits. This means that there are less tax dollars available for things like schools and roads. The poor and the middle class are hurt the most during a recession because they have the least amount of money to start with. When people lose their jobs, they have to spend less money. This means that they can't afford to buy things like clothes and food. The middle class is also hurt because they can't afford to save for retirement or their children's education. The government also has to cut back on services during a recession, which hurts everyone. A recession is a difficult time for everyone, but the poorest and the middle class are hurt the most.

Which jobs are safest in a recession?

A recession is defined as a significant decline in economic activity spread across the economy, lasting more than a few months. Recessions generally occur when there is a widespread drop in spending (an aggregate demand shock). This could be caused by a number of factors, including a fall in consumer confidence, a rise in interest rates, or a major financial crisis. The jobs that are typically most affected by a recession are those that are tied to consumer spending, such as retail and tourism. These sectors tend to see a decline in demand as people tighten their belts and reduce their spending. Other sectors that are often affected by a recession include manufacturing, construction and mining. These sectors are typically more sensitive to economic conditions, as they are more likely to be reliant on business investment. So, which jobs are safest in a recession? Jobs that are essential, such as healthcare and education, are typically less affected by a recession. This is because people will still need these services, even when they are cutting back on other spending. Jobs that are less dependent on consumer spending, such as those in the public sector, are also typically more stable during a recession. Finally, jobs that are based on exports or that are less cyclical in nature, such as technology, can also be more recession-proof. In general, the best advice for weathering a recession is to have a diversified portfolio of skills and experiences. This will give you the flexibility to adapt to changes in the labour market and make you more attractive to employers. The jobs that are most in-demand during a recession may not be the same as those that are in-demand during an economic boom, so it's important to be able to adapt your skillset to the current conditions.

What happens to the average person during a recession?

A recession is a general downturn in any economy. A recession is typically accompanied by a drop in the stock market, an increase in unemployment, and a decrease in consumer spending. The average person during a recession may experience a loss of income, job loss, or foreclosure. A recession can last for a few months or several years. The most recent recession in the United States began in December

2007 and ended in June 2009. The average person during a recession may feel a sense of hopelessness, as if their financial situation is never going to improve. It is important to remember that a recession is a temporary downturn in the economy, and it will eventually recover. During a recession, people may be more likely to experience anxiety and depression. It is important to seek help from a mental health professional if you are feeling overwhelmed. A recession can be a difficult time for everyone, but there are ways to weather the storm. Try to cut back on non-essential expenses, and focus on building up your savings. If you are faced with job loss, try to find ways to supplement your income. You can also take this opportunity to reassess your goals and make changes to your lifestyle. A recession doesn't have to be a disaster, it can be a chance to make positive changes in your life.

Do people work harder in a recession?

In a recession, people are usually worried about job security and their personal finances. This can lead to people working harder in an attempt to save money and keep their job. Sometimes people will take on extra shifts or take on extra projects to try and make more money. While people may work harder during a recession, this doesn't always mean that they are productive. Some people may find that they are working more hours but not getting as much done. This can be due to stress and anxiety about the future. It can also be difficult to focus when you're worried about your financial situation. There are a few ways to try and stay productive during a recession. First, it's important to take breaks and take care of yourself. If you're stressed, you're not going to be as productive. Second, try to set realistic goals. If you're constantly putting pressure on yourself to achieve unrealistic goals, you're going to be overwhelmed and stressed. Third, don't be afraid to ask for help. If you're feeling overwhelmed, talk to a friend or family member. Sometimes it can be helpful to have an outside perspective. While a recession can be a difficult time, there are ways to manage it. If you're finding yourself struggling, reach out for help. There are also many online resources and articles that can offer advice on how to cope with a recession.

What defines a job recession?

A job recession, generally speaking, is when there is a sustained period of job losses. This could be due to a number of different factors, such as a decrease in demand for a certain product or service, or an increase in automation. There is no set definition for how long a job recession must last in order to be considered such, but it is generally agreed that it must last for at least a few months. There are a few different ways to measure a job recession. One is to simply look at the number of people who are unemployed. If this number is increasing month after month, then it is likely that we are in a job recession. Another way to measure a job recession is to look at the number of job postings. If there are fewer job postings than there were in the past, or if the number of job postings is not keeping up with the number of people unemployed, then this is another sign that we are in a job recession. A job recession can have a number of different effects on the economy. One of the most obvious is that it can lead to an increase in poverty levels. This is because people who are unemployed cannot earn an income, and so they may have to rely on government benefits or charity in order to get by. This can also lead to an increase in crime rates, as people may turn to criminal activity in order to make ends meet. A job recession can also have a number of psychological effects on people. Those who have lost their jobs may feel discouraged and may struggle to find new employment. This can lead to feelings of isolation and hopelessness. It is important to remember that a job recession is not permanent, and that there will eventually be a recovery. However, in the meantime, it is important to support those who have lost their jobs and to help them to find new employment.

While the current recession has not been as severe as some in the past, it has nonetheless been difficult for many people. The good news is that the economy appears to be slowly improving, and hopefully the worst is behind us.

How long does a recession lost?

A recession is a period of economic decline during which trade and investment decrease. The causes of recessions are often complex and differ from one country to another. Most recessions last for around a year and have a milder effect on advanced economies than on developing countries. However, the global recession that started in 2008 was unusually severe, lasting for more than four years and causing widespread damage to economies around the world. The impact of a recession can be felt in many different ways. For households, it can lead to poorer living standards and a rise in unemployment. For businesses, it can mean lower profits and slower growth. And for governments, it can result in lower tax revenues and higher spending on things like unemployment benefits. While the exact duration of a recession can vary, most last for around a year. However, the global recession that started in 2008 was unusually severe, lasting for more than four years and causing widespread damage to economies around the world. The United States, for example, lost around 8.7 million jobs during this period. The good news is that economies usually bounce back after a recession. In most cases, growth returns within a couple of years. But it can take longer for unemployment to return to pre-recession levels. This process is often referred to as "recovery". So how long does it take for an economy to recover from a recession? It depends. For advanced economies, the average duration of recovery is around two years. But for developing countries, it can take much longer. The global recession of 2008, for example, is still being felt by many economies today. The bottom line is that recessions are a normal part of the economic cycle. They cause pain in the short-term, but economies usually rebound. The key is to make sure that policy-makers are prepared for when the next one strikes.

Is a recession coming in 2023?

The short answer is: nobody knows. The long answer is: it depends. One thing we can say for certain is that the economy has been on an upswing for the past few years. That's not to say that there haven't been hiccups along the way – but overall, things have been good. This has led some people to believe that a recession is coming in 2023. The thinking goes like this: the economy has been doing well for a while now, so it's bound to swing back the other way at some point. However, there's no guarantee that this will happen. It's entirely possible that the economy will continue to do well into the future, without any major setbacks. So, what can we say about the possibility of a recession in 2023? The truth is, nobody knows for sure. It's impossible to say with 100% certainty whether or not a recession will occur in any given year. However, there are certain indicators that we can look at to get a sense of whether or not a recession might be on the horizon. For example, one sign that a recession might be coming is if there is a sudden decrease in consumer spending. This can be caused by a number of factors, such as a decrease in wages, an increase in taxes, or a decrease in confidence in the economy. Another sign that a recession might be coming is an increase in borrowing costs. This happens when the interest rates that lenders charge on loans start to go up. This can make it more difficult for businesses and consumers to borrow money, which can lead to a decrease in economic activity. Of course, these are just a few of the many indicators that economists look at when trying to predict a recession. So, while we can't say for certain whether or not a recession will occur in 2023, there are certain signs that we can look at to get a sense of whether or not it might be on the horizon.

How do you prepare for a job loss in a potential recession?

The threat of a recession is always looming, and it can be difficult to prepare for something that may or may not happen. However, there are some things you can do to ensure that you are as prepared as possible for a job loss in a potential recession. The first step is to ensure that you have a strong financial foundation. This means having an emergency fund of at least three to six months of living expenses. This will help you to cover your basic needs if you do lose your job. It is also important to have a diversified income stream. This means having more than one source of income, so that if one is lost, you still have others to fall back on. For example, you might have a full-time job, but also earn money from freelancing or renting out a room in your home. It is also a good idea to have a "Plan B" in case of a recession. This could mean going back to school to get a new degree or certification, or starting your own business. Having a Plan B gives you something to fall back on if you do lose your job. No one knows exactly what will happen in the event of a recession, but by having a solid financial foundation and a Plan B, you can increase your chances of weathering the storm.

How does a company survive a recession?

In order to survive a recession, a company must be able to adapt to the changing market. This may mean reducing costs in order to stay afloat, or it could mean finding new ways to generate revenue. For example, a company might diversify its product line in order to appeal to a wider range of customers. The most important thing for a company to do in a recession is to keep its customers happy. This means continuing to provide high-quality products and services, even if it means operating at a loss in the short-term. If a company can weather the storm and keep its customers satisfied, it will be in a much better position when the economy eventually recovers.

How do you prepare employees for a recession?

As the head of a company, it is your responsibility to ensure that your employees are prepared for a recession. Here are a few ways to do that: 1. Keep them informed:Make sure your employees are aware of the potential for a recession and what that could mean for the company. Keep them updated on any changes in the company's financial situation and let them know what steps you're taking to prepare for a recession. 2. Encourage saving:Encourage your employees to save money and to live within their means. Help them to understand the importance of having an emergency fund and suggest ways to cut spending. 3. Help them to be proactive:Encourage your employees to be proactive in their jobs. Help them to understand the importance of being valuable to the company and of finding ways to improve their skills. 4. Be understanding:Be understanding of the fact that your employees may be worried about a potential recession. Listen to their concerns and address them openly and honestly. 5. Keep morale high:It's important to keep morale high during a potential recession. Encourage your employees to stay positive and to focus on the company's goals. Help them to see the potential for growth even during tough times.

How to get rich during a recession?

There's no doubt that we're in the midst of a recession. Jobs are being lost, businesses are shutting down, and people are feeling the pinch. But what does that mean for those of us who are looking to get rich? The reality is that recessions present opportunities for those who are willing to take risks. While others are going through the motions, the individuals who are making the most of this time are the ones who are investing in themselves and their businesses. So, how can you get rich during a recession? 1. Invest in yourself The first step to getting rich during a recession is to invest in yourself. This means taking the time to learn new skills, researching opportunities, and networking with like-minded individuals. 2. Take advantage of opportunities While others are busy bemoaning the state of the economy, those who are getting rich are busy taking advantage of opportunities. This could mean starting a business, investing in real estate, or finding ways to make money that don't rely on traditional job security. 3. Be willing to take risks The key to getting rich during a recession is to be willing to take risks. This doesn't mean making foolish decisions, but it does mean recognizing that there are opportunities to be had if you're willing to step outside of your comfort zone. 4. Stay focused on your goals It's easy to get caught up in the negative news cycle and allow yourself to be worried about the state of the economy. However, if you want to get rich during a recession, it's important to stay focused on your goals. This means staying disciplined with your spending, investing in the right opportunities, and staying positive despite the challenges. 5. Help others While it's important to focus on your own goals, it's also important to remember that we're all in this together. During a recession, it's important to help others where you can. This could mean offering advice, networking, or simply lending a listening ear. Recessions offer opportunities for those who are willing to take risks. By investing in yourself, taking advantage of opportunities, and staying focused on your goals, you can set yourself up for success.

What goes up the most during a recession?

The first question that many people ask during a recession is "what can I do to make the most money?" The answer to that question is not as simple as it may seem. There are a number of things that go up during a recession, and it really depends on what your goals are. If you're looking to make a quick buck, then you might want to consider investing in commodities. Commodities are things like oil, gas, gold, and silver. They tend to do well during a recession because people are looking for ways to preserve their wealth. Another option is to invest in stocks. This can be a bit more risky, but if you choose the right companies, you can make a lot of money. During a recession, many companies go out of business, but some actually thrive. If you're able to find the companies that are doing well, you can make a lot of money. Another option is to start your own business. This is probably the most risky option, but it can also be the most rewarding. During a recession, people are looking for ways to save money, and starting your own business can help you do that. No matter what you decide to do, remember that a recession can be a great time to make money. You just have to be willing to take some risks.

In conclusion, it is clear that recession is a time of great economic turmoil. Many people lose their jobs, their homes, and their savings. However, there are also many opportunities during a recession. Those who are willing to take risks can find new jobs and new businesses. The key to weathering a recession is to be flexible and adapt to the changing economy.

Who makes the most money during recession?

A recession is typically defined as two consecutive quarters of negative economic growth, as measured by a country's gross domestic product (GDP). While the main effects of a recession are typically felt by consumers and businesses, there are some groups of people who actually stand to make a profit during this time. Here are a few examples: 1. Hedge fund managers: While the stock market may be took a nosedive, savvy hedge fund managers know how to take advantage of the volatile market conditions to make a profit. 2. Debt collectors: With more people losing their jobs or falling behind on their bills, there is an increase in demand for debt collectors. 3. Pawnbrokers: When people are in need of quick cash, they may turn to pawning their belongings. 4. Discount retailers: As consumers become more price-conscious, discount retailers such as Walmart and Target see an uptick in business. 5. Funeral directors: Sadly, the death rate usually increases during a recession, as people succumb to stress-related illnesses or commit suicide. So there you have it – a few groups of people who actually benefit from a recession. While the majority of people are struggling to make ends meet, these people are actually making a killing.

What jobs are most affected by a recession?

A recession can have a big impact on employment, with job losses across a wide range of industries. The most affected industries are often those that are most sensitive to economic conditions, such as manufacturing, construction, and retail. While job losses in these industries can be deeply felt by those affected, it's important to remember that recessions don't last forever. The economy will eventually rebound and jobs will come back. In the meantime, there are a few things that can be done to help weather the storm. For those who have lost their job, it's important to stay positive and keep looking for work. It may take some time to find a new job, but eventually you will. Utilize your network of friends and family to help you in your job search. They may be able to help you find leads or connect you with someone who can help. There are also a number of government programs that can help during a recession. Unemployment benefits can provide some financial stability while you look for a new job. And, if you're having trouble making ends meet, there may be programs available to help with things like food, housing, and healthcare. If you're still employed, it's important to be mindful of the impact that a recession can have on your company. There may be a reduction in hours or pay, and layoffs are always a possibility. It's important to stay focused on your work and to be as productive as possible. If you can, try to avoid taking on any extra debt during this time. While a recession can be a difficult time for everyone, remember that it won't last forever. The economy will eventually rebound and things will start to improve. In the meantime, stay positive and do what you can to weather the storm.

What jobs are good in a bad economy?

In a bad economy, it can be hard to find a good job. But there are some jobs that are more likely to be available, and some that are more likely to be in demand. Here are some examples of good jobs in a bad economy: 1. Jobs that are essential to the functioning of society: Jobs that are essential to the functioning of society are always in demand, no matter the state of the economy. This includes jobs like teachers, police officers, firefighters, and nurses. These jobs are important to the community and will always be needed, so they are more likely to be available during a recession. 2. Jobs that are in high demand: Jobs that are in high demand are also more likely to be available during a recession. This includes jobs like healthcare workers, transportation workers, and construction workers. These jobs are necessary to keep the economy moving, so they are less likely to be affected by a recession. 3. Jobs that are less likely to be affected by a recession: There are some jobs that are less likely to be affected by a recession. This includes jobs like information technology workers, scientists, and engineers. These jobs are essential to the advancement of society and the economy, so they are less likely to be impacted by a recession.

Who to survive a recession?

When it comes to surviving a recession, there are a few key things you can do to help make it through tough economic times. One of the most important things you can do is to make sure you have an emergency fund to fall back on. This will help you cover unexpected expenses and help you keep up with your bills if you lose your job or have your hours cut back. Another key thing to do is to cut back on your spending. This doesn't mean you have to completely stop spending money on things you enjoy, but you may want to reconsider any unnecessary purchases. Instead, focus on spending your money on essential items like food and rent. You may also want to try to save up as much money as possible so you have a cushion to fall back on if you do lose your job. Finally, it's important to stay positive and remember that recessions don't last forever. Times may be tough, but if you can focus on making it through the difficult times, you'll be in a much better position when the economy improves.

Does a recession affect the rich?

A recession is defined as a decline in gross domestic product (GDP) for two or more consecutive quarters. A recession typically features high unemployment, slowing corporate profit growth, and declining home prices. In the United States, the last recession began in December 2007 and ended in June 2009. During that time, the unemployment rate nearly doubled, hitting a high of 10 percent. Meanwhile, corporate profits declined and home prices fell by more than 30 percent. So, does a recession affect the rich? The answer is yes and no. On the one hand, a recession does affect the rich. A decline in GDP typically leads to a decline in stock prices, which can hurt the portfolios of the wealthy. A recession can also lead to job losses, even among high-income earners. On the other hand, the rich are typically less affected by a recession than the poor. This is because the wealthy have a higher savings rate and are more likely to have money invested in assets that hold their value, such as stocks and real estate. In the end, whether a recession affects the rich depends on the individual. Some may be hurt by a recession, while others may not.

Who gets hurt in a recession and why?

A recession is an economic downturn that can last for months or even years. It is typically characterized by reduced spending, increased unemployment, and lower production and investment. A recession can have a ripple effect on the economy, affecting businesses, consumers, and the government. Consumers are typically the first to feel the effects of a recession. Families may cut back on spending, especially on non-essential items, and consumers may also save more and spend less. This reduced spending can lead to layoffs and higher unemployment. Businesses may also suffer during a recession. They may see reduced demand for their products and services, and may have to cut costs or lay off employees. Lower production can lead to lower profits and, in some cases, business bankruptcy. The government may also be affected by a recession. Tax revenues may fall, and the government may have to cut spending or raise taxes. This can lead to higher deficits and debt levels. A recession can have a ripple effect on the economy, causing hardship for businesses, consumers, and the government.

What would be worse than a recession?

There have been many periods of recession throughout history. Each one has had different causes and different effects on different parts of the world. But what would be worse than a recession? There are a few things that could be worse than a recession. One of those things would be a complete economic collapse. A complete economic collapse would mean that the world's economy would stop functioning. This would be much worse than a recession because it would lead to widespread poverty and starvation. Another thing that could be worse than a recession is a global pandemic. A global pandemic would kill millions of people and would cause widespread panic and chaos. So, while a recession is bad, there are things that are much worse. A recession can be difficult to deal with, but it is not the end of the world. There are ways to recover from a recession and there are ways to prevent one from happening again. But, if a complete economic collapse or a global pandemic were to happen, those would be much worse than a recession.

The current recession has been hard on everyone, but there are ways to get through it. By being mindful of your spending, looking for ways to save money, and being creative in your approach to making money, you can weather the storm. There may be some tough times ahead, but if we all work together, we can get through it.

Will recession last into 2024?

The Great Recession was a global economic downturn that started in December 2007 and lasted until June 2009. It was the longest and deepest recession since World War II. In the United States, the recession lasted 18 months, from December 2007 to June 2009. Most economists agree that the Great Recession was caused by a combination of factors, including: - The bursting of the housing bubble - The subprime mortgage crisis - The collapse of Lehman Brothers - The European debt crisis While the Great Recession officially ended in 2009, many economists believe that its effects are still being felt today. In particular, many Americans are still struggling to recover from the loss of jobs and income during the recession. There is no simple answer to the question of whether or not the recession will continue into 2024. However, there are a number of factors that will play a role in determining the answer. - The strength of the current economic recovery: The current recovery from the Great Recession has been much slower than other recoveries from past economic downturns. This could be a sign that the economy is still weak and vulnerable to another recession. - The size of the federal government debt: The federal government debt has ballooned to nearly $20 trillion, and it continues to grow. This large debt could put significant strain on the economy and lead to another recession. - The risk of a trade war: The Trump administration has been engaged in a trade war with China, and there is a risk that this could escalate and lead to a recession. - The political environment: The current political environment in the United States is highly polarized. This could lead to policy gridlock and an inability to address economic challenges, which could in turn lead to another recession. These are just a few of the factors that will play a role in whether or not the recession will last into 2024. It is impossible to say with certainty what the future holds, but it is important to be aware of the risks that could lead to another downturn.

Should I hold more cash during recession?

There is no one-size-fits-all answer to this question, as the amount of cash you should hold during a recession depends on your individual circumstances and goals. However, there are a few things to consider that may help you make your decision. Your first priority during a recession should be preserving the cash you have. If you have cash on hand, you'll be in a much better position to weather the storm than if you're relying on loans or credit lines. That means cutting back on unnecessary expenses and keeping a close eye on your budget. You should also think about how you would use your cash if you had to suddenly make a large purchase, like a new car or a down payment on a house. If you don't have enough cash saved up to cover a large purchase, you may need to consider borrowing money or using credit. Finally, you should remember that recessions don't last forever. eventually, the economy will rebound and your financial situation will improve. If you can hang on to your cash during the tough times, you'll be in a much better position to take advantage of the opportunities that come with a recovery.

How much cash should I have in a recession?

The answer to the question "How much cash should I have in a recession?" is complex and depends on your individual financial situation. In general, it's a good idea to have a cash cushion equal to three to six months of living expenses. This will help you cover unexpected expenses and make ends meet if you lose your job or have a significant drop in income. Some people recommend saving even more in a recession, especially if you're already debt-free. Having a larger cash cushion gives you more flexibility to weather a prolonged economic downturn. It can also help you take advantage of opportunities that arise during a recession, such as investing in a depressed real estate market. Of course, saving more cash comes at a cost. You may have to forego some current consumption to build up your cash reserves. And, if you're already carrying debt, you'll need to focus on paying that off before you can start saving more. Ultimately, how much cash you should have in a recession depends on your personal circumstances and financial goals.

Who earned most money in 2008 financial crisis?

In 2008, the financial crisis hit and everyone was feeling the effects. Many people lost their jobs, their homes, and their savings. But some people still came out ahead. Who were these people? The 2008 financial crisis was caused by a number of factors, but one of the main culprits was the housing market. When housing prices began to decline, it put a strain on the entire economy. Banks and other financial institutions were forced to write down billions of dollars in bad loans, and this led to a ripple effect throughout the economy. Many people lost their jobs as a result of the crisis. Companies were forced to lay off workers, and many people were left unemployed. But there were some people who were able to weather the storm and even came out ahead. One group of people who did well during the crisis were hedge fund managers. hedge funds are investment vehicles that are often used to speculate on economic trends. Some hedge fund managers were able to correctly predict the housing market crash, and they made a fortune as a result. Another group of people who did well during the crisis were those who invested in gold. Gold prices soared during the crisis as investors sought a safe haven for their money. Those who had invested in gold before the crisis began were able to make a lot of money. Finally, another group of people who did well during the crisis were those who held onto their jobs. While many people lost their jobs, those who kept theirs often saw their wages increase. This is because companies were desperate to keep their workers, and they were willing to pay them more money to stay. The 2008 financial crisis was a difficult time for many people. But there were some people who were able to make a lot of money. These people were often those who were willing to take risks, and they were rewarded for their smart investments.

What does a recession mean for HR?

A recession is defined as a significant decline in economic activity lasting more than a few months, typically visible in real GDP, real income, employment, industrial production, and wholesale-retail sales. A recession begins when the economy reaches a peak of activity and ends as the economy reaches its trough. Between the peak and the trough, the economy is in a downturn. The National Bureau of Economic Research (NBER) defines a recession as "a significant decline in economic activity spread across the economy, lasting more than a few months, normally visible in real GDP, real income, employment, industrial production, and wholesale-retail sales." A recession is typically caused by a combination of factors, including tight monetary policy, high interest rates, an increase in the cost of oil, or a bursting of an economic bubble. A recession most often follows a period of extended economic expansion, known as an economic boom. Recessions can have a significant impact on businesses, especially those in industries that are particularly vulnerable to economic downturns, such as manufacturing, construction, and retail. layoffs and reduction in hours are common during recessions. As businesses scale back their operations, demand for goods and services declines, which can lead to further job losses and an increase in unemployment. Recessions can also have an impact on workers, even those who keep their jobs. Wages may stagnate or even decline during a recession, as businesses attempt to cut costs. Workers may also see their hours reduced or be asked to take unpaid leave. All of these factors can lead to increased stress and anxiety, as well as decreased motivation and productivity. While a recession can be a difficult time for businesses and workers, there are also opportunities that can arise. businesses may be able to take advantage of lower costs for materials and labor. And, workers who are able to keep their jobs may have a chance to learn new skills or take on additional responsibilities. In the end, how a business or worker weathers a recession depends on a number of factors, including the severity of the recession, the business's or worker's particular industry, and the individual's skills and experience. But, by understanding what a recession is and how it can impact businesses and workers, HR professionals can be better prepared to manage the challenges and opportunities that come with an economic downturn.

What does a recession look like for me?

A recession is generally defined as two consecutive quarters of negative economic growth, as measured by a country's gross domestic product (GDP). A recession is typically characterized by a decrease in spending and investment, as well as a rise in unemployment. For me, a recession would likely mean a decrease in my income and spending. I would be less likely to travel or make large purchases, and I would probably spend more time looking for ways to save money. I would also be more likely to lose my job, or see my hours reduced at work. In a recession, unemployment would likely rise, which would mean more competition for jobs. A recession can also have ripple effects beyond just employment and spending. For example, it can lead to an increase in crime, as people become desperate for money. It can also put strain on social programs, as more people rely on them for assistance. And, of course, a recession can also have a psychological impact, leading to an increase in anxiety and depression. In short, a recession would likely be a tough time for me, and for many people like me. But it's important to remember that a recession is also an opportunity to tighten our belts, save money, and prepare for the future.

What is a bank run?

In order to understand what a bank run is, it is important to first understand how banks work. When individuals deposit money into a bank, they are essentially lending that money to the bank. The bank then uses that money to loan out to other individuals or businesses. The money that the bank loans out is typically at a higher interest rate than what was given to the bank by the depositor. This difference in interest rates is how the bank makes a profit. Banks are also required to keep a certain percentage of their deposits on hand, in what is known as a reserve. The reserve requirement is typically around 10%, meaning that for every $100 that is deposited, the bank can only loan out $90. The other $10 must be kept in the reserve. This is in place to ensure that the bank has enough money on hand to cover any withdrawals that might be made. When individuals or businesses loan money from the bank, they are essentially taking out a short-term loan. The loan will need to be repaid within a certain timeframe, typically within a year. If the borrower is unable to repay the loan, the bank may work with them to extend the loan or may foreclose on any collateral that was put up for the loan. A bank run occurs when a large number of people go to the bank to withdraw their money at the same time. This usually happens when people become nervous about the stability of the bank and believe that their money will be safer if they have it in cash. When a bank run happens, it can put the bank in a difficult situation. If too many people withdraw their money, the bank may not have enough cash on hand to cover all of the withdrawals. This can lead to the bank insolvency and even failure. A bank run can also have a ripple effect on the economy. If people lose confidence in the banking system, it can lead to a decrease in spending and investment, which can in turn lead to a recession.

When it comes to weathering a recession, it is important to remember that everyone is in it together. Governments, financial institutions, businesses, and consumers all have a role to play in ensure a recession is as short and painless as possible. By working together and making smart decisions, we can all help get the economy back on track.

What is a bank run and why is it a problem?

A bank run happens when a large number of people withdraw their money from a bank all at once because they are worried about the bank's solvency. This can trigger a self-fulfilling panic, where the bank actually becomes insolvent because of the large number of withdrawals. A bank run is a problem because it can cause a bank to fail. When a bank fails, people can lose their savings, and the economy can be adversely affected. A bank run can also lead to a financial crisis.

What are bank runs examples?

When people lose confidence in a financial institution, they may try to take their money out all at once. This is called a bank run, and it can lead to the failure of the bank. One famous example of a bank run occurred during the Great Depression in the United States. People became worried that their money would not be safe in the banks, so they began withdrawing their money. This caused a wave of bank failures, which made the Depression even worse. Banking panics can also happen in other ways besides bank runs. For example, the recent financial crisis was caused in part by a panic in the market for a type of financial instrument called mortgage-backed securities. In general, a bank run happens when there is a loss of confidence in the banking system. This can happen for a variety of reasons, such as a scandal at a bank, rumors about a bank's financial health, or a general economic downturn. When people lose confidence in the banks, they may try to take their money out, which can lead to problems for the bank and the wider economy.

What do banks do during a bank run?

What do banks do during a bank run? A bank run occurs when a large number of people withdraw their money from a bank, because they think the bank will become insolvent. This can create a self-fulfilling prophecy, in which the bank actually becomes insolvent because so many people have withdrawn their money. Banks typically have a reserve of cash on hand to cover withdrawals. However, if the demand for cash is too high, the bank may not have enough cash to meet all of the withdrawals. In this case, the bank may try to obtain emergency funding from the central bank. The bank may also impose restrictions on withdrawals, such as limiting the amount of cash that can be withdrawn per day. This is intended to prevent a run on the bank by limiting the amount of cash that can be withdrawn. If the bank does become insolvent, depositors may not be able to get all of their money back. Depositors with insured accounts are protected up to a certain amount, but uninsured depositors may lose all of their money.

What is the biggest bank run in history?

A bank run is when a large number of people withdraw their money from a bank at the same time because they think the bank might fail. It can create a self-fulfilling prophecy, because if enough people think the bank is going to fail, then it might actually fail. The biggest bank run in history happened in the United States in the early 1930s, during the Great Depression. People were withdrawing their money from banks because they were worried about the banks failing. This caused a lot of banks to actually fail, and it made the Great Depression even worse. There have been other big bank runs in history, but none that have been as big or as damaging as the one in the 1930s. Today, banks are much better regulated and they have more money to protect themselves from runs. However, it's still possible for a run to happen if enough people get scared about the possibility of a bank failure.

Why do people do bank runs?

A bank run is a sudden withdrawal of deposits by lots of people. They happen when people get worried that their money is not safe in the bank, and so they take their money out. This can cause a bank to go bankrupt. There are a few reasons why people might do bank runs. One reason is that they might have heard a rumour that the bank is going to close down, so they want to get their money out before it's too late. Another reason is that they might have seen other people withdrawing their money, and so they decide to do the same. Sometimes, people might do bank runs because they need the money urgently and they don't want to wait for the bank to give them their money back. Whatever the reason, bank runs can be very dangerous. They can cause a lot of damage to the economy, and they can even lead to a financial crisis.

What happens after a bank run?

A bank run is when a large number of people withdraw their money from a bank all at once because they are worried about the bank's solvency. This can cause a financial crisis because it can lead to the failure of the bank. When a bank fails, the people who have deposited money in the bank lose their money. This can cause a lot of financial hardship for the people affected. In addition, the failure of a bank can also cause a ripple effect through the economy. When a bank fails, it can cause other businesses to fail as well. This can lead to an economic recession. A recession is a period of economic decline. During a recession, businesses close, unemployment increases, and people have less money to spend. A recession can last for several months or even years. The effects of a recession can be very severe. Businesses can go bankrupt, people can lose their jobs, and families can fall into poverty. A recession can also lead to social unrest and violence. Thus, it is very important to avoid a bank run. To avoid a bank run, the government may need to provide financial assistance to the bank. The government may also need to take over the bank and run it as a nationalized bank.

What happens to my money if the banks collapse?

When it comes to our money, we all like to think that it's safe and sound in the bank. But what happens to our money if the banks collapse? In the event of a bank failure, the FDIC (Federal Deposit Insurance Corporation) will step in to protect depositors. The FDIC is an independent agency of the US government that insures deposits in banks and savings associations. FDIC insurance is backed by the full faith and credit of the United States government. This means that the US government stands behind the FDIC and will provide the resources necessary to pay insured deposits if a bank fails. The FDIC insures deposits up to $250,000 per depositor, per bank. This limit applies to all of a depositor's deposits at that particular bank, including deposits in checking accounts, savings accounts, money market deposit accounts, and certificates of deposit. If you have more than $250,000 at one FDIC-insured bank, you can spread your money among several different banks to be fully protected. In the event of a bank failure, the FDIC will typically pay out insured deposits within a few days. However, if you have a large amount of money in an account, it may take longer to get your money back. If the FDIC is unable to pay all insured deposits, the US government will be responsible for making up the difference. While this has never happened, it is important to know that the US government stands behind the FDIC and will make sure that depositors get their money back in the event of a bank failure. So, while it is unlikely that the banks will collapse, it is important to know what would happen to your money if they did. The FDIC is there to protect you and your deposits, so you can rest assured that your money is safe and sound in the bank.

We are currently in the midst of a recession, and it is having a major impact on our economy. The stock market has tanked, jobs are being lost, and businesses are struggling. The recession is also causing problems for families, as many are struggling to make ends meet. The government is working to try to improve the economy, but it will take time. In the meantime, we must all do our part to try to weather the storm.

How do you stop a bank run?

How do you stop a bank run? The easiest way to stop a bank run is to have the right policies and regulations in place. In the United States, the Federal Reserve is responsible for ensuring that banks have enough money to meet customer demand. The Federal Reserve does this by setting the reserve requirement, which is the amount of money that banks must keep on hand to meet customer withdrawals. If the reserve requirement is too low, banks may not have enough money to meet customer demand and a run may occur. The other way to stop a bank run is to have strong customer confidence in the bank. This can be achieved through good customer service, transparency, and effective communication.

What is the difference between bank runs and bank fails?

Banking recession is a situation where the banking system or a particular bank is facing severe financial losses. This usually happens when there is a run on the bank, where depositors withdraw large sums of money in a very short period of time. This creates a vicious cycle, as the bank then has to use its reserves to pay out the withdrawals, which then leads to more people withdrawing money, and so on. Eventually, the bank runs out of money and is forced to close its doors. A bank fail is slightly different, in that it occurs when a bank is unable to meet its financial obligations. This can be due to a variety of reasons, such as bad investment decisions, heavy losses in trading, or simply because it has too many non-performing loans on its books. Unlike a bank run, a bank fail does not necessarily mean that depositors will lose all their money, as the government usually steps in to bail out the bank. However, it can still lead to a lot of financial instability and is usually avoided at all cost.

What is another word for bank runs?

A bank run happens when a large number of people withdraw their money from the bank at the same time because they think the bank is going to fail. This can create a self-fulfilling prophecy, where the bank actually does fail because so many people have withdrawn their money. A bank run is also sometimes called a run on the bank.

How do banks really make money?

How do banks really make money? It's a bit of a mystery, isn't it? We all use banks, but how do they make their money? Most of us think that banks make their money by lending money to people and charging them interest. And that is true, to a certain extent. But that's not the whole story. Banks also make money from something called the "float." The float is the money that banks have on hand that they have not loaned out. The float earns interest for the bank, and so it's a nice little Earner. Banks also make money from fees. They charge us fees for everything from using our debit cards to withdrawing cash from an ATM. They also charge businesses fees for things like processing credit card transactions. All of these fees add up, and they are a healthy chunk of change for the banks. Finally, banks make money fromInvestment Income. This is the money they earn from investing our deposits in things like stocks, bonds, and other assets. Investment income can be quite substantial, and it's a big part of how banks make their money. So there you have it. Now you know the three ways that banks make money: from lending, from the float, and from investment income.

What is the central issue that causes bank runs and panics?

When the economy is in a recession, people lose faith in the stability of the financial system. This can lead to bank runs, where people try to withdraw their money from the bank all at once. This can also lead to panics, where people don't want to lend money or invest because they are worried about the future. The central issue that causes these problems is that people lose faith in the economy and the financial system. recessions happen when there is a drop in economic activity. This can be caused by a number of factors, such as a decrease in consumer confidence or an increase in interest rates. When people lose faith in the stability of the economy, they are less likely to lend money or invest. This can lead to a decrease in economic activity, which can lead to a recession.

What group is responsible for stepping in to prevent a bank run?

When a bank run is about to happen or is happening, the Federal Reserve is responsible for stepping in and acting as the "lender of last resort." This means that they will provide the financial institution with the necessary funds to prevent the collapse of the bank. The goal is to stabilize the financial system and prevent a domino effect of other banks collapsing. The Federal Reserve can also take other measures such as lowering interest rates or increasing the money supply.

Who owes World Bank the most?

The World Bank is an international financial institution that provides loans to countries for capital projects. These loans are often used to fund infrastructure projects such as roads, bridges, and schools. The countries that borrow from the World Bank are typically developing nations that have trouble accessing traditional forms of financing. The World Bank is one of the largest lenders to developing countries. In 2016, the World Bank lent $61.2 billion to developing countries. The majority of this money went to middle-income countries, with $34.5 billion going to low-income countries. The top 10 borrowers from the World Bank in 2016 were: 1. China - $1.8 billion 2. India - $1.4 billion 3. Turkey - $845 million 4. Venezuela - $825 million 5. Brazil - $740 million 6. Colombia - $735 million 7. Philippines - $665 million 8. Peru - $635 million 9. Mexico - $605 million 10. South Africa - $565 million As you can see, China and India owe the most money to the World Bank. This is not surprising, given their populations and the fact that they are both rapidly-developing countries. What is surprising is that Venezuela owes so much money to the World Bank, given its current economic situation. The World Bank is one of the most important sources of financing for developing countries. It is important to understand who the biggest borrowers are in order to understand the global economy.

The Great Recession was a time of great economic hardship for many Americans. Millions of people lost their jobs and homes, and the economy suffered greatly. However, the country has since recovered and is now doing better than ever. The recession was a difficult time for everyone, but we have come out stronger as a result.

Why do most people keep their money in the bank?

When it comes to keeping our money safe, most of us tend to play it safe by keeping our money in the bank. There are several reasons why this is the case, but the main reason is because banks are seen as being trustworthy and reliable. We know that our money will be safe in the bank, and we can access it whenever we need to. Another reason why people keep their money in the bank is because it's a convenient way to store our money. We don't have to worry about hiding our cash somewhere in our home, and we can easily transfer money to our bank account if we need to. Lastly, keeping our money in the bank also gives us peace of mind. We know that our money is not susceptible to theft or loss, and we can rest assured knowing that our savings are in a safe place.

What were bank runs during the Great Depression?

During the Great Depression, bank runs were common. A bank run occurs when a large number of people withdraw their money from a bank all at once. This can happen when people become worried that the bank may not have enough money to pay all of its customers. Bank runs can also happen when people are simply panicking and withdrawing their money for no particular reason. During the Great Depression, bank runs were very common. People would line up outside of banks and wait for their turn to withdraw their money. Some people would even camp out overnight to make sure they got their money. The reason for this was that people were worried that the banks would not have enough money to pay all of their customers. This caused a lot of banks to close down because they could not handle the demand. The government tried to stop bank runs by guaranteeing that all deposits were safe. They also set up a system where people could get their money if they needed it. This did not stop all bank runs, but it did help to calm some of the panic.

Can a bank survive a bank run?

The term "bank run" describes a situation where a large number of people believe that a particular bank is in financial trouble and withdraw their money from the bank all at once. This can create a self-fulfilling prophecy, where the withdrawal of funds causes the bank to actually become insolvent. Can a bank survive a bank run? It depends. If the bank has enough cash on hand to meet the demands of its depositors, then it can weather the storm. However, if the bank does not have enough cash, then it may be forced to close its doors. There are a few things that can help a bank survive a bank run. First, the bank may try to persuade its depositors that it is not in financial trouble and that their money is safe. Second, the bank may offer to pay higher interest rates to depositors who keep their money in the bank. Finally, the bank may ask for a loan from the government or another financial institution. While a bank run can be a scary event, it is important to remember that not all banks are in danger of failing. Only banks that are already in a weakened financial state are at risk of failing during a bank run. If you are concerned about your bank's financial stability, you can check its ratings with an independent financial rating agency.

How long does a bank have to come after you?

Most people think that once they default on a loan, the bank will come after them immediately. However, this is not always the case. Banks have what is called a "statute of limitations", which is the amount of time they have to sue you for the debt. This varies from state to state, but is typically between 3-10 years. So, if you default on a loan, the bank may not come after you right away. However, this does not mean that you do not owe the debt. The bank can still attempt to collect the debt through other means, such as calling you or sending you letters. It is important to note that even if the bank does not sue you within the statute of limitations, this does not mean that the debt is erased. The debt will still show up on your credit report, and the bank can still attempt to collect the debt.

Should I withdraw my money from the bank?

A recession is typically defined as two consecutive quarters of negative economic growth, as measured by a country's gross domestic product (GDP). In the United States, a recession is also typically characterized by high unemployment, declining home values, and decreased consumer spending. Withdrawing your money from the bank may seem like a good idea in the midst of an economic downturn, but it could actually do more harm than good. Here are a few things to consider before making a decision: The first thing to understand is that your money is likely safer in the bank than it is in your home. While it's true that banks are not immune to economic downturns, they are highly regulated and typically have a lot of safety measures in place to protect your money. In the event of a bank failure, the FDIC (Federal Deposit Insurance Corporation) insures deposits up to $250,000 per account, per bank. So, if you have your money spread out across different accounts and/or different banks, it's unlikely that you would lose all of your money. secondly, withdrawing your money from the bank could actually put you at a greater risk of becoming a victim of crime. If you have a large amount of cash on hand, you become an easy target for thieves and other criminals. This is especially true if you keep your cash in a safe at home. If your home were to be broken into, the chances are good that the thieves would find your safe and take your money. Finally, withdrawing your money from the bank could have a negative impact on your credit score. This is because one of the criteria that lenders look at when considering a loan is your credit history. If you have a history of taking your money out of the bank and/or closing your accounts, it could signal to lenders that you're not a reliable borrower. In the end, whether or not you withdraw your money from the bank during a recession is a personal decision. However, it's important to understand the potential risks involved before making a decision. If you're still not sure what to do, it's always a good idea to speak with a financial advisor to get professional guidance.

Can the bank take your money if the bank fails?

In the event of a bank failure, the FDIC (Federal Deposit Insurance Corporation) will protect your money up to $250,000. The FDIC insures deposits in checking accounts, savings accounts, money market deposit accounts, and certificates of deposit. In the event of a bank failure, the FDIC will protect your money up to $250,000. The FDIC is an independent agency of the United States government that protects deposited money in banks in the event of their failure. The FDIC insures deposits in checking accounts, savings accounts, money market deposit accounts, and certificates of deposit. The FDIC does not insure investment products, such as stocks, bonds, mutual funds, life insurance policies, annuities, or municipal bonds. If you have more than $250,000 in deposits, you may still be protected, but you will need to check with your bank to see if it is a member of the FDIC. The bottom line is that if your bank fails, you should not lose any of your deposited money as long as it is within the FDIC limit.

Do you lose all your money when a bank collapses?

When a bank collapses, people can lose their money in a few different ways. The most common way is if they have money deposited in the bank that isn't covered by insurance. In this case, the FDIC (Federal Deposit Insurance Corporation) might reimburse people for some of their lost money, but it's never guaranteed. Another way people can lose money when a bank collapses is if they have a loan with the bank. In this case, the bank might not be able to give the person their money back, or the person might have to wait a long time to get their money back. Lastly, people can lose money if they invest in the bank. For example, if someone owns stock in the bank, the value of that stock might go down if the bank collapses. In short, people can lose money in a variety of ways if a bank collapses. The best way to protect yourself is to make sure your money is deposited in an insured bank, and to only invest in solid banks.

An American recession is typically defined as two consecutive quarters of decline in the gross domestic product. However, the effects of a recession can be felt even if the GDP is only slightly negative for a period of time. A recession can cause a drop in the stock market, an increase in unemployment, and a decrease in consumer spending. All of these factors can lead to a decrease in the standard of living for Americans.

Have Questions / Comments?

This book was designed to cover as much as possible but I know I have probably missed something, or some new amazing discovery that has just come out.

If you notice something missing or have a question that I failed to answer, please get in touch and let me know. If I can, I will email you an answer and also update the book so others can also benefit from it.

Thanks For Being Incredible :)

Submit Your Questions / Comments At:

https://BornIncredible.com/questions/

Get Another Book Free

We love writing and have produced a huge number of books.

For being one of our amazing readers, we would love to offer you another book we have created, 100% free.

To claim this limited time special offer, simply go to the site below and enter your name and email address.

You will then receive one of my great books, direct to your email account, 100% free!

https://BornIncredible.com/ free-book-offer/

Also by Luna Z. Rainstorm

Recession-Proof Your Life: The Ultimate Guide to Financial
Stability During Economic Downturns